SENSE OF HUMOUR, SENSE OF JUSTICE

Fred Rumsey

FAIRFIELD BOOKS

This book is dedicated to my wife Coleen

Fairfield Books
17 George's Road, Bath BA1 6EY
Tel 01225-335813

Most of the photographs in the book come from Fred Rumsey's personal collection.
The following appear by kind permission of the copyright holders:
page 53 – Getty Images
pages 106 (Mike Page), 180 and 209 (Godfrey Evans) – PA Images
page 198 – Burton Mail

First published 2019

ISBN: 978 1 9996558 4 6

Printed and bound in Great Britain by
CPI Antony Rowe, Bumpers Way, Chippenham SN14 6LH

Contents

Publisher's Foreword

When Fred came to me with the idea of writing this book, I did not realise what a story he had to tell.

I knew him as a fun-loving, larger-than-life fast bowler of the 1960s – probably the fastest left-armer to bowl for England – and I knew that he had played a leading role in the formation of the Professional Cricketers' Association.

What I did not realise was that the creation of the PCA was entirely his idea and that, for about a year, he was a lone figure drumming up support for it in the face of opposition from the cricketing establishment at Lord's.

Nor did I know that, as the result of another of his visionary initiatives, he was the first public relations officer employed by a county cricket club, raising money for Somerset from local businesses in ways that were new to the game at that time.

Furthermore, he played a significant part in modernising the Lord's Taverners charity in the 1970s; he established a long-running cricket festival in Barbados and was even the ground-breaking pioneer of the Caribbean's inter-island football tournament.

It is quite a story and, now that he has finally got round to telling it, he has revealed a fresh talent – as a natural writer, with an easy-to-read style, mixing effortlessly the fun that he has had through his life with the abiding sense of right and wrong, of social justice, that he learned from his parents in the East End of London.

It has been a privilege to see this book into print – and a great pleasure to spend so much time with one of post-war English cricket's most charismatic characters.

Stephen Chalke

Bath, March 2019

EARLY YEARS

FRED

Drawn by the art teacher
at Westbury Junior School

Introduction

Who in their right mind would run 37 yards at pace, deliver a leather ball at around 90 miles an hour to a distance of about 20 yards, walk back and do it another five times before getting a three or four minute break to do six knee bends in a fielding position called the slips? The procedure can last for an hour, sometimes even longer, and can be repeated twice or maybe three times in a day, three or four days a week, at least 20 weeks a year and as many years as the body and mind will allow.

Me, I was that idiot. And if stupidity is the theme, it is compounded by the fact that I decided to throw caution to the wind, take on the cricket establishment and form a union. It was called an Association but, like all employee-founded bodies, there was a certain air of militancy about it.

The union thing happened in 1967. However, before that ...

1

Born a cockney

I was born in Flamborough Street, Limehouse, Stepney, into good London stock, so I am a full-blooded cockney. My father Fred worked in the docks as a stevedore, and my mother Katherine, before she married and had my sister Jean, worked in the rag trade somewhere in Whitechapel.

The stevedores were the loaders and unloaders of ships, whereas the dockers mostly worked on the quayside. The stevedores were skilled workers. If you loaded a ship badly, it could lose balance and break at sea; some captains would only let their ships be loaded if stevedores were available. In more recent years, now that everything is in containers, all the jobs concerning the loading and unloading of ships are performed by dock-workers.

I believe the origin of the word 'stevedore' is Spanish, and one of its meanings is to stuff. I am sure that is what my father said *they* could do with the job on more than one occasion!

I came into this world a minute before midnight on 4 December 1935. The bells of St Mary le Bow announced my arrival shortly after, confirming my cockney status.

My parents moved to Barking when I was a year old, but I actually don't remember much until I was about three.

There is no formal introduction to a mother and father, or any older sibling. They are just there. It was the same with a cricket ball and bat, a sense of humour and a militant attitude.

2

A small boy with a big label

It was not clear to me what was happening. My sister Jean had just tied a big label through the hole in my jacket lapel. The label had writing on it. I could not read what it said because I was only three years old. She was six, but I doubt if she could read it either. So I did not bother to ask. Between giving me cuddles and packing clothes, my mother was crying. This I also could not understand. No one had slapped her, told her off or taken away her toys. It upset me to think that my mummy was crying, so I was very close to crying too. My little mind was very confused; it was most unsettling.

The date was September 1939.

I learned later that England had declared war on Germany and, although I did not know it then, my father was going to be away for a long time. Although his age delayed his call-up, I was not going to see him for over five years. He joined the First Army as a sapper and, after training, went through North Africa, Sicily and on to Italy where he stayed until the end of the conflict.

During this time the family home was an end-of-terrace house in Craven Gardens, Barking, where I had lived since the age of one. As a cockney, born in Flamborough Street, I thought and spoke like a cockney and developed a wicked sense of humour. I needed it when I was taken to the railway station. 'Evacuation' sounded very nasty, like someone sticking a needle into my arm or other places. I soon found out that it was not inoculation, but in its way it was just as bad.

Operation Pied Piper, which began on 1 September 1939, was designed to protect people, especially children, from the expected German bombing of cities. Officially more than three and a half million people were relocated, but at least a third of the whole population experienced some effect from this vast movement. Many children were parted from their parents. My sister and I were two of them.

We were taken to Barking railway station by my mother and, amidst a lot of tears and cuddles, handed over to some unknown people. We carried, hanging around our necks, a small square cardboard box containing a gas mask, and on the lapel of each of our coats was attached a name card. Jean and I held each other's hands, trying not to be parted. It was a good job that I had the label on because a lot of people kept looking at it.

There was so much jostling, and suddenly there was no sign of Jean. I was on my own, and it was an awful feeling. I was crying, but then so many people around me were crying. Finally she reappeared, and we had a cuddle. I was missing my mother very much, but at least I had stopped crying.

I was told later about a mother watching her two tots march off down the road. She saw them step out of the line and rush up to a policeman standing in the middle of the road. "Bye-bye, Daddy," they said. The policeman looked down, smiled and said, "Now be good, kiddies." The children then got back in line and, as they did so, the mother saw tears rolling down the policeman's cheeks.

I cannot remember a lot about the journey except that we went by train and that I was missing my mother even more. Had my sister not been with me, I do not think I would have coped very well. After a long journey we arrived at our destination: Wootton Bassett in Wiltshire.

We were handed over to a young couple who were going to look after us. The mother was a school teacher, who taught Jean whilst she was there. I was too young to go to school, but I have a feeling that my English improved during my stay. Very quickly a ball and a bat found their way into my hands and, whilst I was there, I had my fourth birthday.

After a few months, much to my delight, my mother appeared on the scene. Apparently my father had been called up and was in training somewhere in England. She stayed for a few months and then decided to take us back to London. The expected bombing had not happened, so in the summer of 1940 she took us home to Barking.

I was pleased that she did. Not being aware of the dangers but being surrounded by all that I knew, I was happy.

3

The Blitz

The Blitz began during the afternoon of 7 September 1940. From four to six o'clock, 348 German bombers, escorted by 617 fighters, blasted London. Two hours later, guided by the fires started by the first assault, a second group of raiders commenced another attack that lasted until 4.30 the following morning.

Through the summer the Luftwaffe had targeted RAF airfields and radar stations in preparation for an invasion of Britain. Now, with those plans put on hold, Hitler had turned his attention to destroying London in an attempt to demoralise the population and force the British to come to terms.

There were clearly grounds for evacuation. Free travel and billeting allowance were offered to those who made private arrangements. They were also given to children, the elderly, the disabled, pregnant women, the ill or those who had lost their homes (some 250,000 in the first six weeks in

London). By the combination of all the state and private efforts, London's population was reduced by almost a quarter.

From that first day of the Blitz London was bombed, either day or night, on each of the next 57 days, and the attacks continued until the following May when Hitler switched his attention to the invasion of Russia. Fires consumed many portions of the city. Residents sought shelter wherever they could find it, many fleeing to the underground stations that housed as many as 177,000 people during the night. My birth place, Stepney, got a real pounding because it was near the docks. Forty per cent of its housing was destroyed.

In the worst single incident, several hundred people were killed in Canning Town when a bomb destroyed a school that was being used as an air raid shelter. Londoners and the world were introduced to a new weapon of terror and destruction in the arsenal of twentieth-century warfare.

My mother decided that we would remain in London, which we did throughout the eight months of the Blitz. We did not sleep in our beds but retired every night to an Anderson shelter which had been built in the garden. Made of corrugated metal sheets, it was buried four feet under the ground, with stone steps going down to the door and the arched roof covered with a layer of soil. Many people planted vegetables and flowers on top of them; residents even held competitions for the prettiest shelter. By the time the Blitz began, over two million shelters had been erected. I can still remember how dank and musty it felt. We had a little kerosene lamp and, if it rained, the water ran down the steps into the shelter. To this day I can smell it.

I assume my mother was scared, but she did not show it to us. If a bomb had landed straight on top of us, we would have been dead, but the shelter protected us from the blasts which killed a lot of people. To me, as a four-year-old, I did not fully appreciate the danger.

Anderson shelter

14 Craven Gardens

The Blitz ended on 11 May 1941 at which point, having kept us in London throughout, my mother decided that we should be evacuated again. This time she came with my sister and me. We still had our gas mask boxes but no labels.

Wheatley in Oxfordshire was our destination. It does not hold good memories for me because it was the first time I attended school. We were allocated a large five-bedroomed house in the main thoroughfare, which we shared with another evacuated family. There was a big garden where I used to catch the butterflies that fluttered around a yellow laburnum, and I played football. I still had my ball and bat, and I used to get Jean to bowl under-arm to me. The extra space enabled me to play a few more shots.

We were in Wheatley for about a year before returning to Craven Gardens. By now I was, by all accounts, a cheeky little sod. However, my mother and sister adored me and, being their only little boy, I was grossly spoilt.

This time, instead of going into the Anderson shelter every time the siren warned of an air attack, we would sit under the dining room table until the All Clear sounded. Why we did that, I have never worked out. If we had received a direct hit on the house the table would have been smashed into splinters, along with us.

The war provided me with a new pastime – shrapnel collecting. As soon as the All Clear siren sounded, I was off like a shot to beat the other boys to collect bits of metal that had dropped from the sky. They were part of the

My sister Jean and me

exploding shells fired by the anti-aircraft guns. These precious pieces of metal were like gold dust to the young boys in and around the east side of London. They were admired, traded and played for in a game similar to marbles. Some were so hot that gloves were required to collect them.

One day I was out running the streets, my eyes darting this way and that in the hope of finding the silver metal, when I came across a whole host of boys doing the same thing. I immediately took off to find virgin ground and ended up on some waste land. What I found there was far more exciting than the shrapnel. A German fighter plane had been shot down, and the pilot was standing on his parachute in the centre of the clearing with his hands in the air. About twenty to thirty local men, some I knew, were approaching him, carrying all types of gardening implements: from scythes to forks, from hoes to spades. I do not know what good the tools would have been if the German had used his gun. The capture was so civilised; no one hit the pilot or even jostled him. They handed him over to the local Home Guard who had appeared on the scene and who took him under arrest.

The fact that no one hit him was an enigma that has stayed with me all my life. The pilot was part of a force wreaking devastation on these people's society, yet not one took personal revenge.

4

Six years of war

"I have told you before: if you break a window in the parlour, the cost will come out of your pocket money." My mother from the kitchen. She never did understand the importance of the exercise I was performing, but I put that down to the fact that she was a woman and that cricket was not very high on her agenda.

I still had my cricket bat and ball, but for years the coal shovel, a worn tennis ball and I were inseparable. There was a certain skill to it, but mostly it was a matter of practice. The white pebbledash wall of 14 Craven Gardens got a severe pounding as I laid the foundations for my batting skills. The blade of the shovel was about five inches wide and about six to seven inches long. The handle was no more than 18 inches long but the balance, ah ... the balance. I cannot remember ever having a bat with such a perfect pick-up – not that I ever really noticed such things in later years!

Most of the fluff on the tennis ball had been worn away before it came into my possession. The back garden wall had done the rest. The pebbledash caused the ball to return at unpredictable angles, making the next hit more difficult. I had to let the ball bounce, then play a return shot which would hit the wall without bouncing, for the wall then to return it and so on. On average I could return the ball 40 to 50 times without missing; at my best it could be between 70 and 80. I might be lying if I said that I ever reached a century. Only a limited number of strokes could be applied in this exercise – one to be exact, the straight drive. Any variation, say an off-drive or an on-drive, meant the returned ball would end up in either the dense growth of the rose bed or the black dust of the coal bunker.

Although cricket was my first love, I appeared to have a natural penchant for all sports, particularly those played with a round ball. I attended Westbury Infant and Junior School, where they encouraged us to play sport whenever we were not in scholarly pursuits.

It was about this time that football – soccer – came into my life with a vengeance. I had already been kicking a ball about with my pals but not in a controlled way. Westbury gave me the grounding in the principles required for good team-work. Basically, I was a selfish player and had to have that attribute knocked out of me. I still believe in arrogance in sport, but when in a team it is important to play for that team and the other players within it. Having said that, I never played with or against anyone who was better than me – in my opinion!

The war continued. In 1944, when I was eight years old, a new weapon began to pepper us in London. It was the V1 flying bomb, also known as the buzz bomb or doodlebug. At its peak, more than one hundred V1s a day were fired at south-east England, though a great number did not make their target.

The doodlebug had a distinctive sound; it was a loud drone. When it ran out of fuel, the sound stopped. That was when you started to panic.

I was late for school on one occasion and not in any particular hurry to get there, when I heard the drone. The doodlebug appeared to be travelling in the same direction that I was taking. I had just been considering a large bomb crater, taking comfort in the fact that the bomb had not landed on my home, when the drone got louder. It is fair to say that I broke the junior 440-yard record in my attempt to get to the safety of the school shelter. About 50 yards from the entrance the engine of the doodlebug stopped. I could hear the swoosh of the bomb dropping from the sky. I took off at the top concrete step into the shelter, landing very painfully twelve steps down. As I hit the ground the bomb exploded, shaking the whole building. Bruises apart, I was in one piece and felt pleased with my lot, until one of the teachers chastised me for being late.

Then the Germans introduced the V2, the worst weapon of all. There was no way of knowing when they were coming; they came straight down like whispering death. Our estate was not touched, but we had factories nearby that were targeted, including Ford and a munitions factory where my mother worked. There was a church in Barking that was wiped out by a V2, and a couple of doodlebugs landed in the park.

Together with the Blitz, the V-bombs resulted in the creation of hard, emotionless young Londoners who became far too used to the idea of death.

A policeman inspects the remains of an unexploded V2 bomb

16

It was around us every day. I would go to school in the morning, and the boy in the next desk would be missing. The teacher would explain that he had been killed, and we would just carry on. I was aware that I had hardened myself to death; I made sure that it was not going to upset me emotionally. We all did, the boys and the girls. It was part of your life. You shut out the thought that it was going to be you.

A war child is a different person from a child brought up in peace. The war went on for years, not just a week. Yet somehow the hatred was not for the German people; it was for the aeroplanes and the doodlebugs.

When we went shopping, I was my mother's bag carrier. Shopping was not the comfort that it is today. It was queues, coupons and full-pack marching. One day, as we were heading for the shops, I was only feet away from a young man in his late teens who threw himself in front of a double-decker bus. He was pushed at least twenty yards along the tarmac before finally being run over by the bus's enormous wheel. My mother tried to shield me from the horror, covering my eyes, but she was too late; I had seen the whole thing happening. At the time I had no idea why he did what he did. I felt little or no emotion; to me it was just another fatal event. Later my mother heard that he had not been accepted into the armed services and, as she put it, "It had played on his mind."

If Hitler's intention was for the bombing to demoralise the people and to break their spirit, he failed because it had the opposite effect. It made people harder, more patriotic, more determined to pull together for the country.

5

Homecoming

I was still pounding the pebbledash wall of 14 Craven Gardens with my coal shovel and now almost bare tennis ball. It was 1945, I was nine years old, and I had not seen my father for over five years. To be brought up by two women, my mother and sister, had its advantages. Although I was not aware at the time the discipline I received was quite relaxed. I got away with murder, my mother would say. "Wait until your father comes home," was a constant threat. So much so, that I began to fear the very idea of my father returning and applying his discipline to my happy environment.

He was demobbed in 1945, and it was with some apprehension that I welcomed him home. My fears were allayed when one of his first questions was "How's your cricket?" But I did not get on well with him during the early period of his return home. He was a stranger to me, and I felt at the time that he was also a stranger to my mother.

Jean, my mother and me

My father in uniform

It must have been extremely difficult for returning servicemen to pick up where they had left off five years previously. There were rows and shouting matches, something I had never heard before in my life. Whatever caused the rows I will never know, but it was as if they hated each other. After each row there was silence; they did not talk to each other for days. It occurred to me at the time that they both had used up all the words available to them; that was why they had nothing to say.

This lasted about a year. Then slowly we all got back to loving each other.

I enjoyed my childhood. I adored my mother and sister, and I learned to respect my father. When they settled down, life at home was delightful.

My father's father, another Fred, had been Amateur Heavyweight Boxing Champion in 1904; he used to box exhibition matches with the professional champion Bombardier Billy Wells who later in life banged the gong at the start of J Arthur Rank films. But both my grandfather and grandmother died young, and my father as the eldest was left on his own to bring up four brothers and two sisters. He was a Victorian in attitudes, believing in family, order, discipline, but his discipline was always extremely fair. He never laid a hand on me, and he was not petty. If he had a headache he would not discipline me because of that – but he would if I walked over his garden.

He had been a sergeant-major in the army. They wanted to promote him to captain, but he refused. I think he accepted his social position. When they invaded Italy, he was put in charge of loading and unloading all the ships – first at Bari, then at Rome, Venice and Genoa.

He loved playing cards. He taught Jean and me games like Canasta and Solo. I think he was a lot cleverer than he let on. You could see that from the way he played cards.

When I was about 14, I started smoking – Senior Service, as my father did. A packet cost one shilling and ten pence, which was more than I could afford with my pocket money. My father used to keep his money, florins and half-crowns, in the pocket of his jacket, and I used to 'borrow' from it. I took the odd cigarette, too. I did not think of it as stealing; I thought borrowing from your father was acceptable. It went on for several months. I never smoked at home so I thought my father did not know.

One day he said he wanted a word with me in the front room which, as in most houses, was kept for special occasions. "You smoke, don't you?" he said. "It does seem silly if you smoke that you only do it outside the home. From now on, I am allowing you to smoke at home, and I am going to increase your pocket money so that you can afford two packets a week. I hope that helps to ease your position."

19

I got up to go. "There is one more thing," he said. "Having increased your pocket money, will you please stop helping yourself from my pockets?" I felt so embarrassed; he had known about it for months.

My mother was different. She was a delightful person, with a fabulous sense of humour, almost wicked. Her lovely spirit was passed on to my sister. I cannot remember any of my family ever criticising another soul. If ever somebody said something negative about a person, my mother in particular would find a good point in that person's character. I grew up not knowing there were villains in the outside world, and that did not prepare me for life. I am sad to say that my family were rare in this aspect. Life is just not what they believed it to be – more is the pity!

Just before my father returned home, the whole of London celebrated VE Day. This was Victory in Europe. Every street in every town threw a party. Craven Gardens was no exception; we had a fabulous day, there was bunting everywhere. The mums cooked pies, made sandwiches, baked cakes and set jellies. The kids sat at long trestle tables and were waited on hand and foot. It was on that very day that I tasted my first banana and pineapple slice. My uncle Alf had returned from sea with a whole load of tropical fruit and had chosen VE Day to come to us to deliver it. I can remember being blissfully happy and not really knowing why. During most of my life, I had been bombarded by bombs, doodlebugs and rockets. I had no idea what peace was all about, but I celebrated with everybody.

Sport had taken a bit of a back seat for me during these celebrations, although the number of activities had increased. To me soccer was a year-round sport, to be played anywhere I could lay my jacket as a goal post. Cricket and tennis were restricted to the summer, although indoor cricket schools for winter practice were beginning to become popular. Basketball and table tennis could be played all year round, so I did. I also invented a game called 'Beat the Bus'. I would wait outside Westbury School for my homeward-bound bus to arrive but, instead of getting on it, I would stand there until the conductor rang the bell, then I would run home by a different route and try to beat the bus to the stop of what would have been my disembarkation. To me it was not that important that I won; I believed that this would increase my stamina. It did and, of course, I did win most times.

The country was trying to get back to normal. I remember sweets coming off rationing, then going back on again because we all pigged out and the shops ran out. Dads came home, and discipline increased. My studies and sport were going well at Westbury. I even managed to pass the scholarship, an exam taken at eleven before the 11-plus was invented.

VE Day Party in Craven Gardens
In the upper picture I am towards the left, standing up with my back to the camera
In the lower picture I am on the far left in the middle row, wearing a paper hat;
my sister Jean is bottom right, also with a paper hat

Westbury Junior School Cricket Champions 1947
I am sitting in the middle row, second from the right

I played soccer whenever time allowed and captained Westbury to the local junior schools final – which we lost. I never did captain the cricket team at Westbury, although we won the Junior Schools Championship in 1947.

Our house was on a small estate not far from the river Thames, at its junction with the river Roding. There are three streets, or to be accurate Gardens, and they were all named after cigarettes: Westminster, Waverley and Craven. It was from these three Gardens that we used to pick our local soccer team to play in Greatfields Park.

Although my mother and father were delighted that I had passed the scholarship, I was not such a happy chappy. The school chosen for me to continue my education, Coopers' Company School, was based in Bow, forty-five minutes away by bus and underground train. If that was not enough, I would know no one there. However, the biggest crime of all: it was a rugby-playing school. What was going to happen to my beloved soccer?

I was nearly twelve years old when I started my first term at Coopers and, although I enjoyed the rugby, I still played soccer on a Sunday, in the park with my mates. By this time we were quite organised and played matches against other groups. One day a mother brought her young son, bedecked in football gear, and asked if he could play with us. He could not have been more than seven or eight years old. We were not too keen, but she assured us that he would be able to cope.

On practice day it was usual to have two captains who would pick their team players alternately. The first week 'The Youngster', as we had chosen to call him, was the last pick. He was not very big but that did not seem to matter to him because no one got anywhere near him. It was like he had the ball on an invisible piece of string. His ability to hold and shield the ball was way beyond his years. In about three weeks he went from last pick to first.

His name was Bobby Moore. He lived at 43 Waverley Gardens, and his garden almost backed onto mine. Like me he went to Westbury School and, when he left, the masters predicted a great cricket career for him. Strange, because they predicted a great soccer career for me!

He was a quiet boy, he never showed a lot of emotion, but he had a confidence. To be a good sportsman, you have to be arrogant. If you don't believe in yourself, who is going to believe in you? There was never a batsman I did not believe I could get out. He had that, too, even at that age, but he was not big-headed.

In 2007 a statue of Bobby Moore was unveiled outside the rebuilt Wembley Stadium. One of the best defenders of all time, the only England captain ever to receive the World Cup, an enduring national icon – and all from Greatfields Park.

6

Coopers' Company School

I enjoyed my time at Coopers once I had come to accept that, for me, soccer was a sport of my past. It was an independent school but, not long before I went there, the local authority arranged to pay some of the expenses if the school took a number of scholarship boys, of which I was one. I never had any sense that, as the son of a stevedore, I was unacceptable to the boys with wealthier parents – nor were they unacceptable to me!

My first two terms were in the winter when the rugby bug was firmly planted into my brain. I skippered our year group team, which never lost a game in five years, but I only played in the first two years. After that I became their travelling linesman, because I had a strange complaint where the knobs below my knees went soft. The headmaster banned me from playing, and I had to go twice a week for treatment, having electric plates placed on the muscles above the knees. Then one day, after about two years of this, the doctor said he had been sent a new paste that I was to rub into the skin. Within a week the problem went away.

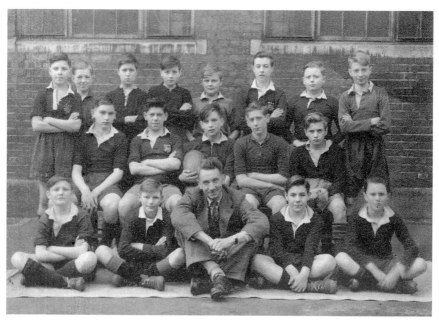

Captain of the Under-13 rugby team at Coopers
I represented the school at cricket, rugby, table tennis, mixed hockey,
chess, athletics, swimming – everything except badminton

Like Westbury, Coopers promoted sport and recreational activities with as much gusto as they did academic studies. Fencing and chess were compulsory for first-year students. After you had learned to fence at foil, and you knew the moves at chess, you could either drop them or join the school clubs for those activities. I had too much on my plate so I dropped both, though I did play for the school chess team sometimes. We had an annual 250-board match against Harrow, where we had to travel to them as our hall was not large enough.

I was in for a big surprise on the first day of the summer term. Three mesh-framed cricket nets faced me as I walked into the playground. Being a first-year student they were out of bounds to me. The school playing fields were a long tube ride away, and we only visited them once a week.

I was missing the fun of playing cricket more regularly so I decided to do something about it. The school cricket coach was a technician in the science laboratory. He played quite a good standard of cricket for Becontree, a club not far from my home, and he had the ability to teach. At the time I was a slow left-arm bowler who batted a bit. I started to talk to him about grip, line and position at the wicket. It was not long before he invited me to perform in the nets. At the first available break in schooling I was with him on the matting. He watched me for a while with a pensive look on his face.

"Do you turn the ball as much on grass?" he asked.

"Yes," I replied.

That was the end of the conversation and the end of break.

Later that afternoon a message arrived to my form room with instructions for me to report to the nets after school. There the coach introduced me to the cricket master, Mr Hodge. There were a number of bigger boys in sports gear, some with pads on. I later learned that they were the Under-15 team. I was asked to bowl at those padded up and, if I were a modest man, I would not tell you that I dismissed all of them more than once.

I was then selected to play for the Under-15 XI in their game later that week. During the first month of that 1948 summer term I played for every cricket team in the school: from the Under-13½ XI to the 1st XI. I spent more time on the cricket field than I did in the classroom. I was quite tall so playing against boys of 18 did not faze me – except when I got hit in the box when I was not wearing one!

I enjoyed my school life. In the third form the rugby master was my form master, and I worked very hard for him, coming top of the class. But, after that, I found it difficult to concentrate on the subject on hand. I became an expert at day dreaming; some of the thoughts that came to mind amazed me.

I was, however, an avid reader and not just pulp fiction. I had read most of the Greek philosophers by the time I was 15. I am not saying that I understood them, just that I read them. The half-hour journey on the underground train helped; it gave me time to read.

I was bowled over by the ability of the great writers to put words together and explain their thoughts. This mostly applied to the poets, old and modern. My bible was Alfred Lord Tennyson; I have still got my battered old collection of his poems. I could recite whole verses of 'Maud'.

> The fancy flatter'd my mind,
> And again seem'd overbold;
> Now I thought that she cared for me,
> Now I thought she was kind
> Only because she was cold.

It has a beautiful rhythm, and it sums up unrequited love perfectly: a man not getting anywhere.

The more you read this book, however, the quicker you will come to the conclusion that not much of this great literary talent rubbed off on me.

I also developed a talent for crossword puzzles. I used to buy the *Daily Telegraph* and, once the compiler was known and I could identify his thinking, they were not too difficult to complete. I got to the stage where I could do them without filling in the answers.

I took part in the school plays. In 'Treasure Island' I was Ben Gunn, with a long white beard, with Long John Silver played by Bernard Bresslaw, who went on to appear in many of the 'Carry On' films. He was two years older than me and a good opening bowler in the cricket team.

I took up photography. A friend, Ron Holcombe, and I used to get on our bikes and cycle all over the place, taking pictures. We built an enlarger, balancing an old camera with a good lens on a pile of books, and printed our pictures on photographic paper.

A photograph of me, sitting in a tree in Epping Forest, taken by Ron and developed in our dark room. We were sticklers for good definition.

The headmaster had banned me from most sport. He said I could play cricket as long as I batted with a runner, but the cricket master ignored that. Away from school I went to the Eastbury Youth Club where I played table tennis and basketball. We became national junior champions at basketball. When the Harlem Globetrotters came over to play at the Wembley Arena, we were the ballboys. We gave exhibitions before they went on.

Cricket was always the number one sport for me, though. I played as often as I could, and I became a junior member of Essex County Cricket Club. I cycled to matches, even the thirty miles to Southend. I was there as a 12-year-old in 1948 when the Australians scored 721 in a day.

As I aged and grew in size, my game improved. I became a cocky lad with an attitude. The school's technician cricket coach thought the time had come for me to get more experience in the wider world of cricket so he invited me to join Becontree Cricket Club. They played in Becontree Park, not that far from my home.

I soon got into the routine of playing for the school first team on Saturday morning, Becontree in the afternoon and Becontree on Sunday. All my cricket gear was contained in a sausage bag which I would hoist on to my shoulder and carry to where I was required. If a school match on Saturday morning was to be played in my vicinity, I would meet the bus at an agreed place. I was always late, believing in my arrogance that they would never leave me behind. On one occasion I was due to meet the bus at Heathway Station and, upon arriving, late as usual, I went up to the bus with the intention of boarding. Mr Hodge the cricket master was blocking my way.

"Where do you think you are going, Rumsey?" he said.

"To play cricket," I replied.

"Not in this team," he retorted. "Get off the bus."

The moment I stepped off the platform he rang the bell. As the bus left me and my sausage bag standing forlornly on the pavement outside Heathway Station, I reflected on a lesson learned – but one that was always difficult to practise.

Essex County Cricket Club offered me three trials while I was at Coopers' Company School. The first was at Abbey School in Barking when I was 12; all the other trialists attending were over 15. The second was at Fairlop School when I was 13. Only four young cricketers were invited and the organiser was Bill Morris, an Essex player who spent a considerable amount of time coaching the four of us in the finer arts of batting. The third and final trial was at Trevor Bailey's indoor cricket school in Ilford when I was 14. It was quite a daunting task having to face Trevor bowling at you in his nets. He was at the time a very successful England all-rounder, and the pace at which he bowled was not something a 14-year-old batsman would relish.

CRICKETERS PREPARE

W. B. Morris, the Essex County cricketer, is coaching promising Essex juniors at Fairlop School during the Easter school holidays. Our photograph shows him giving tips on batting style to P. M. Mann. Middle of the three boys looking on is Ivor Hart, Ilford County High School pupil, who last year was the youngest member of the Essex County Schoolboys XI.
Photo: Wastell, Longwood Gardens.

It's me next to the batsman – I'm not sure my forward defensive was ever that straight

27

The outcome of all three trials was plain and simple: "You are much too young, come back when you are older." I never did go back. However, seven years later, as an amateur I did play for Essex 2nd XI a few times. In later life Trevor and I became great friends, but he never indicated that he thought Essex had missed much by not signing me up when they had the opportunity.

I started in the 3rd XI at Becontree and by 1952, when I was 16, I had progressed to the 1st. In 1951 the 3rds were playing Downshall 2nd XI. Downshall were bowled out for 31. We hit the runs off quickly, so technically the game was over. However, both captains decided to carry on, and I managed to score my first hundred in match cricket, 101 to be exact. I bring this information to your attention with a great deal of emphasis because it was not an event that was repeated very often during the rest of my career.

I was still bowling slow left-arm but occasionally, when the situation demanded, I would go off a longer run and bowl around the wicket at pace. Being idle I preferred slow bowling, but in the end that was not to be.

7

Merchant banking

I left school a wiser, albeit unqualified, young man. I did not get passes in enough subjects to be awarded the matriculation certificate so I left school uncertified.

I joined a merchant bank in the City of London called Ullman & Co, based in Gracechurch Street, near the Monument. It employed about 70 people who dealt mostly with foreign exchange and investment. I started in the filing department, moved to book-keeping and ended up in foreign exchange.

One day I was left on my own in the foreign exchange department, operating the switches that provided direct lines to Europe's major exchange dealers, when I bought the wrong currency at the wrong price, losing about £3,000, more than six times my annual salary. Cap in hand, I went to the senior dealer for my just desserts. His name was Dawes, and he was a partner in the firm. His severe look over the top of his glasses left me without any doubt as to what I was in for. He leapt out of his chair, walked past me and settled himself in my seat in front of the direct-line switches. He then proceeded to deal in numerous currencies over the next hour, recouping my loss and earning a little more.

"Don't say a word to the others when they come back," he said to me. "You are allowed that one mistake. Anyway, I enjoyed the exercise."

He carried on: "It also gives me the opportunity to ask you to play cricket for my team next Sunday without the chance of a refusal, if you know what I mean!" I played for him in the grounds of his house in Surrey, scored a fifty and heard no more about my gaffe.

Playing in that same game was a lively colleague from the bank called Ron Schwendener. He was the person responsible for my moving from Becontree Cricket Club to their neighbours Goodmayes, who played in Goodmayes Park. According to the ladies of the bank, he was quite a dashingly handsome fellow. He and I used to take the younger girls from the bank for drinks after work. These excursions amounted to nothing but were great fun at the time. He, however, along with a bunch of similar-minded pals, used to spend a lot of his leisure time at holiday camps where it was his practice to take his pyjama top and tooth brush to the evening dances. He carefully folded the pyjama top on the chair next to him and placed the tooth brush on top. Apparently this produced a great deal of success.

During the winters I turned out every Saturday for the Old Cooperians Rugby Club. Our home ground was at Grange Farm, a sports complex in Chigwell that was constructed to provide accommodation for over 2,000 foreign students during the Festival of Britain. The school used the facilities for all its sporting activities, so it was natural for the Old Boys to follow suit. Most of the matches were against other Old Boy sides in and about London.

One major weakness of the complex, at that time, was the lack of changing and showering facilities. We used to change in an old barn owned by Ye Olde Kings Head, an excellent watering hole just outside the ground. There were no showers there, either, but the after-match refreshment was at an extremely high level. It was traditional in those days for there to be a kitty of ten shillings a head to buy jugs of beer for both sides. My problem was that I was not a big beer drinker; even then I preferred a glass of wine. Wine was not sold at the bar, but Ye Olde Kings Head had an excellent restaurant, so I was allowed to pick a bottle off the wine list for my ten shillings and that was my lot for the evening.

I played fly-half at school, or sometimes inside-centre, but the Old Boys saw me as a back-row forward, middle of the back row to be precise, what they now call number eight. It is a position that is always on the move, which did not suit my lazy nature. If they are not corner-flagging in defence, they are tidying behind the three-quarters when attacking. This was further aggravated by the fact that at six foot four inches in height I was the tallest forward in the pack so you can guess who had to do all the jumping in the line-outs. At 18 years of age I did seriously consider early retirement, but I liked the life style too much, particularly that bottle of Chablis after the game.

8

National Service

I left the bank in early May 1954 at the request of Her Majesty's Government. Conscription called me, and I opted to spend my two years in the Royal Air Force. At the medical it was established that the only rare thing about me was my blood: B negative.

AC2 FE Rumsey 2721828

My first posting, as AC2 FE Rumsey 2721828, was to RAF Wilmslow for square bashing. This is the part of service life that brainwashes you to accept orders from a superior rank, however stupid those orders may be. It never ceased to amaze me how readily national servicemen accepted these instructions, even though their own intelligence and education was at a far better level. The need to salute and genuflect is understandable in service life, but the practice is abhorrent.

Is that the aroma of injustice that I smell? Early signs of militancy were beginning to appear.

There was a sergeant who used to order us about, albeit in a very pleasant manner. I asked him to join us all for drinks one evening. He declined. "I have got to go to the education centre," he said, "to do me maths and me English." One of my pals said, "I think you have them in the wrong order, sergeant." "No," he replied. "Me maths and me English."

The discipline applied both on and off the square. I learned to march in formation, fold and wrap my blankets in a tidy parcel to be placed at the foot of my bed and, outside of the sleeping quarters, to cover everything that did not move with white paint.

No leave was allowed during the three months of basic training, so I assumed that I would be confined to barracks for the whole period. We were trained in groups of about 30 airmen. Each group was called a flight and was headed up by a corporal. From the day we arrived all the flight corporals shouted abusive instructions at us and made themselves as objectionable as they possibly could, but underneath all the bluster they really loved us!

One day in early June my flight corporal ordered me to report to the Camp Commanding Officer. He was concerned because he had no idea why the CO wanted to see me, and neither did I. The CO was a Group Captain, and from the moment I set foot in his office he was full of smiles.

"I have been told that you have some talent on the cricket field."

"Some, sir," I replied in all modesty, having no idea where his information had come from.

"Good," he said. "We need you to do a public relations job for us with the local mayor."

I really was confused by this time. I had no idea what on earth I could do to improve the image of RAF Wilmslow with the local mayor. It turned out that the mayor was the Mayor of Macclesfield, not Wilmslow, and was a keen supporter of Macclesfield Cricket Club. He wanted the CO to release me at weekends to play for them in the local league.

"Will you do it, Rumsey?" asked the CO.

"Of course, sir," I replied, giving him my best smile.

"You will be granted a 48-hour pass each weekend for the rest of your stay here," he continued. "Should you have any problems, let me know."

I had a sneaking suspicion that the lads back in the barracks were not going to be too pleased when they heard about it. I did not dare to think what the corporal might say.

The whole idea worked very well. I played for Macclesfield, this pleased the Mayor, which in turn pleased the CO, who now had a soft spot for our flight. In addition I was able to return to Essex on some Sundays to play for my new club, Goodmayes.

At this stage of my cricket life I was mostly batting and bowling slow left-arm, but this comfortable position was about to change. One Sunday in July, Goodmayes were playing another Essex club, Hadleigh & Thundersley. The rain had been coming down in buckets and as a result, with start time approaching, only seven Goodmayes players had put in an appearance. Then the weather eased, and it began to look like we would start on time or very close to it. Runners were sent out to find players, and a decision was taken to bat if we won the toss. This the captain achieved.

The wicket was rain-soaked, and within twenty minutes we were four down. More of our players had arrived by this time so at least we would bat to eleven – not that that made a lot of difference because we were all out for 87. I had managed to scrape together 47 of those, with the next highest scorer being extras with 11.

Of the three selected seam bowlers only one had shown. The captain asked me if I had ever bowled seam. This I confirmed with a great deal of reluctance and was told that I was to open with the regular opener, George Turner. I only knew how to bowl left-arm round the wicket, so I straightened my run-up and lengthened it to about 15 yards. It was a strange sensation to come charging in to bowl, so my balance was wrong and the first ball went for wides down the leg side: four, to be exact. I caught on quickly and, once I got the radar working, the wet wicket did the rest. I ended up taking seven wickets for three runs and, with my pal George Turner's three for 11, we bowled out the opposition for 27. They scored only 14 runs with the bat, their highest scorer Mr Extras with 13. Needless to say, I was never allowed to bowl slow left-arm again.

I was sent from RAF Wilmslow to RAF Yatesbury to be trained in radar. There was little time for sport there, as the course was quite intensive. Weekend passes were available, so I continued to play cricket for Goodmayes when possible. After training I was posted to RAF Chenies, a village close to Hemel Hempstead, about 30 miles from my home. It was a radar station whose prime activity was to identify hostile aircraft and scramble friendly aircraft to intercept. It also had a chain home beam which kept a watch on a radius of about 60 miles.

It was a split camp. The radar station was a few miles from the barracks and under the strict security of the RAF Police and guard dogs. At the barracks, however, it was completely the reverse. The fence outside my billet was a shrub about a foot high. This did lead to certain nocturnal activity, on which I will not dwell. I was part of a small group of airmen who spent most of their leisure time together. On a weekly basis we would visit the nearby towns in an old London taxi. The cab belonged to Freddy Fox, an old school chum of mine. Most of us had a girl in each port, so to speak, so, when the station held a dance

Rumsey 7 for 3 and 47 runs in one-man victory!

SEVEN wickets for three runs, and 47 out of a total of 87 by Rumsey of Goodmayes, made the defeat of Hadleigh and Thundersley first eleven at Goodmayes Park on Sunday almost a one-man job! Goodmayes batted first on a rain-soaked wicket and wickets tumbled swiftly until Rumsey, batting number six, made a hard-hit 47, next best being extras—13.

Hadleigh needed 88 but collapsed utterly against Rumsey, who was well supported by Turner (3—11).

So fiery and unplayable was Rumsey that of Hadleigh's total of 27 only 14 were scored with the bat. Top scorer made only five and extras accounted for 13.

Goodmayes won by 60 runs.

GOODMAYES

Green c Lambkin b Watkins		3
Schwendener b Watkins		2
Pecover c & b Holmes		9
Mason run out		0
Fry b Watkins		0
Rumsey b Homewood		47
Anthony c Sheppard b Holmes		0
Brassington lbw b Holmes		6
Clements c Sheppard b Homewood		9
Maxwell not out		0
Turner st Smith b Homewood		0
Extras		11
Total		87

Bowling: Holmes 3—33, Watkins 3—27, Homewood 3—7, Hambridge 0—9.

HADLEIGH & THUNDERSLEY

Watson c Anthony b Rumsey		0
Smith b Turner		0
Lambkin c Fry b Rumsey		0
Eley c Pecover b Rumsey		0
Sheppard b Rumsey		1
Homewood c Mason b Rumsey		5
Hambridge b Turner		0
Farnham c Clements b Rumsey		0
Nichols c Fry b Turner		4
Watkins not out		3
Holmes b Rumsey		1
Extras		13
Total		27

Bowling: Turner 3—11, Rumsey 7—3.

July 1954 – my first game as a fast bowler

and invited the girls from all the local towns, we had to feign duty to avoid the possibility of the girls meeting up and identifying us as common beaus.

Between us we ran most of the sport on the camp. Rocky Pearce was a boxing trainer so he set up an amateur boxing team to fight against other RAF stations and in local tournaments. I was his heavyweight and therefore got special food at the cookhouse. The only problem we had was to find someone to fight me. There was no super-heavyweight division at that time and, at six foot four inches and weighing 16 stone, I was not particularly fancied by 14-stone heavyweights, making it extremely difficult for me to find an opponent. I was on the bill to fight at Watford Town Hall on one occasion, and Rocky had trained me pretty hard. After weighing in, along with six other heavyweights, I was told that I would not be required: again nobody would fight me. This tolled the death knell for my boxing career, and I was bitterly disappointed. Not because I would miss the action (I hardly had any) but because I was not going to get all the great food that Rocky had arranged for me.

The camp was small and had a Squadron Leader as its Commanding Officer. Most of the personnel worked in radar at the security station, doing eight-hour shifts. Because of the intensity of the work, a lot of leisure time was made available. Although of a lowly rank – senior aircraftsman (SAC) – I was asked by the CO to captain both the station's cricket and rugby teams. This decision was most unusual because the sides included young officers. The teams were selected by the camp adjutant and me. In fact, I did all the selecting; he never once suggested a name. But, for the sake of protocol, to protect my position as an aircraftsman, we maintained the impression that he was the chief selector.

RAF Chenies was part of Fighter Command, and therefore we played a lot of cricket matches against other Command teams. One such match was away to RAF Hillingdon, whose captain was a Squadron Leader. It was obvious that he was not too keen to have me, a lowly SAC, leading the opposition, particularly with officers in the side. He was further irritated by losing the toss and having to field. His displeasure was heightened even further by the fact that I scored a hundred and at tea was able to declare our innings closed with a considerable score on the board.

The normal practice at tea was for the two captains to sit together with the rest of the players taking pot luck. Not at Hillingdon! It was made clear to me that I was not welcome at the side of my opposition skipper. In fact, I was not welcome to sit on the table with the officers. The three officers playing for Chenies were ordered to sit with the Squadron Leader, and they did so with a great deal of reluctance. I was just about to tuck in to my curled-up cucumber sandwiches when the booming voice of Wing Commander

Edwards, who was playing for Hillingdon, asked my neighbour to move. He plonked himself down with his own cucumber sandwiches and cup of tea.

With a knowing wink he said, "I thought that the mountain should come to Mohammed." I chanced a glance at the Squadron Leader. If looks could kill, the Wing Commander would be dead. After tea I managed to take five wickets in Hillingdon's innings, including the Squadron Leader's, and much to his disgust we won quite easily.

It is fair to say that the attitude of that Hillingdon officer did not sit well with my views on equality.

The following day the adjutant called me to his office. "Well done with the victory at Hillingdon," he said. "The CO is delighted. It also appears that you have become a big hit with Wing Commander Edwards. He has asked the CO to release you to play for the Command in Bognor Regis." It came to light then that the Wing Commander was the cricket captain of Fighter Command and quite a big mover in RAF cricket circles. The adjutant continued, "The CO has agreed and intends to fly you from Bovingdon to Tangmere on Wednesday."

Unfortunately, there was an exercise at Bovingdon on the Wednesday, and I had to go by train. The match at Bognor was against Flying Training Command, a one-day match that greatly suffered from the English weather.

Of our Fighter Command team that day eight had either played or would go on to play county cricket: Tom Hall (Derbyshire & Somerset), John Naylor (Yorkshire), Ron Tindall (Surrey), Les Savill (Essex), Brian Langford (Somerset), David Allen (Gloucestershire), Geoff Millman (Nottinghamshire) and Fred Rumsey (all stops to Derbyshire). The latter three also played for England – quite a formidable side.

9

Back to civilian life

In the spring of 1956 I was back on the streets a free man. I cannot say that I hated National Service, but it did disrupt not only my career but also the careers of thousands of others. I wanted to go back to the bank and continue working in foreign exchange. However, the department was already oversubscribed, and the alternative jobs on offer were not to my liking. In the end Ullman & Co and I parted company amicably for the second time.

The old adage used when applying for a job, 'I like meeting people', was actually true of me. After a lot of soul-searching I decided that a salesman's life was the one for me. I had no idea how to go about obtaining a position, or indeed what product I wanted to sell, so I placed my future in the capable hands of the local employment exchange. I wanted to continue to work in the City, but jobs outside of finance were limited.

It became clear that to achieve the dizzy heights of salesman, a certain amount of training was required. A few companies were mooted by the employment exchange, but I liked the suggestion of working in Gresham Street, in the heart of the City, for a gloving company called Fownes. They appeared to like me, and within days I was in the leather department as an assistant to the buyer, training for a life on the road. I was not to know at the time that this decision was going to change my life radically.

Not only did I change my job but I also changed my cricket club. I had been advised by a number of people, including my pals at Goodmayes, that I should seek a club of a better standard. I enjoyed playing at Goodmayes but I was sure that this advice was correct, so I made advances towards Wanstead, one of the better London sides north of the Thames. They already had a quick bowler called Barry Knight who was playing quite a lot of cricket for Essex 2nd XI but they took me on and, after a couple of games in the club's second team, I became a fixture in the first. I was, at the time, bowling at pace around the wicket until an umpire advised me to go over the wicket. That move improved my line immeasurably, increased my pace and provided a lot more accuracy. Whoever that was, thank you.

My cricket appeared to improve the further up the ladder I went. The moves from Becontree to Goodmayes to Wanstead were having an effect. The basic change in level was less like a leap, more like a stride; there was no doubt that I improved with each move. I later found that the climb from club cricket to second-eleven county cricket was also a small step, like stepping from the road onto a kerb, but the jump from second-eleven to first-class cricket was like leaping onto the roof of a house.

The higher standard of players at Wanstead, friend and foe, also had an effect. The fielding was better – more catches. The bowling was better – more concentration needed. The batting was better – more guile required.

My role in the team changed from what it had been at Goodmayes. The batters in the Wanstead side were all of minor county standard. Barry Knight, an all-rounder who would go on to play for England, went in at number four or five. John Taylor, a keeper who played for Essex 2nd XI and was only kept out of the 1st XI by Brian 'Tonker' Taylor the future Essex captain, went in at number six. The earliest I could get in was seven or eight so I had less batting and more bowling. I was the quickest of the bowlers, and from that point in my life I became more of a bowler.

My parents started to watch me play when I moved to Wanstead. There was a much better club atmosphere there than at the previous clubs. My sister Jean also attended until she was roped in to score for the 2nd XI. In time she moved up to the 1st XI, developing her own system of coloured pens, and she stayed with them till she died in 2014. She organised fund-raising events; she set up a youth section. She kept a scrapbook of all my cricket; she knew my record in the game better than I did.

My father was a good cricketer in his day, and he was asked if he would stand as umpire for some of the Sunday matches. It was during one of these games that, after a very loud and boisterous lbw appeal from me, "Howzat, Dad?", he uttered the now infamous reply, "That is out, son!"

The year finished on a high note. I was happy at work, leisure and play. On 4 December 1956 I celebrated my 21st birthday and started a love affair with sparkling wine, in particular champagne, which has lasted to this day.

Jean in the Wanstead scorebox
She would do anything to help under-privileged children. She was such a likeable person, kind to everybody. She inherited that from my mum; my daughter Claire is like that, too. When she died, the Wanstead first team captain called her 'the heartbeat of the club'.

SENT TO WORCESTER

*Playing for Wanstead in the summer of 1957,
with no thought of becoming a professional cricketer*

*On the left is Brian Brummell, who played table tennis for England.
I'm second from the right; somewhere behind me, obscured, is Barry Knight.*

10

Essex 2nd XI

Having reached 21 I did not feel that I had come of age. I still held childish thoughts and ideas. Ambitions were for those who hungered for success or even power. The idea of me wanting those things was ludicrous. My life at that time was full of contentment. I enjoyed my lot: the job, playing cricket and rugby, the relationship with my family. I even had a girl friend, Violet Hayzer, who was called Lolly by her friends because of her resemblance to Gina Lollobrigida – I should be so lucky!

The idea of playing sport for a living had never entered my head. I was, however, competitive and liked a challenge. I suppose that was the reason for my climbing up to the higher echelons of club cricket and joining Wanstead. The summer of 1957 was the beginning of representative cricket for me, with an invitation to play for an Essex Club & Ground XI against Tate & Lyle.

The Essex team consisted of nine county 2nd XI players, a Leyton Orient footballer Dave Sexton and me. We won the game by 127 runs. I scored 39, batting at number six, and took four for 22 when opening the bowling. Within weeks I was playing regularly for Essex 2nd XI – as an amateur. I know that I was an amateur because my initials were in front of my name on the scorecard. The professional either had no initials or they came after his name. What a ridiculous practice! Shades of RAF Hillingdon and the Squadron Leader who would not join me, a lowly ranker, for tea.

This segregation of amateur and professional cricketers was a practice dating back to days of yore. In 1806 Lord Frederick Beauclerk came up with the idea that Gentlemen v Players would make an interesting match, with a return match in the same year. The return game was also entitled Gentlemen v Players. Why not Players v Gentlemen, just for a change?

The difference between the two was defined by the English class structure of the time, with the Players deemed to be working-class wage-earners and the Gentlemen members of the middle and upper classes, usually products of the English public school system. Whereas the Players were paid wages by their county clubs or fees by match organisers, the Gentlemen claimed expenses. The whole subject of expenses was controversial, and it was believed that some of the leading amateurs were paid more for playing cricket than any professional.

In later years the two fixtures were played at Lord's and Scarborough and were used as Test trials by the England selectors. Between 1954 and 1962 18 matches were played, the Players winning 12 with the other six drawn. I wonder if that drubbing had anything to do with the MCC's decision, on

31 January 1963, to abolish amateurism and for everybody, Gentlemen and Players, to become Cricketers.

In May 1958 I found myself selected for a Club Cricket Conference Under-24 XI to play against the Royal Military Academy, Sandhurst. Club Cricket Conference is an association of over 1,000 clubs in the south of England. I cannot remember anything about the game itself, but I do know how proud I felt on being selected. It certainly did no harm to my ego.

It is said that to get the best out of a fast bowler he must hunt with a partner. Some of the greatest fast bowlers of all time did so: Lindwall & Miller, Hall & Griffith, Trueman & Statham, Lillee & Thomson. The West Indies doubled up on that with Malcolm Marshall, Michael Holding, Andy Roberts and Joel Garner all in the same team.

At Wanstead there was Barry Knight, who was in and out of the Essex county side at the time, Mike Jones and Bob Campbell. All were good opening bowlers, but I never really struck up a partnership with any of them. I have often wondered why Barry and I managed to get selected for England, whereas the other two appeared not to have the opportunity. There were a lot of talented club cricketers who were the equal of the people I played with in county second eleven cricket.

There is no doubt in my mind that, if England adopted the pyramid system played in most other cricket-playing nations, we would be the strongest cricket nation in the world. There should be a direct line from club to county to region to England. At the moment we have a closed-shop system where an aspiring cricketer has to relinquish his career and join a first-class county to establish whether or not he has the talent to play the game for a living. A great number of good club cricketers will not do that and, even if they did, a couple of bad seasons could see them released from contract with no apparent way back. Allan Border went through such a scenario in Australia. Having had a bad season in state cricket, he was dropped back into club cricket, but such is their system that, by scoring a few hundreds for his club side during the next season, he was back in the state team and then on to the national side.

Our current system of 18 counties allows for about 250 players in the first-class cricket scene. With about 60 overseas players in that number, our Test selectors have less than 200 available to pick from. Of that 200, more than half will not be good enough, leaving fewer than 100, which is a very small number to select from when 840,000 were playing the game in England and Wales in 2014. The obvious answer to the problem is to introduce a system that provides a greater opportunity for more people to play first-class cricket – indeed, a pyramid system.

I am reminded of a poem that I loved at this time, Gray's 'Elegy Written in a Country Churchyard':

Full many a gem of purest ray serene,
The dark unfathomed caves of ocean bear:
Full many a flower is born to blush unseen,
And waste its sweetness on the desert air.

Those lines could easily have been written for those players who have not been allowed to bloom because of the closed-shop nature of our cricket system.

Alfred Lord Tennyson was my favourite poet, though, and he had the extra appeal that he provided Hampshire and England with a cricket captain, his grandson Lionel Hallam Tennyson, the 3rd Baron Tennyson. One of my favourite cricket stories concerns the baron and a Hampshire seam bowler called 'Lofty' Herman. At tea on the final day of a county match, which was going badly for Hampshire, his Lordship told Lofty, who batted at number eleven, that, if he had go out to the wicket, he should make some subtle reference to the light, to try to get the game called off. It was at a time when only the umpires could make a decision as to whether or not play was possible.

Sure enough, Lofty had to bat. As he approached the wicket Lionel Tennyson called out, "I trust that you have remembered our conversation at tea, Herman" – to which Lofty replied, "I can hear you, my Lord, but I cannot see you!"

11

To Worcester

Fownes Gloves is an old established gloving company. In the 1950s, along with Morley and Dents, they dominated the English glove-making scene. Gloves were more fashionable in those days, not just for warmth in the winter but also for special occasions. Women were the biggest users, with their long chamois leather, rouched fabric, usually cotton or nylon, cape leather and suede. Men had their own fashion rules. It was unheard of for a man to wear an overcoat without a good pair of gloves.

As part of my training I was expected to attend high-street shops and stores with armloads of samples to tempt the buyers to purchase our gloves for the forthcoming season. With Fownes it was less like selling, more like representing – the gloves had a tendency to sell themselves. The country was covered by about a dozen top salesmen, all of whom understood the gloving industry inside and out. On one occasion, when it was necessary for the south-eastern representative to have a medical operation, I was asked to take his place for a few months.

The company car was a monster called an Austin Westminster. It and I took some time to get to know each other; it had a gear change attached to the steering column and chose occasionally to miss out gears on the way up or down. To make matters worse, it was in the depths of winter – ice, snow, wind and rain – and I had only just passed my driving test.

I went down to Kent to visit the top store in Maidstone, where I had made an appointment to see the men's and ladies' glove buyers. Burdened with four boxes of samples, I staggered into the store and confronted an extremely well-dressed gentleman in the men's department.

"And what can we do for you?" he asked.

"I am from Fownes Gloves, and I am here to show you our spring collection," I replied.

"Not dressed like that you are not."

I was wearing a nice suit, tie and a Crombie overcoat.

"What is wrong with my dress?" I asked.

"You have the effrontery to come into this store half-dressed and ask me what is wrong. Where are your gloves, and where is your hat?" He was quite scathing.

My first reaction was to pick up my samples and do a runner, but somehow I didn't think that such an action would go down well with this Hitler.

"My gloves are in the car, and I don't own a hat," I stated.

"Well, you should," he replied. "You cannot expect to be selling fashionable items to fashionable stores if you yourself are not fashionably attired." He then ordered, "Come to the hat department."

Within a matter of minutes I was the proud owner of a blue Homburg and silk scarf to go with my navy Crombie coat. What a salesman!

Unfortunately Fownes Gloves' location in the City prevented good access to the Guildhall. They were asked by the City of London, with a suitable inducement, if they were prepared to move to another location so that their building could be razed to the ground to open up the front of the Guildhall. They agreed to do this and decided to locate to Worcester where they owned a factory with considerable available space. One of the directors of the company, a Mr Caldicott who was part of the Fownes family, was asked to supervise the move. He chose me as his personal assistant and, along with Violet Hayzer, we moved to Worcester in the summer of 1958.

Fownes glove factory, Worcester

My career in the gloving company was taking off. After a year in Worcester I was appointed as personal assistant to the new managing director. I was also appointed advertising manager, sales manager and warehouse manager. Each time I was given a new managerial appointment, I was given another member of staff, which resulted in me having less and less to do. My staff and I would meet every morning to discuss the day's activities and by 11 o'clock we were done. I complained to the MD that he could reduce the number of my staff to allow me to do a little more work. He refused my request, saying that he planned a future for me away from the head office. Unbeknown to me, he had earmarked me for the job of MD of a company Fownes was buying in Somerset. He wanted good coverage in those departments that I was managing once I had left.

The new job in Yeovil was not going be available for a year or so, so he suggested that, because I was keen on cricket, I should spend more time playing it, as long as I dealt with Fownes matters at the morning meetings. Mike Jones, my old pal from Wanstead, came originally from Worcester, and he had moved back there to a teaching post. He introduced me to Worcester City Cricket Club, who played on the county's ground at New Road, and he encouraged me to play Worcestershire Club & Ground matches. From that, I moved up to playing for the county second eleven in 1959.

It was the first summer of the Second XI Championship, two-day matches, and I made my debut against Warwickshire 2nd XI at the Mitchells & Butlers ground in Birmingham. Warwickshire had an opening bowler called Jack Bannister who, eight years later, would play a major role in assisting me with the formation of the Professional Cricketers' Association. We lost the match, but I had a reasonable game, taking four wickets in each innings.

I played in three more games as Mr FE Rumsey, the aspiring amateur, and at the end of the season Worcestershire offered me a two-year contract to turn professional. The remuneration was £300 for each of the two seasons. I was earning over six times that amount at Fownes, with greater opportunities to come, so I was in a dilemma.

Violet Hayzer had chosen to return to London to further her career there, so at least I was a single entity. The balance sheet came down in favour of my having a go at professional cricket. I suppose my love for the game and my attachment to bat and ball overrode the common sense of what my brain was telling me. Fownes' Managing Director was disappointed but he wished me well, and the wrench to leave that fold the following April was immense. The MD was even prepared to hold my position open for a couple of years in case I had a change of heart, an action I thought to be exemplary.

Whilst working at Fownes I started playing rugby for Worcester RFC. I suppose I played the best rugby of my career at that time, and it included one game for the North Midlands, a very powerful county team. My career at Worcester began with the usual match in the second team, the 'A' XV. They had four sides if I remember correctly, and I guess at the time they played in the country's third tier of rugby, against teams such as Birmingham,

NO STOPPING BIG FRED!

The proximity of the line indicates that the Stourbridge defender is going to have a job to stop Fred Rumsey scoring for Worcester. In fact, he didn't stop him—this was the second of Worcester's five tries in their 17—6 victory at Bevere last Saturday. A clever break by Brian Wilkes had given Rumsey his chance. Up in support are Tony Collins (left) and Mike Daniel centre).

Hereford, Stourbridge, Hinckley and Sale. The following week I was picked to play lock forward, number eight, for the 1st XV. The normal number eight, Jimmy Bennett, had been selected to play for the North Midlands. Although I had a good game I did not expect to be selected for the following week's match when Bennett returned but, to my surprise, I was in and he was out.

He was the under-manager of The Star, Worcester's top hotel, so I decided to pay him a visit to suggest that I withdraw. I was expecting quite a hostile reception, but he could not have been more courteous and would not hear of my withdrawal.

"What will you do?" I asked.

"I will tell them where to stick their rugby club," he replied with a grin. He did, and he never played for Worcester again. Like so many people I met in Worcester he became a friend and remained so until his death.

I also struck up a friendship with another back-row forward, Jeremy Richardson. Although he was a little younger than me, we became kindred spirits on and off the field. We both had small vans which we would push to the limit. One away game, in Cardiff, we were on our way home in Jeremy's van, having enjoyed the after-match celebrations, when we were pulled over by the police. We were concerned about Jeremy's intake of alcohol.

"Do you realise that you were exceeding the speed limit?" the officer asked Jeremy.

"Yes, officer," was his reply. "I was taking a run at this hill in front of us."

"What, for three miles?" the officer retorted, and he sent us on our way with a smile.

The Worcestershire and Herefordshire Rugby Football Union was part of the North Midlands Rugby Union and played at Minor County level. Both Jeremy and I were often selected to play for their county side, a proving ground for aspiring rugby players and a stepping stone to the full county side. I was getting some aggravation from the Worcestershire County Cricket Club about possible injury, but I was determined to become a full county rugby player.

My chance came when I was asked to play in the first trial match of the season, but I had a pulled hamstring and had to cry off. My disappointment was enormous but was soon quelled by an invitation to play for the Rest XV in the second trial. I had a reasonable game, but I was only selected as travelling reserve for the first game against Warwickshire in Coventry. Brian Wightman, the Moseley number eight, was the normal lock and he had played for England, so it was with some reluctance that I had to accept the fact that he would be selected before me. However, for some reason,

Wightman was unavailable, and I was told as I got on the team bus that I was playing. My joy was short-lived when I saw the Warwickshire pack I was up against: Phil Judd, Mike McLean, Bert Godwin, John Price, Tom Pargetter, John Owen, Stan Purdy and Peter Robbins – all but one were internationals. The fact that we lost and that I was black and blue all over did not matter a jot to me. I had played my first and, as it turned out, my last county rugby match.

Mike Smith, the England cricket captain, was an excellent rugby player. In fact, he played once for England, making him one of the very few dual internationals. I first watched him play rugby in a varsity match at Twickenham. He partnered the Welsh scrum-half Onllwyn Brace at half-back, and the ball passing was mesmeric. It was more like the Harlem Globetrotters playing basketball than a rugby match. I played rugby against him once when Worcester played at Hinckley, and I cannot remember ever laying a hand on him. At that time England's scrum half was Dickie Jeeps, whose style of play was orthodox, similar to Mike, which could have been why Mike had a limited rugby career. In my opinion it is better to have a pair with one orthodox and one unorthodox. Ironically, Onllwyn Brace's style was unorthodox, similar to that of Cliff Morgan; it was a pity that they could not have been transposed.

That game against Mike Smith was important to me because it was my rugby crossroads. The following day I travelled to Warrington to attend a rugby league trial. In those days the idea of a rugby union player having a trial with a rugby league club was a dastardly affront to the controllers of the union game. I had contacted George Duckworth, a former England wicket-keeper who was involved with the Warrington club, and requested a trial, and he obliged. When I got to Warrington I was given a pair of running spikes and was asked to warm up on a cinder track at the back of changing rooms. The coaches then matched me with a number of other players, mostly three-quarters, on 50-yard dashes. After extensive activity and some ball passing, I was asked into an office to discuss their offer. First, they told me that I would be playing on the wing, not something I had ever considered before; secondly, that I could not expect a signing-on fee, which did not impress me much; thirdly, what the match fee would be.

Jeremy Richardson, who had accompanied me on the trip, pressed me for my decision. We had spent the previous night sleeping in my Sunbeam Talbot, exhaust fumes and all, so I was not up to making a clear decision about my future.

The next day I was, and I did. I never played rugby football again.

12

Worcestershire's number five seamer

My life changed the moment I walked into the New Road ground in early April 1960. I had discarded the security of being surrounded by a safe job, great prospects and a future pension, for a job where I had to survive on my wits, my ability and the decisions of others. My new colleagues were all in the same boat, developing a wonderful atmosphere of apprehension which was infectious. No more sales talk and profit margins; more cricket, politics, sex and religion!

Playing cricket every day, either in the nets or on the field, gave me a focus on how I performed. I had an easy and comfortable run=up, but I always felt that something was lacking at the point of delivery. I used to watch other fast bowlers but could never find a difference between their action and mine, until I studied Fred Trueman. The newspapers used to publish photographs of fast bowlers' actions in a 20-frame display. It was apparent in Fred's display that, just before delivery, there appeared to be a pause where his body continued through the action but his bowling arm was held back. As his front shoulder went through and pulled down, it created a lot of tension on the bowling arm, the result of which was somewhat like a ruler being jammed into a desk to create a whiplash. By using this method he could generate more pace. I tried to copy it without success and decided, for fear of upsetting my current action, to put it on the back burner for a future date.

For the first time in my career I was being coached by a former Test cricketer. His name was Charles Hallows, a left-hand batsman who had played for Lancashire and England in the '20s and '30s, the only cricketer ever to score 1,000 runs in May. Now before you grab for your *Wisden*, let me explain. On 30 May 1928 Charlie – Mr Hallows, as I called him – had scored 768 runs, requiring 232 to reach the magic figure. He actually scored 232 and was out the next ball, the only man ever to score exactly 1,000 runs in May.

His knowledge of fast bowling was limited, but his advice on how a batsman would play against a left-arm-over bowler was invaluable. He maintained that a right-hand bat had to open himself up to face a left-arm-over bowler, and this action made him vulnerable to balls bowled across him. Geoff Boycott did not enjoy playing against that line; he was always checking the position of his stumps relative to the position of his feet.

Those early days as a young professional were the happiest working days of my life. I was playing the game I loved for a living, with people I respected and in some cases admired. The fact that the remuneration was poor was accepted and went with the territory. It is fair to say that Don Kenyon, the club captain at that time, was not over-enamoured of me, nor I with him. Somehow we just did not gel. I was a lad about town, a bit of a playboy, and he did not see that going well for my quick bowling. His personality and mine were like two poles that repel. But the rest of the squad were friendly and helpful, and I made a number of lifelong friends.

A typical Worcestershire first team in 1960 would be Don Kenyon, Martin Horton, Ron Headley, Dick Richardson, George Dews, Bob Broadbent, Roy Booth, Doug Slade, Len Coldwell, Jack Flavell and either John Aldridge or Derek Pearson. The second team was captained by Joe Lister, the Secretary, and would be picked from Laddie Outschoorn, Dick Devereux, John Sedgley, Alan Ormrod, Alan Spencer, Brian Spittle, Jim Standen, Trefor Davies, Peter Robinson, John Elliot, Norman Gifford and me.

As a seam bowler I was starting out in fifth place behind Flavell, Coldwell, Pearson and Aldridge.

During the season certain players swapped between the teams, particularly the younger ones who were given opportunities in the first team. My chance came on Saturday 25 June against Cambridge University at New Road, my first ever first-class match. Cambridge were put in to bat by Don Kenyon, and their openers were Tony Lewis, who would go on to captain England, and Roger Prideaux, who would also play for England and would work with me as the first Chairman of the Cricketers' Association.

Tony Lewis hit me to leg for two fours as a welcome to the first-class game. So I spreadeagled his stumps just to warn him what to expect in the future. With my first first-class wicket under my belt, I was ready to face the world.

The first county championship match came quicker than I expected, on the following Wednesday, when I was chosen as the third seamer after Jack Flavell and John Aldridge. We were playing Glamorgan at Stourbridge, and my first championship wicket came when I bowled Alan Jones for 72. Five more first-team matches followed that summer, including a first appearance at Lord's against Middlesex.

It was around this time that I bought my first drophead motor car, a Standard Eight coupé that was at least 20 years old and very close to its last legs. Not only was it a drophead, it had a dropped floor as well. It had been messing me around, starting, not starting, not firing on all plugs, that sort of thing. Not wanting it to leave me stranded, I took it to a repair garage and asked the engineer to solve my problem, mentioning the spark plugs. After a 15-minute inspection he came into the waiting room, carrying a plastic box. "You were right," he said. "It is a spark plug problem." He emptied the plastic box full of spark plugs onto a small table. "Take those, and go and find a decent engine to fit them!"

STARS OF THE FUTURE?

Don Kenyon, Worcestershire's captain (right), chats with four young men of whom the County have great hopes—Treffor Davies, Norman Gifford, Jim Standen and Fred Rumsey. All were promoted from the second XI for to-day's game with Cambridge University and for Rumsey it was his first appearance in a first-class match.

Worcestershire at Lord's, August 1960

Back: W Faithfull (scorer), RGA Headley, N Gifford (12th man),
LJ Coldwell, FE Rumsey, DW Richardson, DNF Slade, T Davies
Front: R Booth, MJ Horton, D Kenyon (captain), G Dews, JA Flavell

Eight of us played Test cricket: seven for England, one for the West Indies.

The winter was an opportunity to earn some additional income although jobs were not that easy to come by. In the three winters I spent in Worcester after I left Fownes, I had five different jobs. I sold and cleaned carpets – I used to sell broadloom and stitched body carpets, fitting them all over Worcester. Sometimes they were so comfortable I would fall asleep whilst fitting them, particularly when I was suffering from a late-night hangover. I was an assistant electrician – I made chandeliers out of cartwheels for Berni Inns. Their restaurants came with their own pre-stylised interiors with Tudor-looking false oak beams, white walls and, of course, my chandeliers. I was a builder's labourer – I helped construct a new telephone exchange in the centre of Worcester. I worked for Kay's mail order house – one of over 200 processors dealing with customers' postal orders, where for the only time in my life I had to clock in and out. We were allowed 15 minutes for a morning break in the company canteen. There were three sections with over seventy people in each and on the first day, seconds before the bell rang for my section's break, I got the shock of my life when there was the rasping sound of seventy chairs being pushed back. All seventy pairs of eyes must have been fixed on the clock. And, finally, I sold wool shoddy to the hop growers and plastic netting to the market gardeners – the wool shoddy provided the hop growers with organic fertiliser to augment the chemicals in the soil; the red and green plastic netting gave the sprouts and carrots a stronger and better colour.

All this made me a true 'Jack of all trades, master of none'. Apart from enjoying the rugby which I was still playing at that time, winter was a pain, and I could only look forward to April and a return to New Road.

13

The summer of 1961

The summer of 1961 heralded the arrival of the Australian touring team, captained by Richie Benaud. As was traditional at the time, the tourists played against Worcestershire in their opening game. It was too much for me to expect to be playing in the match, with the might of our opening bowling attack all available and fit. I did, however, have two important duties to perform: (1) car park attendant in an adjacent field to the ground, and (2) assistant twelfth man to the Australian team.

It was in this latter capacity that I met and became friendly with Bobby Simpson. Bobby had been playing at Test level for Australia for a few years and was a delightfully communicative sort of man. Although he was still to score a Test hundred, he had an enormous knowledge of the game and was prepared to impart it to a young English sprog. The batting details did not interest me too much, nor his leg spin, but his position on the field at first slip did. In the 1960s he was the number one slip catcher in world cricket. Phil Sharpe and Colin Cowdrey could run him close but he would catch five out of six, where they caught four out of five; anything above two out of three was good. He stressed the importance of being relaxed, even though concentrating hard, but more importantly the fielder must have soft hands.

"Let the ball come to you, never chase it," he would say. "Watch it from the bowler's hand at first slip and off the bat at second slip." I had reason to remember these lessons because, although I fielded third man and fine leg at that time, it was not always going to be the case.

Bobby Simpson catching David Allen in the Old Trafford Test that summer. Richie Benaud said it was one of the best catches he ever saw.

The session as a car park attendant in the farmer's field developed into more than I had bargained for. Apparently, the farmer had sprayed the field with insecticide, and it got into my blood stream via a small cut I had in the lower region of my left leg. I went to my local GP who gave me some pills and told me to rest it as much as I could. My nausea was too strong for that so I presented myself at the hospital and asked for Mr Dee, an orthopaedic surgeon whom I knew to be a Worcestershire member. He told me off for going direct, took one look at my leg and confined me to hospital for ten days whilst penicillin concentrated the poison into a small area of my shin. I was amused by the light-hearted bickering of the young, pretty nurses as to which of them would carry out my bed baths. Recently, at the age of 82 years, I was once again confined to a hospital bed, but this time the nurses threw the bowl of hot water onto the bedside cabinet and said, "Do it yourself!"

I was not allowed to stand up for the whole of this period and, once the surgeon was ready, he cut the poison out without a full anaesthetic. The process was simple: a leather tongue for me to bite down on, one heavy sand bag on my foot, one heavy sand bag above the cutting area, two delightful nurses spreadeagled over my lower regions and a firm two-handed hold on the iron rails of the headboard. As he cut into the leg, the iron rails of the headboard bent inwards. The operation was successful although I was told afterwards that, had they not treated it so quickly, there was a danger that the bone would have become infected. If that had happened, you would not be reading this book.

I was out of cricket until the end of May, and my first match back was an extremely pleasing occasion. Tom Graveney had had a falling out with Gloucestershire and, as a result, he had chosen to join Worcestershire. The outdated practice of a player needing special registration if he wanted to move from county to county was still going strong. It did not matter that both Worcestershire and Tom Graveney wanted him to play first-class cricket. A peeved Gloucestershire committee did not, and they were going to block it. I was certain that this was an illegal practice. I could not believe that a person could be stopped from earning a living in a profession that he was eminently qualified for. My first question would be: why allow him to play Second XI Championship cricket? What is the difference? Anyway, more about that subject later. First-class cricket's loss was my gain as I got the chance to play with one of the greatest English post-war batsmen, albeit in 2nd XI cricket.

I did well in the 2nd XI that summer, taking 37 wickets at the best average in the championship, but my step up to the 1st XI was not so successful, my four games bringing me just one wicket for 211 runs. The last of these games was against Yorkshire at Bradford. Fred Trueman was playing, a man I had admired for years. He was not many years older than me, but he appeared to have been on the cricket scene for ever. He had just bowled Jim Standen and I had to walk past Fred on my way to the wicket. As I got level he said, "Eh up, youngster, what's like coming in ont' middle of hat trick?" It nearly was, too. One run later Brian Close got me out, caught by Sharpe in the slips.

Jim Standen joined Worcestershire at about the same time as I did. He was one of those rare people who played professional football as well as professional cricket – a goalkeeper who started his career with Arsenal, moved to Luton and then on to West Ham where he won an FA Cup medal in 1964. This was followed by another winners' medal in the European Cup Winners' Cup Final in 1965.

At the beginning of the 1961 season he suggested that we should find digs together. We hunted around and settled on living with an elderly couple who operated a successful faggot-and-peas shop in the centre of Worcester. They lived very comfortably above the premises, and our landlady was a fabulous cook. After about a couple of months of her culinary delights, I asked Jim if he liked faggot and peas. "I love them," he replied. "So do I," I said. "I wonder why our landlady does not serve them to us." Within minutes of our discussion she called up to ask if we had a preference for dinner. "Faggot and peas," we both shouted down. Her reply was quick and terse. "There is no way that I'll serve that muck to you two!"

I first came into contact with the Lord's Taverners charity during the 1961 season. Some of the junior staff were asked if they would help fill the Taverners side in a match to be played at New Road. I had no cricket to play on that particular Sunday so I made myself available. Among the show-business celebrities was David Frost, who was quite a good wicket-keeper and very chatty with me at first slip. I suppose he had a great bearing on my future activity with the Taverners, and we remained friends until his death.

I did not play cricket in the Birmingham League, unlike most of the junior staff at Worcetershire, but played some games for Worcester City and others for a village team called The Fox. Mike Jones introduced me to The Fox Inn at Bransford, a typical country pub which satisfied the alcoholic needs of the local population, in this case mostly farmers. Sunday lunch was the popular time to drink at The Fox, and folks would travel from all over the area. However, in the summer, Sunday lunchtime drinking was somewhat curtailed for a number of regulars because The Fox played cricket on that day. A farmer had provided the field, the groundsman at New Road had prepared the wicket, and the old professionals' changing room from the County Ground doubled up as the pavilion. One of the leading lights behind the scenes was Gaffer Jay, a delightful man with a son and three gorgeous daughters. He and one other used to keep the ground in good order. How they talked me into becoming their unpaid professional I will never know, but they did and I had more fun with them than I did at any other time in the whole of my cricket career – they really were nuts.

They were hop farmers mostly, and at hop picking they would work long and late. One match at The Fox was in the middle of harvesting, and a hop farmer George Holloway, a larger-than-life character, had spent over 24 hours awake. We lost the toss and were fielding. At the fall of the first wicket George, who was fielding in the covers, lay down on the ground, stretched out and went to sleep. We played the whole of the innings around him, had tea, started batting, with the opposition also playing around him, and were five down before he finally woke up. With a sheepish grin he returned to the changing room, put on his batting pads, plonked himself into a deck chair and promptly went to sleep again.

This arrangement with The Fox gave me some activity on a Sunday when I was not at the beck and call of the county. With first-class cricket not played in any form on a Sunday, county beneficiaries would play matches to boost their benefit funds. One such game was played at The Fox. A star-studded side, including Tom Graveney, turned out to support Bob Broadbent. I played for Bob and not for The Fox, much to their consternation. In this type of cricket it was traditional for the beneficiary's team to field first. A batsman hit a skier, and I went flat out for the catch, not knowing that Dick Richardson was also going for it. The top of Dick's head hit me squarely on the nose and cheek bone, breaking both. Tom Graveney took me to hospital, and for the second time that season I was confined to a hospital bed for a week. I got a nice note from the Fox team wishing me well, ending with a PS: 'God pays debts without money!'

Whether it was because of my life style, the fact that I was injury prone or just not good enough to be a professional cricketer, Worcestershire decided not to renew my contract at the end of the 1961 season. Joe Lister, the club's Secretary and 2nd XI captain, publicly stated that I would not make an opening bowler in a month of Sundays, or something to that effect.

I had burned my bridges with Fownes Gloves, so there was no going back there.

14

Crucial advice from Roy Tattersall

The problem with writing an autobiography is the number of occasions it is necessary to write about oneself. Even the most egotistically outgoing of people must find it a pain. I know that I do.

Having made that point, I feel that in the next few paragraphs I must give you some idea of how I felt when I received news of my dismissal. It is true I had played first-class cricket, 11 matches in all, and I had played one county rugby match. The rugby was not so much of a problem, but I felt I still had something to offer cricket and my desire to play had not been sated. I decided to write to all the first-class counties, with the exception of Yorkshire (you had to be born there to play for them), in the hope that one of them would take me on their staff. I cannot remember getting a single reply. If I did, it was an emphatic no. A deep depression began to envelop me, and I found it difficult to rationalise my thinking. For some reason I turned to writing poetry.

My mood was dark:

A Troubled Mind

I want not God nor Mother dear
To expiate my blame.
It is in living not in birth
That I have cause to shame.

Far brighter burn the fires in hell
With evil acts of fun.
More fuel for the raging furnace
Are good deeds never done.

I am my own true champion
Who wants I wear a crown.
I am my devil's advocate
Who wants to pull me down.

A dozen faces all of mine
Cry out in single voice
Guilty, guilty, guilty, My Lord
We have no other choice.

The cap is black and raised on high
Beneath the wig my face.
The cap is down I hear no sound
And now this evil place.

FER

During this phase I had an occasion to be on the Severn Bridge in Worcester, watching the swollen river flow beneath the supports. A lorry was passing slowly behind me, and the diver shouted from his cab. "I wouldn't do it, mate, if I were you. Whoever she is, she isn't worth it." The jibe seemed to jolt me out of a dream. Although he was not correct in his assumption, he was certainly right in his philosophy.

I approached the problem from a different angle and decided to remain in cricket but at a lower level. I contacted a number of league clubs who, I thought, might like a young quick bowler on their books. This time I got more than one reply. I decided to accept an offer from Kidderminster, a neighbour of Worcester and in fact a ground which the county used for first-class matches. Kidderminster played in the Birmingham League, one of the strongest leagues in the country, and were normally one of the contenders for the title. Once the announcement that I had joined Kidderminster appeared in the local newspapers I was contacted by Worcestershire and asked if I would continue to play Second XI cricket for them on an ad hoc fee of £5 a match. I saw it as a way back into the game and accepted immediately.

One of my duties at Kidderminster was to provide the team with coaching. Most of the players would attend at some time or other, but work often played havoc with their attendance. One regular attendee was the previous professional, Roy Tattersall, but there was very little I could teach him as he had played as an off-spinner for Lancashire between 1948 and 1960 as well as 16 times for England. In fact, he would have played a lot more for England, had Jim Laker not been around at the same time.

As it turned out, however, there was a lot he could teach me. In his early days he had been a medium-fast bowler, and he was also a great pal of Brian Statham, Fred Trueman's England partner in the fifties and sixties. Apparently he and Statham spent hours together discussing the complex theory of fast and spin bowling. He was not one who just turned up and played his cricket; he watched and absorbed the game.

At the beginning of the first net session of the season Roy asked me if he could continue the coaching of a few young players he had taken under his wing during the previous season. I, of course, agreed, and we became quite a good team, he providing the spin, me the pace. Early on in this partnership Roy was standing behind me. I thought he was watching the batsman. When he asked me why I did not bowl in-swing, I could not answer because I did not know.

"I have never bowled swing," I replied.

"Well, you should with your side-on action," he said. "Show me how you hold the ball." I did, and he laughed. "You'll never swing the ball holding it that far into your palm. It's as if you don't want to let it go. Hold it at the end of your fingers as loosely as you can, with your thumb underneath."

"It will fall out," I said.

"Have a go," he replied.

He took the ball from me and worked a shine on one side, using perspiration and the flannel of his trousers. "Right, hold the ball with the shiny side on the outside. With your action and being left-handed, you should swing the ball in."

I ran in with the ball almost slipping out of my fingers, bowled the normal line and the ball ended up at the back of the net in roughly where third leg slip would be. I could not believe it. I had been bowling in Second XI cricket for three years and had never swung the ball, not even the new ball.

We continued to practise, and my line improved. I started to aim at second slip, which enabled me to get the right line. Why no one had told me this before, I will never know, but it was the turning point of my cricket career and I was delighted.

The theory of Trueman's action to generate more pace had to wait further whilst I carefully honed my new-found ability. All I could say to Roy Tattersall was "Thank you, from the bottom of my heart." Working with him for a whole season proved to me that England had missed a great opportunity by not engaging him in some form of national coaching position.

Although I had a newly found weapon, I had another issue to contend with. That summer the no-ball law was changed from one based on the position of the back foot to one on the front foot. This was the administrators' answer to the problem of dragging, where bowlers adhered to the back-foot regulation but in some cases landed their front foot as much as two feet over the batting crease. As it is only possible to bowl over the front foot, it made the fast bowler that much closer to the poor suffering batsman. Like all the draggers, I had great difficulty adapting to this new rule. It took years rather than months for me to become comfortable with this restriction. I had to develop a new run-up, and from 37 paces that was not easy.

Do not believe any pundit who tells you that it is possible to bowl just as quickly off a short run as it is off a long run. The long run is required to get the bowler to the bowling crease at the correct pace and balance to bowl at his fastest. I was still uncomfortable with the no-ball law when I was picked for my first Test match at Old Trafford two summers later. I asked Syd Buller, one of the umpires, if he would let me know if my front foot was getting close to going over the line. "Yes," he said. "I'll call 'No Ball'."

The season started well for Kidderminster, who won four of their first six games, as did Worcestershire Second XI, so both my teams were doing well. I did not realise how nit-picking league cricket could be until I played in a match against West Bromwich Dartmouth at our home ground. I was running a temperature and feeling unwell so I left the field for about an hour. When I returned and took my sweater off to bowl, the visiting captain, Ron Williams, protested to the umpires on the grounds that I had been resting and was fresh. The umpires consulted and agreed that I could not bowl. Later my captain, Peter Heard, asked again for me to bowl and was refused. At that time the laws of cricket clearly stated: 'A player may bat, bowl or field, even though a substitute has acted for him previously.' The protest did West Bromwich Dartmouth no good, though, as they lost the match by eight wickets.

Kidderminster, Birmingham League champions in 1962
back: Roy Tattersall, David Bennett, Mike Evers, Fred Rumsey, Ken Harding, John Elliott
front: Trevor Larkham, Peter Harris, Peter Heard, Tony Smith, Paul Booton

I enjoyed playing for Kidderminster. Every player in the side had played Second XI county cricket and four of us had played in the first-class game, one of whom was a former Test player. Kidderminster's wicket-keeper, John Elliott, was on the staff at Worcestershire and was understudy to Roy Booth, the regular first-team keeper, for years. In fact, his loyalty to the club went further than that when he took on the chairmanship in later life.

One of my winter jobs while I was on the staff at Worcester had been selling and cleaning carpets for a man, Tom Winwood, who had played for Worcestershire in the 1930s. Having learned all about carpets from him, I decided to hire an empty shop and set up on my own, selling by day and cleaning carpets in pubs and hotels by night.

For a while, when I had nowhere to live, I was sleeping in the back of my van, which I had made comfortable by fitting a carpet. I did not care that I had no home. I was young, I was fit, and I was saving money. When I was on the staff at Worcester, I often used to park at the back of the pavilion at the ground so I would be on hand for the morning.

Sometimes, when I was in the van, I would have company for the night. On one occasion, however, the two of us could not use the back of the van as I was carrying my carpet-cleaning machine, a great thing called a Columbus Dixon with rotating brush heads and a tank full of cleaner. So we decided to spend the night under the covers of the cricket square. Unfortunately one of the groundsmen spotted us, and it may have been this that led to my receiving a lecture from Charles Hallows. As a coach he may not have taught me anything about fast bowling, but he was a gentleman, a man you could respect.

We were playing Northamptonshire 2nd XI at Northampton. Before the game started, he asked me to walk around the ground for a quiet chat.

"It's been brought to my attention," he said, "that you spend too much time with ladies."

"Yes, Mr Hallows," I said.

"I've also heard that you like a drink or two."

"Yes, Mr Hallows."

Then he started on about my van in the car park.

"The committee have got to hear about your activities, and I have been asked to speak to you."

All round the ground he gave me chapter and verse about how a playboy image would affect my future playing career. Then, when we got back to the pavilion, he said, "All right, you can go now."

I went to walk up the steps, well and truly chastised, then he quietly called me back. He put his arm around my shoulder and whispered in my ear. "Youngster, I do hope you have understood what I have been saying to you."

I said, "Yes, Mr Hallows."

He said, "I am not asking you to give it all up. I am just asking you to talk less about it."

I played ten Second XI Championship matches for Worcestershire in 1962, which helped to keep me in trim form. This fact, together with my new-found ability to swing the ball, inspired the county to show fresh interest in me. In early July Jack Flavell severed his Achilles tendon and was out for the season; he ended up getting a job as a milkman to help improve his walking. Then Len Coldwell twisted his ankle and, with Worcestershire pushing for their first-ever championship title, they asked Kidderminster to release me. Kidderminster were pushing for their own title and they were not keen, but finally they agreed that I could play – but only in mid-week fixtures.

My first game back was at Gloucester, starting on Wednesday 18 July. Although we lost the match, I managed to notch up seven wickets, including five for 37 in the first innings. Talk had started, in the dressing room and the press, about me returning to the Worcestershire staff. So, thanks to Roy Tattersall, my gamble was paying off.

Len Coldwell returned from injury, and it was four weeks before my second chance came. This time Len Coldwell was selected to play for England so I was called up to play against Derbyshire at Chesterfield. By now I was beginning to take control of the swinging ball. I was much more confident about holding the ball with my finger tips which, by the way, I did not do all the time.

John Aldridge, Derek Pearson and I had all left Worcestershire, and that summer the county recruited Bob Carter from Warwickshire as its back-up to Flavell and Coldwell.

Outside of Test matches the game at Chesterfield was the most important of my career. Derbyshire ended a rain-affected first day on 88 for one, with Jim Standen taking the only wicket. On the second day Derbyshire declared at lunchtime at 172 for nine: Carter four for 80 off 29 overs, Rumsey four for 46 off 26. Don Kenyon declared Worcestershire's innings closed at 212 for four, and at close of play Derbyshire were 18 for no wicket.

The fireworks started on the third day. Derbyshire were bowled out for 150: Carter two for 56 off 22 overs, Rumsey seven for 50 off 23 overs. At one stage I had four wickets for two runs. Worcestershire, needing to score 111 in 125 minutes, finished on 103 for nine, eight runs short. One more victory that summer would have put us above Yorkshire as county champions – so those eight runs turned out to be crucial, as did the failure to beat Leicestershire in the next game, starting on the Saturday. Len Coldwell was still away with England but, when Worcestershire asked Kidderminster for my services, they got an emphatic no, not under any circumstances. Kidderminster were narrowly leading the Birmingham League's top division with only two games to go. There was no way they would release their only professional, and no one would expect them to.

The season ended with Worcestershire as runners-up in the championship, the county's highest ever position. The Second XI won its championship, and Kidderminster won the Birmingham League. Quite a successful season, especially for me, as in my two first-class games I had taken 18 wickets for 170 runs. I was almost certain that the county would recall me on a more permanent basis.

As expected and after a lot of media pressure, Worcestershire decided to offer me a contract to rejoin them. I asked for a meeting with Joe Lister, the Secretary, who had been one of the group who had fired me. I was way past any aggravated thinking, I was just pleased to have the chance to get back into the sport.

SCORE CARD PRICE 4d.   Toss won by DERBYSHIRE

This Card does not necessarily include the fall of the last wicket

DERBYSHIRE v. WORCESTERSHIRE

Queens Park, Chesterfield Aug. 15th, 16th, 17th, 1962

Hours of Play—   Lunch—1.30 p.m.

First Day 11.30 to 7.0   Second Day 11.30 to 7.0   Third Day 11.0 to 4.30 or 5.0

Scorers—T G Ryde and W Faithfull

DERBYSHIRE	First Innings		Second Innings	
1 Lee C	b Standen	22	b Rumsey	31
2 Hall I	c Broadbent b Carter	40	c Booth b Rumsey	18
3 Johnson H L	b Rumsey	24	c and b Rumsey	5
4 Oates W F	c Booth b Rumsey	5	b Rumsey	13
5† D B Carr	lbw b Rumsey	7	c Graveney b Carter	2
6 Morgan D C	c Kenyon b Carter	37	c Broadbent b Gifford	30
7 Buxton I R	b Rumsey	7	lbw b Carter	29
8 Smith E	b Carter	13	b Rumsey	2
9‡ Taylor R W	c Slade b Carter	2	c Booth b Rumsey	1
10 Rhodes H J	not out	3	not out	4
11 Jackson H L	not out	2	b Rumsey	10
Extras—b-4 lb-5 w- nb1		10	b-2 lb-3 w- nb-	5

Umpires—Oldfield N and Parks J H

Average runs per over 2.38 9 wkts dec. Total 172   Total 150

Fall of Wickets—1st Innings   2nd Innings

1	2	3	4	5	6	7	8	9	10	1	2	3	4	5	6	7	8	9	10
56	89	99	105	120	138	164	167	168		48	53	54	71	71	127	133	133	136	150

Bowling Analysis—	O	M	R	W	O	M	R	W
Carter	29	4	80	4	22	6	56	2
Rumsey	26	7	46	4	23	10	50	7
Horten	4	2	8	0	..	..	..	..
Gifford	4	3	2	0	4	4	0	1
Standen	9	3	26	1	10	2	24	0
Slade	..	..	..	..	11	7	15	0

WORCESTER	First Innings		Second Innings	
1† Kenyon D	b Jackson	26	b Rhodes	2
2 Horton M J	c and b Morgan	24	c Rhodes b Buxton	7
3 Richardson D W	c Lee b Morgan	89	b Buxton	0
4 Graveney T W	c Jackson b Smith	33	lbw b Rhodes	20
5 Broadbent R G	not out	23	lbw b Rhodes	22
6‡ Booth R	not out	8	lbw b Rhodes	24
7 Slade D N F			c Taylor b Rhodes	0
8 Standen J			c Smith b Morgan	10
9 Rumsey F			b Rhodes	4
10 Gifford N			not out	10
11 Carter R G M			not out	1
Extras —b-2 lb-7 w- nb-		9	b- lb-3 w- nb-	3

† Captain   ‡ Wicket-keeper

Average runs per over 2.80 4 wkts dec. Total 212   Total 103

Fall of Wickets—1st Innings   2nd Innings

1	2	3	4	5	6	7	8	9	10	1	2	3	4	5	6	7	8	9	10
40	73	157	202							8	8	10	33	69	69	84	92	92	

Bowling Analysis—	O	M	R	W	O	M	R	W
Jackson	18	4	57	1	..	..	..	..
Rhodes	21	8	39	0	17	4	30	6
Buxton	5	1	14	0	15	7	41	2
Morgan	17	8	59	2	5	1	15	1
Lee	4	1	7	0	3	1	14	0
Smith	8	1	27	1	..	..	..	..
	..	..	..	..	..	..	..	..

Worcestershire Second XI, champions in 1962
back: A. Ross-Slater (scorer), John Elliott, Winston Davis, Fred Rumsey, Michael Downs, Peter Robinson, Ken Arch, Ted Hemsley, Charles Hallows (coach)   front: Roy Tattersall, Bob Carter, Dick Devereux, Joe Lister (captain), Doug Slade, Duncan Fearnley, Alan Ormrod

Joe Lister presented the contract offer and, much to his surprise, I presented my own conditions. I pointed out that I would be 27 by the time the season came around and that it would be pointless spending another year playing Second XI cricket purely as a back-up player. I must be guaranteed a number of matches in the first team to help me develop and to enable the Worcestershire selectors to assess my worth correctly. He did not think that the club would accept my terms but said that he would put them to the committee and come back to me.

I did not hear anything for a couple of weeks but, in the meantime, I had been contacted by Harold Stephenson, the Somerset captain, who asked if I would consider joining his county. I put the same conditions to him, and he could not see a problem with them. He told me that he would be in touch.

Worcestershire then contacted me, confirming that the committee was not prepared to accept my conditions but that the offer of a contract was still open. I turned it down. Two months later I still had not heard from Harold Stephenson and was becoming concerned for I had no other irons in the fire. I took it upon myself to try to contact Harold and phoned the Somerset office, only to be told that he was away on holiday and could he, Richard Robinson the Secretary, help. After I had explained to him Harold's chat with me, he suggested that I should travel down to Taunton with some gear for a run-out in the indoor school.

When I arrived Richard Robinson said, "I vaguely remember Steve telling me something about this," which at the time seemed very laid back to me. I did my stint in the indoor school and reported to his office.

"I understand that you have some conditions relative to joining us. I do hope that they are not too dictatorial," he asked. After I had explained them to him he said, "In principle we can accept those, but you must give us the opportunity to drop you if you perform badly." We shook hands on that and I was offered a three-year contract there and then, to commence in April.

*

I had spent almost five years living in and about Worcester. My abodes were many and varied – twelve in all. I began living in a flat on The Cross, slap bang in the middle of town. The apartment was above Foster Bros, the outfitting chain, and Bruce Langstone, Foster's manager, was my landlord. He was an old friend of Mike Jones and an air gunner during World War Two. The cramped turret and cold conditions that he had been subjected to every flight left him with severe arthritis and considerable pain. He grumbled little and was a man of few words, but so too were a lot of his comrades. They sacrificed a great deal for our way of life and should never be forgotten.

Of my other accommodation, suffice it to say that some were hotels, some were rooms and some living with families. John Aldridge, one of my pals on the staff at Worcestershire, invited me to dinner one evening. His then wife, having provided me with a marvellous meal, asked me where I was living. "In my van," I replied. Six months later I left their lovely home.

I lived in half a farm house at one stage. It was very lonely living on my own in the countryside so I had many visitors. One Sunday I decided to cook a lunch for a young lady. My cooking capabilities were very limited – frozen runner beans topped with two fried eggs, egg on cheese on ham on toast, that sort of thing. A Sunday roast was way outside my range so I decided to phone my mother. Twenty telephone calls later, I was the proud presenter of roast chicken stuffed with sage and onion, roast potatoes and parsnips, peas and sprouts. My credibility soared with the lady so I decided to learn more about the art of cooking. I enrolled for a correspondence course in cordon bleu cooking, which culminated in a week at a local technical college to take the exam. Somewhere in one of my many abodes rests a cordon bleu certificate with my name on it.

My penultimate place of residence was the Great Western Hotel, adjacent to Shrub Hill Station. The manager there was far-seeing enough to do a deal with me for the cost of my winter board and lodgings. At my own cost I was to refurbish my room by putting in some complicated electrical wiring, carpeting, wallpapering and decorating throughout. I finished the job in early January when I was suffering from the beginning of one of the coldest winters on record in the United Kingdom. Temperatures plummeted and lakes, canals and rivers began to freeze over. The winter of 1962/63 was called the Big Freeze and, believe me, it was.

I had made friends with a charming and delightful young lady called Alison Westwood, who was at the beginning of a great career in show jumping. You may know her better as Alison Dawes, who had fantastic success with The Maverick. She won over 100 international show-jumping titles and represented Great Britain at the Olympics. In 1962 she rode a mare called Catriona to success in the *Daily Telegraph* Cup. For exercise Alison would let me ride Catriona, and the horse actually developed a crush on me!

Jean Shepherd, Alison's mother, heard that I was living in a hotel near the railway station and insisted that I live with them as a guest at Priors Court, a 17th century house between Tewkesbury and Ledbury. I had stayed at the house on a number of occasions and had heard a lot about it being haunted. My last visit had been on New Year's Eve

Priors Court

when, wearing only a big bath towel and a large safety pin, I had entered the party room at midnight.

Jean's second husband, who had passed away, had noticed something strange about the structure of the house – that the distance between two bedrooms outside the house was at least twelve feet more than the distance inside. He hired a builder to knock through a wall in one of the bedrooms; inside was a room occupied by a chair and the skeleton of a cavalier with his regalia.

The house is reputed to have four ghosts: a woman who was murdered whilst sheltering from a storm, the cavalier, a girl who walks from the courtyard to the orchard and a strange-shaped entity which manifests itself in one of the bedrooms. The Bishop of Worcester has exorcised the place, and skeletons of an old man, a woman and two children were found behind oak panelling. Although there were some strange goings on while I was living in the house, nothing ever threatened, frightened or harmed me.

Jean Shepherd was the driving force behind a pump company based in Birmingham. The Sixties were still sensitive about women holding the reins of industrial businesses, and Jean was aware of this. At any social or business functions she instigated, she asked me to be the upfront host. She would give me the wherewithal to pay all the bills, and I would appear to be the organiser. It was a very pleasing arrangement which provided me with some wonderful nights out, like the Horse and Hound Ball at Grosvenor House.

I felt the wrench when the time came for me to leave Worcester and travel to Taunton. I had enjoyed my time with Worcestershire and would miss quite a number of the players. Most of the younger staff were pals like John Elliott, who went on to become Chairman; Duncan Fearnley, who became a successful bat-maker and also Chairman; Alan Ormrod, who coached Lancashire; Alan Spencer, who had the talent to do so much more; Ron Headley, who played for the West Indies; Norman Gifford, who played for England; Tom Graveney, who would play for England again; Jim Standen and Brian Spittle, who succeeded with their football careers; Peter Robinson, of whom I would see a lot when he too joined Somerset; Dick Richardson, who had played for England and enjoyed life so much; John Aldridge, to whom the game was unfair; Martin Horton, who played for England and was one of the nicest men I ever met; Roy Booth, unlucky not to have played for England; and John Sedgley, who had so much to offer. I knew I would see them all again but not in the same context. I would now be a member of the opposition with an axe to grind.

SOMERSET & ENGLAND

My first day at Taunton

Peter Wight, Fred Rumsey, Haydn Sully, Mervyn Kitchen, Ken Palmer, Peter Eele, Chris Greetham

15

First summer with Somerset

In early April 1963 I reported for net practice and training at the Taunton County Ground, in the centre of the glorious country market town.

The emblem for Somerset is a rampant griffin, and that is just as I felt – raring to go. However, all that enthusiasm was well and truly knocked out of me when I developed a nagging boil-like growth at the base of my spine. I did not want to report sick having only just arrived, but the pain grew worse until it was quite excruciating.

The club doctor referred me to the local hospital who diagnosed the growth as a pilonidal sinus, a small cyst or abscess that occurs in the cleft at the top of the buttocks. Infected pilonidal cysts can become very inflamed, causing a lot of pain. The surgeon can open and drain the poison or operate to remove the entire structure. The physician prescribed the latter, to try to prevent a recurrence at a later date, and I was committed to hospital for the third time in a couple of years. I had thought that my luck was turning with the signing of a three-year contract with Somerset – and now this! I had not been in Taunton a week and here I was, in hospital, awaiting surgery.

The operation was a success, but it left a hole in the base of my spine about as big as half a man's thumb. It was packed with cotton waste, and a large cotton pad was placed on the top. I was told to keep the wound clean and was discharged from hospital with an armful of bandages. I had only been inside for two days, but what surprised me more was that the surgeon allowed me to return to training on the understanding that I changed the dressing after each session.

The club did not retain a masseur or any medical staff whatsoever. I could not change the dressing myself for obvious reasons, so what to do? The problem was solved by my new opening bowling partner Ken Palmer. He loved the idea of removing the waste cotton, cleaning the wound and packing the gauze back into the hole. It appealed to his caring nature! It was the beginning of a great partnership which lasted for six years. I am pleased to say that the sinus has not returned to this day. The hospital and Kenny Palmer did their respective jobs impeccably.

Between the dressings I trained hard and got myself ready for the start of the season. During this period I had the chance to practise slip catching and to develop my theory on Fred Trueman's action.

As Bobby Simpson had told me, a successful slip fielder has to have soft hands. You have to allow the ball to come to you and not for you to go for it, but how should you practise that to effect? The catching cradle is a torture machine and should only be found in the Chamber of Horrors basement at Madame Tussauds. There was more likelihood of a broken finger from that than an improvement in catching ability. Suddenly I got a light in the cloud above my head; a tennis ball was the answer. If a tennis ball is hit hard enough at you from close range, it is necessary for you to allow the ball into your palm in order to catch it. I got hold of a tennis racquet and tennis ball and set to. I was still practising that method of catching up to the time I retired. On one occasion I went to a party in Yorkshire; Phil Sharpe was there and, as you know, I rated him the best slip fielder in England at that time. For a game we started to throw blood oranges at each other to see who would be the first to drop one. It was necessary to follow the line of the orange and catch it about three feet behind your body. It was a good job we caught them all because, otherwise, there would have been a hell of a mess.

Copying Fred Trueman's action was a much greater problem to solve. Somehow I had to allow the front of my body, the side nearer to the batsman, to go through without bringing the bowling arm into action. It was an understatement to say it was difficult. I got aches and pains in different parts of my body, in places I did not even know existed. I was practising in a net on my own; I could not subject a batsman to deliveries that even I had no idea as to where they were going. Then that magic light in the cloud above my head came back again. The best way to develop this new action was initially to bowl short bumpers and work upwards towards a length. I would hold the action for as long as I could whilst my body was going forward and then bring the bowling arm over with all the force I could muster. Eureka! It worked. It took some weeks before I felt comfortable enough to use it in competitive matches, but I had achieved a result and began to bowl at least a yard quicker. Thank you, FS.

The first match of the season was a friendly against Glamorgan. Because my wound had not fully recovered, I was asked to bowl only a few overs and spent most of the match umpiring, something I had never done before. Finally I was declared fit, even though there was still a small hole at the base of my spine, and I was selected for Somerset's first championship match of the season, on 1 May 1963, against Kent at the County Ground, Taunton.

For the first time in my life I was going to be playing first-class cricket without worrying about team selection for the next match. It is not ideal for any sportsman or sportswoman to be worrying about keeping his or her place in the team. For talent to reach its zenith it must be free from concern, something English Test and county cricket selectors should have uppermost in their minds.

Somerset at The Oval, 1963

back: Tommy Tout (scorer), Roy Virgin, Brian Roe, Fred Rumsey, Geoff Hall, Roy Kerslake, Ken Palmer   front: Chris Greetham, Peter Wight, Harold Stephenson (captain), Brian Langford, Graham Atkinson   (Bill Alley was absent)

The Kent match was uneventful, but the second game at Trent Bridge was a different kettle of fish. Nottinghamshire elected to bat, my first over was unremarkable but Kenny Palmer was hit for 18 runs off his first five balls. For some reason he was uncomfortable and asked the captain and me if he could change ends. We both agreed, although I was a little reluctant as the opening bowler usually has choice of ends.

Well, mayhem hit Nottinghamshire. Kenny wrecked their batting with a spell of eight wickets for 28 runs before the rain came to give the batsmen some respite. On returning, he took wicket number nine and, with Bomber Wells now batting, he looked en route for a ten-wicket haul. I was bowling at Bomber with the deliberate intent of not getting him out, but the wider I bowled the further Bomber reached for it until with a despairing lunge he finally made contact and the ball went through to our wicket-keeping captain, Harold Stephenson, who caught it. There was complete silence for a few seconds, then in hardly a whisper Harold appealed. Bomber was given out, and Kenny had missed taking the magic ten-wicket haul. There was some consolation for him; he had taken nine for 57, a career best. The consolation for Harold Stephenson was that Bomber was his 1,000th career victim.

Kenny was a good new-ball partner for me; we complemented each other. I don't know what speed I bowled – somebody studied some frames of film and calculated that it was 93 miles per hour – and Kenny, who was not tall, was a fair bit slower than that, maybe 80 miles per hour. But he was one of the best seam bowlers in England; he was very accurate and he did a lot with the ball. We made a good pair because I was left-arm and swung the ball in, where he was right-arm and moved it away. In one of my early games for Somerset, at Old Trafford, we bowled Lancashire out for 62, and Kenny took seven wickets for 36 runs. I was fielding in the slips to him so I had a good view of his bowling; he was coming over the wicket, pitching the ball on leg stump and hitting the top of off. Before our innings started, the groundsman took me out to look at the marks on the pitch. There was an area on a length, no bigger than a sheet of newspaper, where all Kenny's balls had pitched.

The West Indies touring side visited Somerset at the end of May. The team was captained by one of the great Three Ws, Frank Worrell. Frank was a delightful man to know as was another Barbados all-rounder, Garfield Sobers. They beat us easily by an innings, but I remember being struck by the friendliness of the whole team, including Charlie Griffith, who had the reputation of being a little of a rabble-rouser. Garry scored a hundred with seemingly little effort, opened the bowling with Charlie and took a catch; otherwise he did not do too much.

In June we played Yorkshire at Harrogate. The match was not much to talk about because we lost by an innings and 39 runs. Bill Alley and I went for a quiet drink after the close of the second day. Somehow we ended up in a nightclub in York where we met a couple of young actors, Ian McShane and John Hurt. Both were keen on cricket, and we spent a pleasant half an hour discussing the merits of the game. During the conversation I was flicking over beer mats from the edge of the table and catching them before they grounded. Ian McShane was particularly fascinated.

"How many of those do you think you could catch?" he asked.

"I've no idea," I replied.

"Let's have a challenge," he said and, before I could answer, he had grabbed the beer mats and was flicking and catching. It seems hard to believe now, but we both caught a pile of over forty beer mats until he crashed out at 42, leaving me the champion. I never met Ian again, but John Hurt and I played some Taverners cricket together.

We had made a good start to the season. When Yorkshire came to Taunton the following week, it was a bit of a table-top battle. They were in first place, and we were third. We declared with a first innings lead of 49 and, when they batted again, we had them 118 for five. At this point Fred Trueman came in to join Geoff Boycott and batted for an hour, scoring 13 runs. Harold Stephenson, who had been sensing a victory, told me to shake Fred up a little.

"Have you heard of the fast bowlers' union?" I asked him.

"He's a batsman today," said Harold. "Let him have a couple of bouncers."

I obliged, and all hell let loose. "Do you want to blankety blank die?" said Trueman. "Have you got a death wish or just lost your mind?" he ranted on.

I ignored his tantrums but decided to bowl no more bouncers. However, the next ball was a foot or two short, he turned his back on it and it hit him right at the base of the spine at the top of the buttocks. He threw his bat away in anger, and I learned all about my parents, my mother, family and friends.

Although we had shaken the situation up, Trueman went on to make 42 before I caught him, in the slips, off David Doughty. Boycott batted on and, by the time we finally bowled them out, there was less than an hour to play. Back in the dressing room I was receiving congratulations from the long-suffering batsmen who had often been roughed up by Freddie when the skipper said, "Put the pads on, Rumsey, you are opening the batting."

There was a ghastly silence until Brian Langford, our number ten batsman and off-spinner, started laughing.

"Put your pads on, too, Langford," said the captain. Brian stopped laughing immediately and went a pale shade of yellow.

The two of us nervously followed the Yorkshire team out to the middle. Fred had already paced out his run-up and was standing at the end of it, tossing the new ball up and down, with a menacing glare on his face.

When we reached the wickets Brian Close called out to Fred, "Give me the ball, Fred, and go down to third man."

If the proverbial look could kill, Close would have died on the spot. With a great deal of reluctance and grumbling Fred trudged off to third man. Brian Close tossed the ball to Jackie Hampshire, and the look of relief on Brian Langford's face was a sight to behold. I cannot say that I was unhappy about the situation, either. Doug Padgett was the other opening bowler – a batsman who had been playing for Yorkshire since 1951. After hitting him for one boundary, I became his first victim in county championship cricket.

The following match of the 1963 season was unusual. It was against the Pakistan Eaglets, a touring team of current and potential Test cricketers, all but two of whom went on to full honours. The team included three of the famous Mohammad brothers: Mushtaq, Wazir and Sadiq. Only Hanif was missing – and, if it was not enough for all four brothers of a family to represent their country, they added Shoaib, the son of Hanif, at a later date.

The match was drawn, but interestingly Somerset included a bowler, Vincent Lindo, who had left Nottinghamshire after playing only one first-class match there. Somerset were giving him a run-out to see what he could do. He hit 23 not out, including 22 off one over from Intikhab, took eight wickets for 88 runs in the Eaglets' only innings and was never seen again.

The Somerset playing staff always contained a number of personalities. Not least of these was Bill Alley, an attacking all-rounder. Bill was a hard, tough Aussie, born in Sydney in 1919. As a young man he was a middleweight boxer and was undefeated in 28 contests before having his jaw badly broken in an accident in a cricket net. He was tipped by Don Bradman to play for Australia, but the injury set him back and, when he missed out on selection for the tour of England in 1948, he came over to play for Colne in the Lancashire League. He became the only player in the league's history to score 1,000 runs in each of five consecutive seasons. After Colne he joined Blackpool and in 1957, at the age of 38, he left them to join Somerset on a three-year contract.

His best year came in 1961 when, at the age of 42, he scored 3,019 runs and took 62 wickets. Then the following year he scored 1,915 runs and took 112 wickets. He was dismissed by Somerset at the age of 49, the same year – 1968 – that I chose to leave. I felt they fired him because of his age, which made no sense to me. That summer he played all the games, scored over 1,200 runs and took 36 wickets. In my opinion he was still the best player in the team.

He brought his letter of dismissal to me so that I could see the way the club had informed him that his services were no longer required. It was a terse A5-size letter, fourth carbon copy, hard to read and of little content. Were his 16,644 runs and 738 wickets for the club of no importance? I asked him if he wanted me, as his union representative, to take the matter up with the club.

"No," he said. "In recent years the aches and pains come more often." I have never forgotten what he said next: "My eyesight is starting to go – so I've decided to take up umpiring." He successfully did this, standing in ten Test matches and nine one-day internationals. He died in 2004 at the age of 85.

There are a number of stories about Bill – some I guess fictional, some true. He was an avid talker on and off the field. At one time Brian Close banned the Yorkshire team from speaking to him when he went in to bat. Alec Skelding, former fast bowler and umpire, was an old pal of Bill. On one occasion when Alec was standing, Bill was up to his usual business of talking to all and sundry whilst he was at the wicket. There was an appeal for lbw against Bill. "That's out," said Alec, raising his index finger. As Bill passed him on the way to the pavilion he said, "Where's your white stick, Alec, and your guide dog? Where's your guide dog?" "I got rid of it for yapping," replied Alec, "like I'm getting rid of you!"

A lot of humour existed in the game in days of yore. After an accident in the field Charlie Harris of Nottinghamshire was taken to the local hospital with a suspected dislocated shoulder. He was in a great deal of pain as the medics tried to manoeuvre his arm back into its socket. This was apparent by his loud yelping. A senior sister entered the cubicle and said, "Mr Harris, there is a petite young woman in the next cubicle giving birth to her first baby, and she is not making anywhere near the same fuss as you," to which Charlie replied, "Try putting the bugger back."

It is not my intention to recount all my cricket matches in detail. Suffice to say that certain matches had a great effect on my future. One such game was against Glamorgan at Neath in July 1963. There had been a lot of bad weather about, and we started the match on a very wet wicket. Glamorgan won the toss and chose to bat first, hoping – I assume – that the wet ball would be difficult for us to hold and that it would quickly lose its shine. The conditions, however, were extremely humid and, as I am sure you know, the ball swings a lot more in humid conditions than in bright sunshine. This particular humidity was so thick it could proverbially be cut with a knife. Kenny Palmer, who had just been selected in the twelve to meet the West Indies at Leeds, took the first wicket, then I took the next five for two runs. At this stage Glamorgan, who were third in the championship table, were six wickets down for seven runs. By lunchtime they were all out for 52 – Rumsey six wickets for 24 runs. Our batsmen did not fare much better in our first innings, being bowled out for 156 by close of play. When we resumed the contest on the Monday morning, the conditions had improved a little, but Glamorgan were still six wickets down for 32 within the first hour. Soon after lunch they were all out for 102, giving us victory by an innings and two runs. My match figures were 12 wickets for 59 runs. Wilf Wooller, for many years their captain, was the Secretary of the club, and he ordered the whole Glamorgan team out onto the pitch, practising on the wicket that we had just vacated. Meanwhile, knowing we were going to get a day off, we were enjoying the delights of the swimming pool at the entrance into the ground. A few days later I was awarded my Somerset cap.

A week later we played the return match against Glamorgan at Glastonbury. It was a tame draw with Alan Jones getting his own back for Neath by scoring 187 not out and 105 not out. I have mentioned this match mainly because it reminds me of a very important event in my life.

A few days before the match, I had been asked by a young Glastonbury lady to invite a few of my Somerset colleagues to her 21st birthday party. Not one to disappoint the fairer sex or turn down a party, I accepted. When I arrived with some of my younger Somerset team-mates I was grabbed by the hostess and introduced to one of her best friends. The girl, Coleen, was very beautiful and, before an embarrassing atmosphere could be created, I asked her to dance. It was normal at that time for the band or orchestra to play three quicksteps, three foxtrots and three waltzes. This particular dance sequence was a slow foxtrot.

During the first dance I opened up with three or four of my best lines, but her reaction to my attempts to make conversation was less than warm. In fact, it was extremely cold. I remember saying, "I really don't think we have much in common," and I walked off the dance floor, leaving her standing alone in the middle. I grabbed one of her friends, Anita Jones, asked her to dance and spent the rest of the evening with her. Three years later I married Coleen and have paid for my rudeness ever since!

Harold Stephenson did a lot to make my introduction into Somerset cricket an easy route. He always had the club at heart and was a good enough keeper to have obtained Test match recognition, but he was up against an enormous amount of competition: Godfrey Evans, Roy Swetman, Geoff Millman, John Murray, Keith Andrew and Jimmy Binks. There were many others who, like Steve, were never given the opportunity to show their talents.

Harold Stephenson was not bad as a skipper; he could certainly get you to work for him. I had by now become a regular first slip, so we often had the opportunity for a chat. In one match against Nottinghamshire at Taunton I performed well in the first innings, taking seven wickets for 39 runs. At close of play on the second day the wicket had eased, and Nottinghamshire's second innings had reached 48 for two.

The final day saw Somerset in the field, attempting to bowl out the opposition. I happened to mention to the skipper how flat the wicket was, hoping that he would take me off and put on one of the spinners. He ignored me completely. After another over I suggested that Brian Langford might do better than me. Again I was completely ignored and continued to bowl until lunch time. We left the field and entered the dressing room. I had only made one stride into the room when the skipper turned on me in anger.

"I am the captain of Somerset, not you," he said. "I will decide who is to bowl and when. And, what's more, I suggest you change your clothes because you'll be bowling again immediately after lunch."

I did, and Nottinghamshire were all out for 156, bringing my match tally to 13 wickets for 104 runs. After the game Steve took me to one side and pointed out the value of having in the side a strike bowler who wanted to bowl, whatever the conditions. When there is no help to be had from the pitch or the conditions, a fast bowler is your best weapon. It was a good lesson learned, and I offered no further advice unless asked.

Bowling at Weston-super-Mare, with Roy Virgin at short leg

I lived in Taunton during that first season and was extremely fortunate in having Mervyn Kitchen as my room-mate. Mervyn was a left-hand, top-order batsman who scored 15,213 runs during his career at Somerset. After retirement he went into umpiring, standing in 20 Test matches and 28 one-day internationals. He was a great roomie, attentive, did not snore and had a superb ability to iron shirts without burning them. We roomed together for three summers but he never surpassed that first summer, when I would wake up in the morning to the beautiful aroma of freshly cooked mackerel or whiting; I loved my morning fish. Mervyn would get up at about 5am and go fishing in the Severn Estuary, then cook what he had caught, eat them with me and be ready for nets at 10. It is no wonder that I asked him to be godfather to my elder son.

That first season at Somerset cemented me into the ways of first-class cricket; I felt that I belonged. In the last match, in the first week of September, I passed 100 wickets for the summer. Then I took myself off to Worcester where I was to hibernate until April the following year.

16

Bowling bouncers

Mervyn Kitchen and I had changed our digs. We now lived in the splendour of the Princess Royal, a cider public house no further than a boundary throw from the cricket ground. Whilst we were there, a number of the visiting teams would drop in for a drink. Hardened beer drinkers used to find the rough cider a difficult drink to take. I am sure that a number of our home victories resulted from the hospitality that Mervyn and I offered to the members of our opposition.

My opening match of the 1964 season was against the Australian touring side at Taunton. It was time to rekindle my friendship with Bobby Simpson who had taken on the captaincy. I would like to have seen less of him on the cricket field: in the second innings he notched up 125 runs out of a total of 213 for one wicket, declared. They beat us quite easily, but at least I was able to put Norman O'Neill onto his backside with quite a nasty bouncer, which resulted in him retiring hurt.

I have often been asked what my reaction is to hitting batsmen. It is very simple, really. He has a bat; I have a ball. Given the chance, he would hit my ball out of the ground. The bouncer is a vital part of the fast bowler's armoury; by bringing it in to play, an element of surprise is introduced. Some batsmen will hit a bad bouncer for six or four; some will watch and avoid it. Reg Simpson was the latter type; he never hit a bouncer or got out to one; he just kept his eye on the line and swayed one way or the other. How I hated him! I hold the view that, if you cannot hook, do not hook. The decision is in the batsman's hands.

I hit a few people and broke a few noses. Helmets were not worn in the Sixties. My worst match was at Taunton against Warwickshire in 1966. In the first innings I hit Billy Ibadulla on the chin, and he had to go to the hospital for half a dozen stitches. In the second innings I hit Bryan Richardson in the eye, and he had 27 stitches. Mike Smith was carried off after I had hit him in the back of the knee, and he was given out lbw.

As I left the field I was booed by the Warwickshire supporters. I got some pleasure from that but not from hitting Bryan Richardson. I went to the hospital that evening because I was really concerned about his condition. The physicians were worried whether or not his vision had been damaged. The swelling was so severe they were unable to test his eyes correctly. I spent a very uncomfortable night, only to learn in the morning that the swelling had subsided and he could see. It was a worrying time, but it did not stop me from attacking Peter Walker with a few bouncers in the next match against Glamorgan.

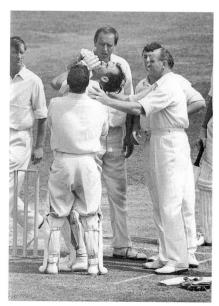

Middlesex's Ron Hooker, going for the hook, is hit in the face.

Protective headgear, although not unheard of, was not used widely until the late 1970s. Patsy Hendren was one of the first to use a self-designed protective hat in the 1930s. There are records of cricketers using towels, scarves and padded caps to protect themselves throughout cricket history. Mike Brearley introduced one of his own design which protected the sides of the head, particularly the temples. The first player to wear a protective helmet in a Test match was the Australian Graham Yallop against the West Indies at Bridgetown in March 1978. Later England's Dennis Amiss popularised it, and soon they were widely worn throughout cricket. The last batsmen at Test match level never to wear a helmet throughout his career was Viv Richards, who retired from the international game in 1992.

Had I been playing at the time of their introduction I would have applauded the decision to wear them. Although my views on batsmen are well known, I do believe that they have a right to protect themselves. Use of the helmet did bring with it a certain legacy: batsmen, who had never previously hooked or pulled, suddenly found the confidence to attempt such strokes. The result of this was some very bad batting which, it is sad to say, has continued to this present day. One of the changes in the game did affect me: the introduction of the male earring. Surely the wearers of this adornment must have understood that it would become an object of attack.

Somerset reached the quarter-final of the Gillette Cup in 1964, when we had a home tie against Sussex, who had won the cup in its first year in 1963.

The evening prior to the match, I was having a quiet glass of Somerset cider in a Taunton hostelry when a few of the Sussex players came into the bar. Having purchased their drinks they occupied a table close to my own. Their discussions moved on to the forthcoming match on the morrow.

"How quick is this new fellow Fred Rumsey?" one of them asked.

The reply came from the only player I recognised in their group.

"Oh, I wouldn't worry about him," said Richard Langridge. "He runs faster than he can bowl." This brought about a few laughs, and they changed the subject.

The following morning Somerset won the toss and elected to field. I had never seen so many people in the ground; it was packed solid. The hubbub died down to silence when Richard Langridge settled into his stance, and I began my run-up for the first ball. It pitched middle and knocked the middle stump cartwheeling towards Peter Eele, our wicket-keeper. There was total silence in the ground. It could not have been for long, but it felt long. Then this enormous roar erupted. A moment like that really makes you tingle: the stumps flying and the crowd yelling.

As Richard Langridge walked past me on his way back to the pavilion, I said to him with wicked pleasure, "You have obviously forgotten how fast I can run!"

I got Ken Suttle out in the same over. At one stage Sussex were 51 for five, but they recovered to 141 all out. We fell short by 16 runs and were knocked out of the 1964 Gillette Cup.

I was having a reasonable season, and certain cricket writers were bringing my name up in association with England. Some were difficult to believe, particularly those who had journeyed from Australia: their motives needed clarification!

We were playing at Worcester in the middle of July. We batted first and were all out with about half an hour left in the day's play. I was surprised to see Martin Horton and Duncan Fearnley come out to the wicket; normally Don Kenyon opened for Worcestershire. Apparently, I heard, Duncan Fearnley had locked himself in one of the the toilets and was standing on the lavatory seat. Don went into the room and said, "I know you are in here, Duncan. There is no point in you hiding. I want you to put your pads on and open the batting. The umpires are getting ready to go out so you had better hurry." There was no love lost between Don Kenyon and me, and he obviously did not want to face me with half an hour to go.

Most fast bowlers enjoy the short spell of a situation like this, and I was no exception. I hit Duncan Fearnley half a dozen times in the first few overs, culminating in one ball which hit him on the head and went one bounce for four leg byes. At first I was looking at the ball and not at Duncan, who was spreadeagled on the ground. Then, when I saw him, I ran towards him, along with Martin Horton.

"What's your name, what's your name?" Martin kept on asking.

"For Christ's sake, it's Duncan," came the reply.

"How are you feeling?" Martin asked.

"Lousy, what do you expect?" was the response.

"Well it could have been worse."

"How do you work that one out?"

"It could have been me."

I did not have the pleasure of getting Kenyon's wicket in that match, but at least we beat them by 83 runs.

We went from Worcester to Hinckley to play against Leicestershire. On the Sunday morning it was announced on the radio that I was included in the twelve for the Fourth Test against Australia at Old Trafford, starting the following Thursday. I was absolutely delighted, and so too were all my teammates. It was not long before the champagne started to flow.

Mum and Dad posing for the local paper with their scrapbook of my cricket

17

Debut for England

"Do you think we'll both play tomorrow?" John Price the Middlesex fast bowler asked.

"Yes is the short answer, Sport," I replied, calling John by his nickname.

"Why are you so definite?"

"I can't see England going into a Test match against Australia with Tom Cartwright opening the bowling, as good as he is. Can you?" I asked. "You will play," I said. "After all, you're the second quickest bowler in England at the moment!"

He ignored my jibe and continued to study the ceiling in deep thought.

We were lying on our beds at the Lymm Hotel, just outside Manchester. It was the eve of the Fourth Test against Australia. From the seven-wicket defeat at Headingley England had left out Jack Flavell, Norman Gifford, Ken Taylor and Fred Trueman. The twelve selected were Ted Dexter (captain), Ken Barrington, Geoff Boycott, Tom Cartwright, John Edrich, John Mortimore, Peter Parfitt, Jim Parks (wicket-keeper), John Price, Mike Smith, Fred Titmus and me.

I was not as confident as my reply indicated. This would be my first Test, if selected, and, although logic indicated that the selectors would leave out a batsman, that assumption could not be relied upon. Selectors are not noted for the great support they give to their selections. Already that summer, in three Tests, 15 players had represented England. Now there would be three or four more, and by the end of the series the number reached 20, the majority of whom played only one or two games. This is not the practice of most other cricket-playing nations.

My prediction proved correct, and both John Price and I were in the team the following day. Mike Smith was the batsman left out, and the Warwickshire captain proved his worth over the next two days as an accommodating twelfth man. The Australian team we were facing was quite a strong one. Although they did not have a fast bowler in their squad, they did have Graham McKenzie. Their full side was Bobby Simpson (captain), Bill Lawry, Ian Redpath, Norman O'Neill, Peter Burge, Brian Booth, Tommy Veivers, Wally Grout, Graham (Garth) McKenzie, Neil Hawke and Grahame Corling. Their twelfth man was Bob Cowper, a man who later became a very close friend.

Ted Dexter lost the toss, and Australia elected to bat. The two umpires were Syd Buller and Fred Price and, as we took the field behind them, I was the last man out. I closed the pavilion gate behind me, and one thought went through my mind. "I've made it. No one can now take the three lions away from me."

Ted Dexter gave me choice of ends, and Fred Price was standing at the wicket waiting for me. I noticed that the bails were not on the stumps and then saw Fred's hands shaking. I took off my large sweater, wrapped it around him and, whilst doing so, I grabbed the two bails out of his hands and put them on the stumps. I do not think anyone else noticed Fred's nervousness. He was 62 years old and was in his 16th summer as a first-class umpire, but the previous match at Headingley had been the first Test in which he had stood. His apprehension was understandable. My only hope was that his nervousness would not stop him from giving an accurate decision, should it be required. I should not have worried as he was not called upon in my first spell.

The pitch played superbly. On reflection it was possibly the best pitch that I ever played on. The ball did not swing at all and, with the Aussies having this nasty habit of playing with a slightly angled bat, runs began to accrue.

The breakthrough did not come till after tea, in the 100th over, when – with the score on 201 – Bill Lawry was run out for 106. It was not until Tom Cartwright trapped Ian Redpath in front for 19 that we bowlers had any reward for our labours. Bobby Simpson reached his hundred just before close, his first in Test cricket, and Australia ended the day on 253 for two. It was not quick scoring, but Australia only needed to draw the game to retain the Ashes.

As if I had not had enough of him during the day I went out for dinner with Bobby that evening. The following day I had my knuckles rapped by the England selectors for fraternising with the enemy.

Day two brought Simmo to the wicket again, this time with Norman O'Neill. O'Neill scored 47 before being bowled by John Price, Peter Burge fell to Tom Cartwright for 34, and Bobby Simpson just kept rolling along. At close he had reached 265, with Australia on 570 for four.

That evening Walter Robins, the chairman of selectors, arrived at Old Trafford. He bemoaned the miserable day he had spent and the tedious journey to Manchester. He commented on how little information he had received about the cricket.

"You bowled too short today," he said to me.

"How do you know?" I replied. "You've been busy all day and travelling."

There was what is called a pregnant silence, and the subject was changed. I do not think that I endeared myself to Mr Robins and his pomposity.

Day three, the Saturday, began, and out came Bobby Simpson again, this time with Brian Booth the other not-out batsman. The weather had not changed, the pitch was still shining at me, and the balls were not swinging. As we continued to toil, there was a commotion coming from the pavilion of all places. It was enough activity to stop play, and I saw what was happening. A young lady was being removed from the front row of the male-dominated seats and was being escorted out of the pavilion. I needed only one look to tell it was a lady I had invited to spend a day at the Test without having given her full instructions about procedure. I suffered for that lapse later, but at least it brought some relief from Bobby Simpson.

Brian Booth was out for 98 with the score at 601. Bobby Simpson went on to 300. Not long after, John Price had him caught behind by Jim Parks for 311, a great innings but appreciated only by Australians. Australia were then 646 for six and, apart from the run out, all the wickets had been taken by John Price and Tom Cartwright. I felt like the poor relation at a rich man's table.

Bobby Simpson acknowledges the applause for his 300.
His 311 remains the highest score in an Old Trafford Test; second highest is
Ken Barrington's 256 in England's innings – it was no match to be a bowler.

Ted Dexter threw the third new ball to me. I think it was the third; I had lost count by then. Wally Grout was facing me on nought not out and – surprise, surprise – the ball started swinging. I got his wicket and that of Tommy Veivers in the same over, and immediately Bobby Simpson declared the innings closed at 656 for eight. I finished with an analysis of 35.5 overs, two wickets for 99 runs. I was the only one of the five main bowlers not to go for 100.

Bobby Simpson's decision to play for at least a draw had got off to a good start. Now it was important for us to play just as sensibly and deny him victory. The pitch was still as good as it was at the start so only bad batting could cause our downfall. Geoff Boycott and John Edrich opened our innings. With only 15 on the board John Edrich was out to Garth McKenzie, and Ted Dexter was on his way to the wicket. Ted as a skipper was like the girl with the curl. When he was good, he was fantastic; when he was bad, he was bloody awful. But he had this air about him; you wanted to play for him. Before he went out to bat at Old Trafford, he said, "If anybody sees me playing a square cut, you have my permission to kick me up the arse when I come back in." We all wanted him to play one.

He and Boycott put on 111 runs before Boycott was bowled for 58. When Ted Dexter had scored about 70, he was caught by Peter Burge in the covers. Ted set off for the pavilion; he must have travelled at least 40 yards when Peter Burge called to Syd Buller, "I'm not sure I caught that, Syd."

"Well, only you would know that," was Syd's reply.

Peter said, "No, I didn't. Call him back."

A bemused Ted Dexter returned to the wicket, and England were 166 for two at close of play. I wonder how often such a sporting decision would occur now.

Day four got off to a good start: no change in the weather and the pitch playing just as well. Ted got his hundred, then Kenny Barrington got his. Towards the end of play, when it looked like they were both going to carry their bats through to close, Ted Dexter was bowled by Tommy Veivers for 174. He had been at the wicket for eight hours and, much to our disappointment, had not played one square cut. He had put on 256 with Kenny Barrington and deserved the standing ovation he received from the crowd and his team as he walked into the dressing room. Kenny Barrington and Peter Parfitt came in at close with 411 for three on the scoreboard and Kenny 153 not out.

Day five's weather was like the other four days and the wicket had not changed. Finally Kenny Barrington was lbw to Garth McKenzie for 256, scored in 11½ hours, by which time the score had reached 589 for six. Garth McKenzie then took the wickets of Fred Titmus, John Mortimore and Tom

Cartwright, finishing with seven for 153 off 60 overs, an epic piece of bowling on that wicket.

The fall of Tom Cartwright brought me to the wicket to partner my bowling colleague John Price. There were only about 30 minutes left in the game, and ideally we should see it out. At this stage of the innings the off-spinner Tommy Veivers had bowled a lot of overs. The world record for the most overs in a Test innings was 98, held by Sonny Ramadhin against England at Edgbaston in 1957, so I asked Syd Buller if he knew how many overs Tommy had bowled.

"Yes," he said. "94."

I said to Tommy, "There is nothing on this game. How would you like to get the world record?"

"Why not?" he said.

I walked down to the other end to explain the situation to John Price.

"We are just going to push down the line for the next few overs to get Tommy the record. Don't play any shots. OK?"

"OK," said Sport.

The 95th over went by without a hitch, and we survived an over from the other end. The first ball of Tommy Veivers 96th over was tossed high in the air. I watched John Price's eyes open like organ stops, and my heart sank. He took a mighty, left-handed swipe, trying to hit the ball into the middle of Manchester. He missed by a mile, and the ball bowled him.

There was complete silence on the pitch. Then Tommy Veivers said, "Jesus Christ, Sport, how could you?"

"Sorry, old boy," came back the embarrassed reply.

At least Sonny Ramadhin could breathe a sigh of relief. He was playing for Lancashire down in Kent. His record still stands today.

The game continued, and guess who came out to bat? You have got it: Bobby Simpson. He and Bill Lawry faced a ferocious two overs from Kenny Barrington and Fred Titmus, scored four runs and left the field after five minutes, the proud retainers of the Ashes. Bobby Simpson was on the field for the whole five days less about fifteen minutes.

As for that pitch, Lancashire were playing Warwickshire in a Gillette Cup semi-final the following day. The two captains, Ken Grieves and Mike Smith, agreed to use the same strip by just repairing the foot holes.

Somerset's next match was not till the Saturday when we were playing Gloucestershire at the Imperial Athletic Ground in Bristol, a match of great significance in my life. I received a telephone call from a young lady, asking if I could leave a ticket for her to watch the game. She said that she had met me at a party in Glastonbury the previous year. I assumed it was Anita, the girl with whom I had spent the evening. I left the ticket, but it was not collected by Anita; it was Coleen who turned up, the pretty lady I had left standing in the middle of the dance floor. As it happened, I had a girl friend from Worcester, Janet, already on the ground so I sat Coleen with her for company. At the end of the day all three of us piled into my red MGA drop-head sports car, which really was only a two-seater, and drove to the centre of Bristol where we dropped Coleen off – however, not before I had arranged to meet her on the Monday evening, the outcome of which you already know.

The selectors were in their usual good form when picking the England team for the last Test at The Oval. John Edrich, John Mortimore and Fred Rumsey were dropped, and Bob Barber, Colin Cowdrey and Fred Trueman came in. Strange, because the Australians picked exactly the same side that they played at Old Trafford. Apart from an injury that prevented Norman O'Neill playing at Headingley, they had fielded the same eleven all series.

18

Wicketless and cold in my second Test

Two new faces joined Somerset in 1965. During the previous year I had been asked by the management if I had come across any slow left-arm bowlers who were not playing first-class cricket. As it happened, I had: Peter Robinson. Peter was a member of the Worcestershire 2nd XI Championship-winning side of 1962. He was always going to struggle to make the first team because of Norman Gifford and Doug Slade. A proposition was put to him, and he joined us for practice at the beginning of April.

Harold Stephenson had missed much of the 1964 season because of trouble with his back, with Bill Alley captaining the team in his absence. The committee were not too happy with this arrangement and decided to invite Colin Atkinson, the deputy headmaster of Millfield School, to take over the reins. This upset Harold Stephenson, who decided during the winter to retire.

This left us without a top-line wicket-keeper so an invitation was sent to Geoff Clayton, of Lancashire, to join the permanent staff. Both these newcomers joined Mervyn and me at the Princess Royal, doubling our band of eager hospitality providers.

Geoff Clayton was an enigma. He had to be ranked among the top six keepers in England but for some reason, which I never discovered, he carried a wooden plank on his shoulder – not a chip, a plank – when it came to his relationships with administration. I had had run-ins with administrations on a number of occasions and there were going to be more in the future, but I would not let my militancy interfere with the way I played cricket. Geoff

Clayton did. I liked him a lot – maybe because he was his own man – but he never gave his immense talent the full opportunity to blossom, which could have been at international level: the England selectors would have been hard put to pick a wicket-keeper who, with studded boots, would trap the new ball when it was thrown short to him from the boundary.

On one occasion, when he thought I should have been bowling faster, he threw the ball at me. It hit me on the back of my head. I said, "There are better ways of making your point, you know."

In an early game against Middlesex at the Imperial Ground he went in as nightwatchman on the first evening and scored a century the next day. He grabbed three victims behind the stumps, contributing enormously to Somerset's nine-wicket win. That was how valuable Geoff Clayton could be.

I was picked to play five Test matches in 1965, although I only played in four, missing nine championship matches for Somerset.

The Test selectors had a reshuffle of their own. Walter Robins, the chairman, and Willie Watson retired. Doug Insole took over as chairman, Alec Bedser continued, and PBH May and Don Kenyon were added to the list. However, although the committee had changed, their policy of shuffling the pack had not. Having won a series in South Africa with John Price, Ian Thomson and David Brown as the new-ball bowlers on the tour, they picked Fred Trueman and me to open the bowling in the First Test against New Zealand at Edgbaston.

I received a few telegrams of congratulations, including one from my beloved Fox Cricket Club: 'Congratulations on your Test call up – if selected would you be able to play in next Sunday's home match?'

On the morning of the first day I was having breakfast in the Raven Hotel in Droitwich, reading an article in the *Daily Telegraph* written by EW Swanton, Jim to his friends, about the forthcoming Test. Now, Jim played three first-class matches for Middlesex as a batsman, all against the universities, amassing 67 runs in five innings; he never bowled his leg-breaks in a first-class game, but that did not stop him from becoming a major expert on all matters cricket. In the article he compared the New Zealand left-armer Richard Collinge and me. He conceded that I was the quicker but, because of where my back foot landed, wide almost on the return crease, he said it would be extremely difficult for me to get an lbw decision. Richard Collinge's back foot, however, landed between the return crease and the stumps, making it more likely that he would obtain lbw decisions. What a load of rubbish! It is said that a little learning is a dangerous thing. Had he followed his scrutiny further through my action he would have noticed that, because I was more side-on, my front foot landed on the batting crease only marginally outside the line of leg stump, giving me a better position than Richard Collinge. He also should have been aware that bowlers bowl off the front not the back foot. I bowled in-swing and, had he bothered to check the previous year's figures, he would have found that 11 of my 80 wickets were lbws. Up to the start of that Test, according to my computer, Richard Collinge had taken 66 first-class wickets and not one of them was an lbw.

I remember complaining to another member of the press corps that his previous day's reporting was inaccurate. He had suggested that one of the wickets I had taken pitched on the leg stump and hit off stump, when it had actually pitched middle and hit leg.

"I don't give a jot what you think," he said. "I don't write to please you. I write for the spectators sitting behind cover, mid-wicket and, in particular, those who aren't at the ground." I never raised the point again.

Back to that front foot. It had its own problems landing so close to the line of the stumps. After delivering the ball from that position, where would the next stride land? Because I was beyond side-on in the delivery, the natural landing spot would be right on a length in line with the stumps. The only problem with that was the effect it had on the umpires. "Don't rough up the wicket for your off-spinner," I was once told. "How do you expect me to give a decision when I can't see the batsman?" was another. Most important of all, it was illegal. I could be taken off for constantly running on the wicket. It was quite an effort of contortion, but I did manage to land far enough out of line to satisfy most umpires.

Nine of the New Zealanders were making their debut in Tests in England; only their captain John Reid and Bert Sutcliffe had played before. Although John Reid was a very competitive player, he did confide to me that a draw against England was like a win to most of his team.

The temperature was really low that first day. The umpires, Charlie Elliott and Fred Price, were wearing their pyjamas under their trousers and two sweaters under their jackets; they looked like Michelin men with their white coats on. Fortunately for me, England won the toss and decided to bat. If all went well, I would not be required until well into the next day, and it did go well. At close of play we were 232 for three, with Kenny Barrington 61 not out.

It was just as cold on the second day. Before play started, the dressing-room attendant informed me that some people were asking for me at the players' entrance. I investigated and found that Gaffer Jay, from the Fox Cricket Club, with two of his children, had brought me a gift. It was a bunch of radishes called 'White Icicle'. They were as hot as chillies, and I loved them. "We thought we would put some fire in your belly as it is such a cold day," said the Gaffer, before taking his seat in one of the stands.

When play got under way Colin Cowdrey was the next man out for 85, we lost our skipper Mike Smith for 0, and we were then 300 for five. The score rose slowly until Fred Trueman was out at 394 for nine. This brought me to the wicket, with Kenny Barrington on 117 not out. Believe it or not, we put on 41, beating England's highest tenth-wicket partnership against New Zealand, of which Kenny scored 20 and I hit 21 not out, including – according to *Wisden* – 'two classic cover drives'. We were finally all out for 435, with Kenny scoring 137 in 7½ hours.

When we took the field I was waiting for Fred to choose his end so that I could take up my fielding position. To my surprise, and I guess Fred's, Mike Smith threw the ball to me, asking me which end I wanted. I could not believe that Fred would not have the first choice and said so to Mike Smith.

"So when did the selectors make you captain?" he asked.

"Sorry, skipper," I said and went off to pace out my run. It did embarrass me a little because I revered Fred.

New Zealand started reasonably well on an unresponsive pitch. It was the type of conditions that suited neither batsman nor bowler. I was fielding at mid-on whilst Fred Trueman was bowling and on his way back, after one delivery, he confided in me, "It's like bowling a doughnut on a shit heap." New Zealand finished the freezing day on 59 for one.

The weather had not improved by the third day. My hands were going blue and spent most of their time in my pockets. We were even offered coffee in the drinks break. It was Saturday, and I could identify my parents in the stand because they were almost the only people in it! It really was that cold.

Fred Trueman was beginning to work up some pace, even though the bounce was low. He gave Bert Sutcliffe a torrid time, at one point suggesting to him, "If you back away any further, you'll be in a bus queue for Birmingham!" It was not long before Fred hit him in the ear with a bouncer, and he retired hurt.

During the lunch break both Fred and I were asked up to the committee room. The hierarchy of both teams were in conference, along with Mike Smith and John Reid, the two captains.

"We are asking both Freds to agree not to bowl bouncers at Bert Sutcliffe, is that correct?" asked Mike Smith.

"You what?" said Fred with added expletive.

"Now hang on, Fred," said Mike, "Hear the whole thing out. If you and Fred agree not to bowl bouncers at him, Bert Sutcliffe will retire from Test cricket at the end of this match."

Reluctantly we both agreed and returned to the dressing room and the match. New Zealand were bowled out for 116 and were forced to follow on.

They batted better in their second innings, being bowled out just before the end of day four for 413. Vic Pollard made an unbeaten 81, with the only other fifty coming from Bert Sutcliffe. Playing with confidence off the front foot, he scored 53 in his last Test innings.

Geoff Boycott and Bob Barber knocked off most of the required 95 runs on the final day, and we beat New Zealand by nine wickets. I am sad to say that I did not take a single wicket in either of the two New Zealand innings, making my selection for the Second Test at Lord's extremely doubtful.

19

A triumphant morning at Lord's

Having not taken a wicket at Edgbaston and knowing what the selectors were like, I was gobsmacked when it was announced that I was in the Test side for Lord's against the New Zealanders. I use this disgusting phrase to highlight its use in the English language. Whoever put gob and smacked together for an expression of surprise needs to be blindfolded, stood against a wall and receive their own special surprise.

Tom Cartwright was out, with John Snow joining Fred Trueman and me in the side. More surprising was the fact that, after scoring 137 at Edgbaston and securing the match for England, Kenny Barrington had been dropped, supposedly for slow play, and Peter Parfitt was back in the team.

It is normal for the team to dine with the selectors on the eve of a Test match. A private room is taken, and conversations about the policy for the following day are aired. Doug Insole, the chairman of selectors, opened the discussions by suggesting that Kenny Barrington had been dropped as a matter of public opinion. "So the press are picking the England side now," I offered and received a nasty kick under the table from the skipper Mike Smith. That match holds other memories for me; it was the first time that I had met a member of the Royal Family, and in this instance it was the Queen.

New Zealand won the toss the next day, elected to bat and then lost four wickets for 28 runs, all taken by me at a personal cost of seven runs (including, I might add, two lbws). I had visions of my name being added to the honours board in the Long Room for taking five wickets in a Test at Lord's. Mike Smith had given me choice of ends again, but this time it did not make me feel as uncomfortable. Reid became John Snow's first Test victim on his debut, but Pollard and Taylor added 92 for the seventh wicket before New Zealand were bowled out for 175. I did not get another wicket so no honours board for me.

RUMSEY THE WRECKER
The new 'fiery Fred' has Tourists reeling

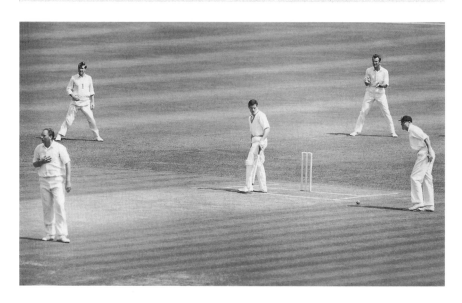

Four wickets before lunch at Lord's v New Zealand, 8 June 1965
Congdon lbw 0, Sinclair bowled 1,
Dowling lbw 12, Morgan caught Parfitt 0.

England v New Zealand, Lord's, June 1965
back: Peter Parfitt, Geoff Boycott, Fred Rumsey, John Snow, Bob Barber, Fred Titmus
front: Jim Parks, Colin Cowdrey, Mike Smith (captain), Ted Dexter, Fred Trueman

When bowling I would take my lunch in the dressing room. It enabled me to effect a full change of clothing. The twelfth man would get the food for me whilst I got on with the disrobing. Mike Brearley was twelfth man on this occasion and, as well as bringing my lunch, he brought his own food. We were tucking in when the dressing-room door opened, and in walked Jim Swanton, bold as brass, without an invitation, as if he owned the place. Without acknowledging me he rounded on Mike Brearley.

"Brearley, now that you are not playing for Middlesex, perhaps you will turn out for the Free Foresters?"

"I don't know about that, Jim," Mike replied. "I don't enjoy those games very much. Most of the players talk with plums in their mouths."

"You do realise, Brearley, that there is such a thing as inverted snobbery," retorted Swanton.

"Jim, that is something you know nothing about," said Mike.

Jim Swanton was pompous but a likeable man. Gubby Allen was a good friend of Jim. They were having dinner together at Jim's home, and right through dinner all Jim could talk about was the expensive embossed wallpaper hanging in his dining room. A few weeks later Gubby invited Jim to his home for dinner. Swanton excused himself from the table and went to the lavatory, only to return to the dining room flushed. "You bugger, Gubby," he spluttered. Gubby Allen had decorated his small room with the same embossed paper.

Jim Laker used to enjoy playing the odd prank on Jim Swanton. One Test match Jim Swanton was climbing the ladder to the commentary box to deliver his lunchtime summary. Jim Laker heard him coming and, as Swanton entered the box, he said into the microphone, "It appears that Jim Swanton is not coming, viewers. He's most likely had too much wine with his lunch so I will present the lunch-time summary." A flustered Jim Swanton grabbed the microphone and spluttered. "I certainly have not been drinking wine, viewers. In fact I haven't had any lunch yet." The producer's voice came through the earphones, "Wrap it up, Jim, we are on air in thirty seconds."

Let's get back to the Lord's Test. We replied to New Zealand's 175 runs by scoring 307 runs in our first innings, with 119 from Colin Cowdrey and 62 from Ted Dexter. Overnight on Saturday New Zealand were 261 for seven.

In the Sixties Test cricket was not played on a Sunday. A lot of the married players took the opportunity to go home to their families. As a bachelor I had no such responsibilities. I was sharing a room in the Great Western Hotel near Paddington with Geoff Boycott. He decided to go back to Yorkshire on the Saturday evening after the cricket. I had no intention of being lonely so I imported Coleen to replace Boycott. On the Sunday evening we were enjoying a bath together when Boycott returned to the suite. After a lot of door banging and hints from me, he got the idea that I didn't want him around for a while. He cleared off, and Coleen left.

I thought that that was the end of the matter until I was summoned the next morning to a meeting with Alec Bedser, who was the selector given the role of team manager for this match. Geoff Boycott, being the great roomie he was, had reported me to him for having a woman in our room.

"I understand that you have had a woman in your bedroom," he said.

I said, "Yes, Mr Bedser."

"That's not good, you know."

"Who's told you?"

"It doesn't matter who's told me. You are a bowler, you need your strength to be bowling in the match."

"Yes, Mr Bedser."

"In my day," he went on, "it was beer for the bowlers and women for the batsmen."

So I said to him, "Well, God bless the all-rounders."

"Bugger off," he said, with a dismissive shake of his head.

As at Edgbaston, New Zealand batted much better in their second innings, scoring 347. We needed 216 to win and, with 76 from Geoffrey Boycott and an unbeaten 80 from Ted Dexter, the main danger to our victory came from the weather. At one stage after long interruptions on both of the final two days, victory was beginning to look doubtful. We won in the end by seven wickets with only 15 minutes to spare. The match was Fred Trueman's last ever appearance for England. He finished with 307 Test wickets, quite a record.

Somerset had three home games before the final Test against New Zealand at Headingley. These were to be played at the Recreation Ground in Bath. A few weeks before the first game the groundsman from Taunton paid an investigatory visit to Bath to check the condition of the pitch. To his horror he discovered that the grass had been allowed to grow a foot high. The result of this is that the roots of the grass rise closer to the surface, loosening the soil and making it difficult to bind.

Apparently the regular groundsman had left the employ of the local authority, and the only replacement they could get was a part-timer who also worked as a patrolman for the Automobile Association. Our groundsman got stuck into the repair and did his best, but there was some apprehension as we went into the first match. On the way from Taunton to Bath I suggested to Peter Robinson that his haul for the three games could be considerable. The Bath pitch was well known for its support for spinners and, with the current condition of the wicket, it could be perfect for him.

In fact, in the first match he bowled only eight overs and did not take a wicket. Worcestershire were bowled out for 143 and 42, and Somerset won by an innings and five runs. I captured Don Kenyon's wicket in both innings, of which one was a duck.

The second match was against Hampshire and, to give the Bath supporters a good chance to watch some first-class cricket during their lunch hour, we had a 2½-hour morning session, with lunch not taken till 2pm. Our skipper Colin Atkinson had some trepidation about batting second on the wicket, and he lost the toss.

"Don't you worry," I said. "I'll get you seven wickets before lunch."

"If you get seven wickets before lunch, I'll buy you a silver bike," he replied.

Bill Alley and I bowled unchanged for the two and a half hours. By lunch time Hampshire were all out for 64, and I had taken my best analysis of eight wickets for 26 runs.

The next day Hampshire were bowled out again by the seamers for 77, and Somerset won by seven wickets. I got my silver bike; it was a brooch about an inch long!

Peter Robinson did not get a bowl in either innings. He did, however, make the best remark of the match. On his way into the pavilion, having been dismissed for 6, he was heard to say, "That AA man should put out one of his road signs: 'Loose Chippings – Drive with Care!'"

Peter is the nephew of Roly Jenkins, a former England leg-spinner. Roly was well known for his observational sense of humour, and it most certainly passed down to Peter. I was in the Worcestershire dressing room on one occasion when Roly blessed us with his presence. We were discussing the merits of a racehorse which was performing at Ascot later that day. I suggested that the odds would be short, due to the horse's recent successes. Roly interrupted me by addressing us all. "There is only one safe way to back a horse, lads, and that's into shafts!" I, for one, took his advice.

I was playing with him in a charity match at his beloved West Bromwich Dartmouth when a reverend gentleman came to the crease. In bun-fight cricket matches like this Roly would drop his bowling arm to almost round arm and turn the ball at right angles. He so mesmerised the batsman that the cleric fell down onto his knees. Roly's immediate response was, "No point in your praying to him, vicar, he can't help you out here."

For the third and final match at Bath, against Nottinghamshire, CRM Atkinson lost the toss again. By close of play on the first day Nottinghamshire had scored 242 all out. This time we were on the receiving end on the wicket and were bowled out for 133 and 62, losing the match by 200 runs. Peter Robinson was rested for the match and, on the way back to Taunton, he asked me to keep my predictions to myself in the future.

"Exactly how many wickets did you get on that spinners' paradise?" he asked.

"Twenty-six," I said.

"Thanks a lot, pal," was his response.

It was all change again at Headingley for the final Test against New Zealand. Fred Trueman, John Snow, Ted Dexter and Geoff Boycott out – to be fair, Dexter and Boycott were unavailable – and John Edrich, Kenny Barrington, Ray Illingworth and David Larter in. With no Trueman and Boycott, maybe they brought in Illingworth because they needed a Yorkshireman in the side at Headingley.

With the score at 13 Bob Barber was out, having scored all the runs. Kenny Barrington joined John Edrich and, by close on the first day, England were 366 for one. Colin Cowdrey had worn his pads for almost six hours so, with 15 minutes to close, a nightwatchman took over. It is fair to say that, although the rest of the team saw a little of the cricket, most of the afternoon was spent watching athletics on television. On occasions we would all turn to the cricket, stand up and give John and Kenny a round of polite applause, then sit down and continue to watch the athletics.

Day two gave little relief to the New Zealand bowlers as John and Kenny piled on the runs. Edrich hit an unbeaten 310, Barrington scored 163, and England declared on 546 for four.

We won by an innings and 187 runs. On the fourth evening New Zealand were 158 for five in their second innings when Fred Titmus asked me whether we had reached the time when, if the game finished, we could stay overnight. After a few enquiries I established that we had and confirmed this to Fred. He promptly changed the angle of his flight, and in one over he took four wickets. In fact, rain came and we did not take the last wicket till the next day.

This was the last Test match played by captain John Reid. He was the one most responsible for establishing New Zealand as a first-class cricketing nation, elevating his players from club cricketers to international players. When he was appointed to the captaincy in 1956, New Zealand had played 42 Tests and won none of them, but he led them to victory against the West Indies in his third game in charge, and he also won twice in South Africa. He was a leading force with both the bat and the ball, a man respected on and off the field and should be regarded as a legend of New Zealand cricket.

20

The end of the road with England

Somerset had two matches to play before the three-match Test series against South Africa started. The first of these was against Northamptonshire, my pal Colin Milburn's team. They won the toss, put us into bat, and we were all out before tea for 121. At close I had taken the only two wickets to fall, including Colin Miburn for 63.

Colin and his captain, Keith Andrew, decided that a bit of gamesmanship was required so they invited me out for a night on the town – we went to a night club in Yeovil. Haydn Sully joined us, a Northamptonshire player who had previously played for Somerset. Between them they piled on the drinks until the early hours. The following morning all three of them were like death warmed up, with hammering headaches. I had to bowl so, within an over or two, I had sweated the poison out and was raring to go. Keith Andrew came in to bat, still nursing a nasty hangover, and left quite quickly by my hand. However, the outcome was not that good for Somerset as we were beaten by an innings and one run.

The second match was against Essex at Westcliff. Essex were a nomadic team, even when at home. I must own up to a certain pleasure at this because some of the wickets were quite lively. Westcliff was a case in point. Having scored 295, we bowled them out for 97 in their first innings, my bag being seven wickets for 34 runs.

Trevor Bailey, the Essex captain, was philosophical about the outcome of the match, as he was about many things. He had a reputation for slow scoring, but that had saved England on many an occasion. Apart from skippering Essex, he was also the club's Secretary, and he explained to me the difficulties of moving around the county for the various home games. Getting the right caterer could be a bind. One food-and-drink provider said to him on one occasion, "Mr Bailey, I love it when you go to the wicket." Feeling quite charmed, Trevor asked, "Is it my stroke play or my defence that you appreciate?" "Oh, nothing like that," said the caterer. "When you go in to bat, my beer tents fill up with people!"

I was in the side for the First Test against South Africa at Lord's as was David Larter, but we had a new partner in David Brown of Warwickshire. Like John Snow in the previous Lord's Test it was his debut. Ted Dexter was still injured – a freak accident with his car had broken his leg – but Geoff Boycott returned in place of Peter Parfitt. This was the 100th Test between the two countries although there was little celebration of that event.

It was a game in which fortunes fluctuated from start to finish, watched by close to 100,000 spectators over the five days. A highlight of the match was the tremendous fielding of the South African players, Colin Bland in particular. His running out of Kenny Barrington, who had made 91, and Jim Parks was exceptional.

As we went into the final day the outcome was difficult to predict. South Africa left England 191 to win in just under four hours, but our batting really never got started. John Edrich was hit on the head by Peter Pollock and was forced to retire, Kenny Barrington fell cheaply and, when Colin Cowdrey was out, it was 135 for six. With John Edrich not returning and David Brown, me and David Larter to come, I do not think that the crowd sensed fabulous victory.

David Brown was out, to make the score 140 for seven, and my worst nightmare visited me as I made my way to the wicket to join Fred Titmus. To my relief it was Graeme Pollock bowling, not his brother Peter, and with one or two close escapes 'Fred and Fred' played out the last overs to complete the survival.

Two of the six wickets I took in the Lord's Test against South Africa
Bob Barber at leg slip knocks up the ball before catching Eddie Barlow;
Ken Barrington holds on to Peter van der Merwe at second slip

My contribution to the batting against South Africa at Lord's

(right) Bowled in the first iunings for 3

(below) Surviving a stumping appeal off Graeme Pollock in a match-saving 0 not out

After a couple of games with Somerset the twelve for the next Test at Trent Bridge was announced. Surprise, surprise, it was the same team that played at Lord's except Peter Parfitt was in for the injured John Edrich and Tom Cartwright for twelfth man Ray Illingworth. Shortly after the twelve had been announced, David Brown withdrew because of injury, and John Snow was added in his stead.

On the Tuesday evening, after the last day of the Somerset v Gloucestershire match, I was resting at Coleen's home in Bristol. I was due to report to Trent Bridge the next day for nets before the Test started on the following day. I was running down the stairs when my left leg collapsed, and I tumbled down a dozen risers to the bottom. There was no additional injury, but my leg was sore. A visit to the doctor diagnosed a spasm in the left hamstring. Apparently, these can occur if the muscle has been overused or is tired. They are short term and, apart from the initial pain, should mend quickly. A good night's sleep and I should be back to normal was the doctor's prognosis.

Out of consideration for England and the selectors, something they never showed in return, I contacted Lord's and made them aware of the problem. Obviously I did not want the team to go into the Second Test without the required number of fast bowlers. They asked Jeff Jones, the Glamorgan left-armer, to report to Trent Bridge, and the selection became thirteen.

When I reported on the Wednesday I had a good run-out in the nets without any problems – the leg felt sore but not weak. It was agreed with the match manager, Peter May, that I would have another net the following morning before announcing my condition. This I did and, apart from feeling sore, the leg felt OK. I declared myself fit and was told by Peter May that I was in the team.

I returned to the dressing room just as the chairman of selectors, Doug Insole, arrived. He asked after my health and, upon being told it was OK, he suggested a walk around the ground.

"Are you going to break down?" was his first question, once we were on the grass.

"I don't think so," I replied, "but you never know with injuries. It could be something entirely different."

He continued, "You do realise that, if you do break down, it could have an enormous effect on your future career."

The idea of missing the final Test against South Africa and the winter tour of Australia did concern me. If it meant that, by withdrawing from one Test, I could secure my future, I had no other course of action but to withdraw. I did, and I never played for England again!

The selectors had summoned David Larter, John Snow, Jeff Jones and me to Trent Bridge. For the final Test at The Oval David Larter was injured, but the other three of us were all discarded, with Brian Statham, David Brown and Ken Higgs coming in. What they achieved with all this swapping around, I have no idea.

Worse was to follow for me when I was not selected for the tour of Australia. Nor was John Snow. Instead, they picked David Larter, Ken Higgs, Jeff Jones and David Brown. They asked me to stay fit in case one of the seam bowlers broke down. In fact, David Larter did, but then they asked Barry Knight to join the tour, not me. I cannot say that I was surprised; the wonders of the England Board of Selectors were long lost to me.

An even bigger puzzle was why the selectors dropped Tom Graveney in February 1963 and did not select him again until June 1966. During that three-year period he twice helped Worcestershire win the championship, once as the leading run-scorer in the country. When the selectors finally came to their senses and recalled him against the West Indies, he scored heavily, including an innings of 165 at The Oval, which one experienced journalist described as 'arguably the best innings of his life'.

21

Friends on the county circuit

Playing counties home and away in three-day matches led to a great number of friendships. My band of friends more or less fell into place automatically, their make-up always including humour, rebellion, independence and a glass of something or other.

David 'Butch' White of Hampshire was one such animal. We had a wicked arrangement: if a match between Somerset and Hampshire was heading for a draw and one of us was at the crease, the other was certain of a wicket if they were bowling at the time. Butch played a couple of Tests for England in the early Sixties. I did not play with him in those Tests, but in that summer of 1965 we played together in three end-of-season games at the Scarborough Cricket Festival. He had six innings in which to take the ten wickets he needed for his 100 for the season, and he managed just one. As we took the field for the last time our captain, JT Murray, asked me to give Butch the slope, which was considerable at Scarborough. I ran in for my first ball and failed to get anywhere near the bowling crease. No wonder Butch only got one wicket; it was like running up the side of Mount Everest.

His Hampshire captain, Colin Ingleby-Mackenzie, was another who had a humorous gleam in his eyes. Hampshire were due to play Sussex on a Saturday, and on the previous evening Colin was at a black-tie function in

Butch White, the Nawab of Pataudi, Mike Page

London. Ted Dexter, the Sussex captain, was at the same do; they were both delayed overnight and travelled together to Hampshire, still in their dinner jackets. They arrived at the ground about an hour before the start. There was no time to change so, much to the delight of the Hampshire and Sussex supporters, they went out to the middle for a black-tie toss. Everybody loved the moment, but guess what? Lord's had them sanctioned.

Mike Page was a Derbyshire batsman with a lot of talent. Somerset played at Buxton one year, and he got hit in the face fielding at short leg and had to go to hospital. When he returned, with a broken nose and stitches above the eyes, Derbyshire were struggling in a run chase and his captain, Derek Morgan, asked him to bat. I was bowling at the time and greeted him with a nasty well-placed bouncer and a pleasant smile. The next year I was playing alongside him for Derbyshire, and we spent a lot of time together. When, as a team, we attended meals in a hotel the noise level could be so high that conversation was impossible. Mike would bang the table with a spoon three times, the noise would die down and he with everyone else in the restaurant would be looking around for the culprit. If the restaurant was too quiet he would get me to stand up and have a loud meaningless row with him, just to get the tongues wagging.

Colin Milburn was one of our happy band. He was naturally humorous. He must have had a serious bone in his body, but I never saw it. We spent a lot of time together, particularly after his motorcar accident when he lost his left eye. When he was playing for Northamptonshire the committee there was of the opinion that he presented the aura of a drinker. Every time he returned to the pavilion, after a two-hour fielding session, he would head straight for the bar and order a pint of bitter. They suggested that, if he had to have a drink, why not drink in half pints. After the next fielding session he

Colin Milburn, Colin Ingleby-Mackenzie, Cec Pepper

entered the pavilion, headed for the bar and ordered two halves of bitter. He lost his false eye in a swimming pool once, and six of us dived in to try to find it. I was the unlucky diver who found it staring back at me.

He asked me to arrange a fund-raising lunch for the Chairman of Northamptonshire, Lyn Wilson, to celebrate their centenary. I asked Tim Rice (lyricist), John Taylor (Welsh rugby international) and Willie Rushton (raconteur) to speak at the occasion. It was very successful, money was raised and the event enjoyed. Not long after the do, we all received an invitation to become honorary life members of the club. Milburn did his nut. "I spent fourteen years at this club, playing my heart out with not so much as a thank you. You lot turn out for a couple of hours and are given honorary membership!"

Another cricketing friend who lost an eye in a motor accident was Mansoor Ali Khan, the Nawab of Pataudi. On 1 July 1961, at the age of 20, he was a passenger in a car which was involved in an accident in Hove. A sliver of glass from the broken windscreen penetrated and permanently damaged his right eye. Six months later he played his first Test in Delhi against England. A year later, at the age of 21, he became the youngest ever Test captain, a record that has only been beaten by Tatenda Taibu of Zimbabwe.

He followed his father, who played cricket for England and India, to the Pataudi title; he was the titular Nawab of Pataudi from 1952 until 1971, when by the 26th Amendment to the Constitution of India the privy purses of the princes were abolished and official recognition of their titles came to an end. It was during this period that he offered me the job of coaching cricket within the Pataudi district. He believed that somewhere in his district there lurked an unfound fast bowler who had not developed because of the flat wickets. I was to receive a moderate remuneration to find and coach such a player. I would live in a palace, "with all the usual trimmings" as he put it. I was going to be required for about four months of the year; the remainder I would be able to travel on Air India to any part of the world free of charge. It was such a tempting offer, but I had only just played for England so unfortunately it came at an inappropriate time. There were other romantic reasons, too, but we will not go into those.

Not all my friends were players. There were one or two umpires who could see the funny side of things. One was an Aussie called Cec Pepper. Garry Sobers, who played against him in league cricket, said of Pepper that "the reason he never played county cricket was probably because of his over-ripe language. He was certainly good enough as a cricketer, but no one wanted to take the chance." It is also said that Sir Don Bradman once remarked that, had Cec's mouth and his attitude been more moderate, he would have been one of the greatest all-rounders the world has ever seen.

We were playing Yorkshire at Scarborough, and I was steaming down the famous slope and hit the batsman's pads with an in-swinger. I appealed firmly enough, but it was turned down by Cec. The very next ball I repeated the procedure, this time appealing a little louder. Cec's cry of "not out" was also louder. The third ball was a repeat of the first two. "Howzat?" I yelled. He shouted loudly back, "Not out." I could not resist it and shouted, "Why not?" "Because there are three stumps down that end, not a row of f---ing pailings."

A news correspondent once said that he could not imagine any match involving Cec Pepper pursuing a peaceful course but added that usually 'there was a lot more humour than anger.'

22

Festival time

Although I never played in another Test match, my bowling kept on improving. The foundation laid by Roy Tattersall in 1962 was paying off for me in 1965. I was beginning to control the swing better. I had given up the idea of bowling away swing, it meant too much of a change in my action. I was a side-on bowler, and I would have had to square my action to bowl away swing. I also noticed the batsmen watching me shine the ball before placing it at the end of my fingers. They were trying to find out on which side the shiny side was placed in my hand. As a deterrent I would throw the ball in the air just before placing it.

By using a two-coloured ball, one side black, the other white, we were able to determine how often the ball turned when it left my hand. Some seam bowlers are able to keep the seam straight after the ball leaves their hand. but I could not. The ball would turn twice after it left my hand which resulted in a late swing. By holding the ball a little firmer with my side-on action, I could bowl it straight; so my philosophy was to bowl a couple straight and the third in-swing, or a couple of in-swing and one straight, or any variation thereof. I never tried to cut the ball off the wicket although sometimes it happened without my trying. If I got into a nice rhythm, balance and line, I would not change it. The only time to play around with your action in the middle is when you are getting no results.

The Scarborough Cricket Festival would occur every year at the end of the season. It was a light-hearted affair, although the cricket could be of a high standard. Music would be played by local brass bands to entertain the crowd and the dignitaries in the VIP tent. The cricket would be taking place at the same time and I found, when bowling, that I would run up to the rhythm of the music, rather than the rhythm of my action, which was quite disconcerting.

Over an 11-day period three three-day matches would be played, involving Test players and other senior first-class cricketers. The opening fixture would be TN Pearce's XI against the tourists, which in 1965 were the South Africans, fresh from winning a series against England for the first time for 30 years. TN Pearce's side was selected and organised by Tom Pearce, who had captained Essex between 1933 and 1950 and was an England Test selector for many years.

All the players in the team, with the exception of David Green, had played Test cricket, six of us in the series against South Africa. Although David Green did not play Test cricket, he had a particular talent that a number of people envied: he could down a pint of bitter in under three seconds. I used to manage him in this, taking the bets in challenges by aspiring opponents. After three or four victories he would visit the men's room, heave away the bulk liquid and return to face more challengers. The South Africans thought they would up the odds by getting him to down Guinness instead of bitter. They bet against him doing this within five seconds, but they failed miserably. It took a long time for them to realise that he did not drink the pint; he just opened his gullet and poured it in.

Mike Smith, England's captain, was in the side, but Trevor Bailey took on that role. I opened the bowling with Butch White, later in the innings renewing my Wanstead partnership with Barry Knight. In a low-scoring game we beat the South Africans in two days. So perhaps the selectors did get it wrong.

The second match of the festival was a historic one. Rothmans, the cigarette manufacturers who were already supporting cricket in a number of ways, decided to sponsor two matches between England and the Rest of the World: the first at Scarborough, the second at Lord's. It was typical of Rothmans' approach that they took no part in selecting the teams, preferring to invest that responsibility in a poll of television viewers conducted by the *Radio Times*. The response was remarkable proof of the interest the fixture aroused, with around 40,000 replies.

Although picked in the twelve Norman O'Neill, the Australian, declined the invitation, in protest at the selection of Charlie Griffith, whose bowling action he considered unfair.

The following twelve players were summoned to represent the Rest of the World XI: Wally Grout (Australia), the Nawab of Pataudi (India), John Reid (New Zealand), Hanif Mohammad (Pakistan), Eddie Barlow and Colin Bland (South Africa) and Garry Sobers, Lance Gibbs, Charlie Griffith, Wes Hall, Conrad Hunte and Rohan Kanhai (West Indies). Quite an imposing bunch of players.

The England team, selected by Brian Sellers, Tom Pearce, Trevor Bailey and Leslie Ames, was: Mike Smith, John Edrich, Bob Barber, Peter Parfitt, Kenny Barrington, Colin Cowdrey, Barry Knight, John Murray, Fred Titmus, Butch White and me.

War had broken out between India and Pakistan. With tensions high, Pakistan invaded the Indian state of Jammu and Kashmir, and India responded with a full military attack in West Pakistan. It was decided by both teams that we would individually sign a petition condemning the action of the two sides, pointing out the comradeship of the Nawab of Pataudi and Hanif Mohammad in the Rest of the World team. The conflict was over soon afterwards, and I have oftened wondered how much influence our petition actually had!

The Nawab of Pataudi, the Indian captain and captain-elect of Sussex, stood down from the first match, allowing John Reid, so recently retired from Test cricket, the honour of leading the side. He won the toss and South Africa and the West Indies, in the shape of Eddie Barlow and Conrad Hunte, opened the batting for the Rest of the World. The wicket was completely dry at one end but a little damp at the other. In poor light all the Rest of the World batsmen were subdued by the English bowling. I worked up a good pace, but it was Barry Knight who worried them most by moving the ball around off the seam. Hunte and Barlow ran beautifully between the wickets and provided a good start but, to the great disappointment of the huge crowd, Sobers and Kanhai never really got going. Without runs from Colin Bland and Charlie Griffith, the Rest of the World might not have made much more than 100, but they were all out for 215 late in the day. Bad light and rain brought proceedings to an end, with England on 10 for no wicket.

Both sides were having a drink in the England dressing room afterwards when Charlie Griffith asked what activities were available in Scarborough that evening. Someone suggested the Black and White Minstrel Show.

"What," said Wes Hall. "No way. We've been living that all day out there."

The second day saw Wes Hall and Charlie Griffith in full flight. John Edrich, who had only just recovered from the hit on the head he had received at the hands of Peter Pollock at Lord's, bravely withstood the onslaught. He and Bob Barber saw the England XI off to a good start. When Bob Barber was out, fending off a nasty bouncer from Charlie Griffith, it brought Peter Parfitt to the wicket. His innings of 71 not out was one of the best I ever saw him play. He was an excellent stroke-maker, and the whole of his repertoire was on show that day. John Edrich scored a battling 51 and, because of the inclement weather, play finished early. Mike Smith declared the innings closed overnight at 160 for two.

The game was marred by Ted Dexter who, on a television programme covering the match, accused Charlie Griffith of throwing every ball he delivered. There had already been something of a witch-hunt during the West Indies tour to England in 1963. Our most senior umpire at the time, Syd Buller, approved Charlie's action during that series but, because he got 32 Test wickets and a scary reputation, the press, like a dog with a bone, would not let the matter go.

Syd Buller was standing in the Rest of the World match and, to put the cat among the pigeons, John Reid put on Charlie Griffith at the end where he would be in full view of Syd Buller. Nothing happened, and Ted Dexter's comments became a storm in a tea cup.

My view was not the same as Ted's. I believed that Charlie bowled his normal delivery but that, when delivering a faster ball like a yorker or bouncer, something was different. What, I do not know. He was only called from square leg twice in his career, which makes the whole subject of his being a 'chucker' rather nebulous.

Conrad Hunte and Eddie Barlow went to town on the third and final day, putting on 100 for the first wicket, and, when John Reid declared, England had a target of 209 for victory. The crowd was looking forward to the prospect of John Edrich & Co taking on Wes Hall, Charlie Griffith and Garry Sobers, not to mention Lance Gibbs, but it was all to no avail. The weather had the final say, and the game finished in a damp draw.

I have achieved many things in my life, but playing in the first ever Rest of the World match is high on the list. I still have the battered tie that Rothmans produced to celebrate the occasion. It is one that I will never part with; maybe it will be worn when I am dressed for my last journey.

The final match at Scarborough was Yorkshire against MCC, and five players were retained from the England side which played against the Rest of the World: Barry Knight, John Murray, Fred Titmus, Butch White and me. In came Alan Jones, David Green, Colin Milburn, Keith Fletcher, Robin Hobbs and Basil D'Oliveira. Fred Titmus was appointed captain, and we batted first. Early on in the innings Fred Trueman hit Alan Jones on the head with a ball only marginally short. Alan was one of the shortest players in first-class cricket, and a ball around the rib-cage to an average-sized batsman was a bouncer to Alan. He shook his head once or twice and continued to bat, getting out soon after to Don Wilson, the Yorkshire slow left-armer. Colin Milburn and David Green steadied the ship, there was good support from Barry Knight, and we were all out for 277 by close of play.

I was upstairs in the pavilion having a drink with the Yorkshire players when Fred Trueman came into the room and made a bee-line for me. "What are you doing for dinner tonight?" he asked.

Now this was a colossal surprise to me. I mean, we were friendly and often had the odd drink together. But dinner?

"I can't tonight," I said. "I have two girls to look after." Coleen and her close friend Anita had travelled to Scarborough to support me.

"Bring them with you," Fred said.

Now I was concerned. Fred was a reasonably generous person, but to take three of the opposition out for dinner on the first evening?

He gave me directions to his country club and arranged a time. We joined him and his first wife Enid who was in good form, attacking him on every subject he discussed. Halfway through the delightful meal he said a strange thing: "I didn't mean to hit him, you know."

I had no idea what he was talking about and said so.

"But Fred Titmus and JT Murray told me you were upset because I'd hit Alan Jones on the head."

"No," I said. "I was aware that the ball was only marginally short and said so at the time."

"Those bastards."

All the Yorkshire team, with the exception of Tony Nicholson, an extremely useful medium-paced bowler, had played or would play for England, but they did not get off to a particularly good start. Ar one stage they were 163 for six, then Jack Hampshire and Jimmy Binks put on 141, and that enabled Brian Close to declare at 312 for seven. MCC finished the day on 59 for three.

One of those three wickets was Colin Milburn who, on his return to the dressing room, stripped off and entered the shower. Having dried himself off, he sprayed a deodorant over every inch of his ample body. For some reason, known only to Colin, he placed the nozzle of the spray between the cheeks of his large posterior and gave a long press. The look of horror on his face was something to behold. He dashed into the wash room, filled a sink with cold water, climbed on and sat in it with his legs dangling over the edge, uttering exquisite sighs of relief.

The following day MCC finished on 214, leaving Yorkshire to score 180 runs for victory. This they did easily by seven wickets.

In the three matches of the festival I had taken eight wickets, bringing my tally for the summer to 119.

Here endeth the Scarborough Festival and the season of 1965.

WINTERS IN SOUTH AFRICA, SUMMERS IN ENGLAND

Deck cricket on the Transvaal Castle

23

On the boat to South Africa

Not to be picked for the final Test at the Oval was a body blow; not to be picked for the tour down under, a nasty uppercut. Then to be on standby for Australia and for the selectors to take someone else was a knockout.

I made inquiries about the possibility of a coaching position abroad and was offered an appointment with the Argentine cricket authority. At that time the Argentine was being encouraged to show more interest in cricket. I accepted the post, but a week later it was cancelled; I never found out why. MCC handled the negotiations, and I imagine that they felt sorry for me because a week later they came up with a job coaching two schools in East London, South Africa.

When I gave the news to Coleen that I was going to South Africa for the winter she was not too pleased.

"I'm not so sure that I'll be around when you return," she said.

"What does that mean?"

"What it says. I have no intention of just hanging around, whilst you go off to a foreign country enjoying yourself unless you can convince me that there is more substance to our relationship and that we will be together permanently on your return."

"It's not a leap year," I said, taking a quick step backwards. "But I accept your proposal as long as you make the arrangements for the wedding on my return."

This she agreed to with the words, "Go sow your wild oats, and we will marry in April!"

There were two popular modes of travel to South Africa, flying and sailing. Flying was expensive. Sailing was longer but more fun; it was an 11-day trip of which at least six days were through the tropics.

I booked my passages with the Union-Castle Line: outward on the *Transvaal Castle*, homeward on the *Windsor Castle*. The *Transvaal Castle*, launched in 1961, was different from the other ships in the fleet in that all its 736 passengers were accommodated in one class rather than being split into first and tourist classes. It was also the first ship in the fleet to use female waiting staff – stewardettes, as they were called.

Colin Milburn had already told me that he was going to be coaching in East London. We decided to share, both on the *Windsor Castle* and at the hotel when we arrived. Well, it was not quite sharing with Colin; he had two-thirds and I had the other third! Two other first-class cricketers, Jim Pressdee (Glamorgan) and Geoff Keith (Hampshire), were on the ship with us; they too had coaching positions in South Africa.

I have never suffered from sea sickness, but I have never experienced anything like the evening when we sailed through the Bay of Biscay. To call it 'rough going' would be an understatement. The ship went up and down, side to side, all at the same time. Meals were taken in two sittings, and Colin and I were on the second roster so we had plenty of opportunity to put a few gin sours into our ample frames. The turbulence had increased by the time the second sitting was called, and out of 350 possible diners only three attended, including Colin and me. By the main course there were just the two of us; by the dessert there was one, me! I was so drunk by then that I was most likely walking in a straight line, my stagger contradicting the ship's roll. The following morning the captain, who was standing in for the regular skipper, apologised for not putting the stabilisers out, confessing that he did not know the ship had them. It cost him a drink all round, an expensive mistake.

Once we got into the tropics the swell subsided, and it was like sailing on glass. The mirror effect of the ocean was only broken by the schools of dolphin racing to keep pace with their bigger metal colleague. It was a wonderful experience, travelling for 11 days whilst on holiday. The captain was mad on cricket and, once he learned that there were four first-class cricketers on board, he challenged the engineers to a game of deck cricket. He asked me to skipper his team and Colin to captain the engineers' side.

For those of you who have never played deck cricket, I will explain. The bats were similar to a normal blade and made of wood. The ball was made of rope and was quite hard. The batsman's crease was about 12 yards from that of the bowler who had to deliver the ball underarm. The wickets were pitched on the narrow side of the ship, allowing a width of about six yards. A net was hung on the outer boundary to stop the ball from going into the ocean. Lines were painted across the width at six yards (a hit past that was one run) and nine yards (two runs). Past the bowler's crease was four – or six if in the air. There were six players in each side: a wicket-keeper and five fielders, all of whom had to bowl.

When Colin's side batted, two of my fielders from the crew placed themselves either side of the wicket just in front of the six-yard line. This was not too bad a position for a normal batsman but for Colin Milburn? I did warn them, but to no avail. One was carried off; the other walked with a limp for a week. Needless to say, Colin's aggressive batting won the match for the engineers, and the ship's captain did not speak to me for a few days. When his petulance subsided we had a return match, and my now wary team triumphed quite comfortably.

Both Colin and I were out-going people. We made a lot of friends on board, from both genders and various ages. After the cricket matches the third engineer became very friendly with us. He was about the same age, and he asked us to do him a favour. Being third engineer he got the worst eight-hour watch: 4pm to 12 midnight. This gave him little opportunity to socialise with the younger passengers on board. Colin's and my job was to fill his large cabin with young people so that he and his watch colleagues could party until the early hours. As we were included in the parties, we did not see much of the ship's activity before lunchtime. We enjoyed the parties enormously but felt that our fitness could be suffering badly. Whilst on the boat we became very friendly with a girl called Ann Kershaw, who lived in East London and was returning home after a period in Europe. We were close to her for most of the voyage and remained so when we arrived.

24

First days in South Africa

We were met in the docks by a former South African first-class umpire who escorted us to our hotel and briefed us on our responsibilities. I was going to be coaching at two schools, Afrikaans-speaking Hoerskool Grens and English-speaking Cambridge. Our host asked if we would like a quick trip around East London to get our bearings. We agreed to this and, after about half an hour, Colin said to our new friend, "This Hou Links must be a very big golf course; I've seen signs to it everywhere." Our host chuckled: "I don't think so. It means 'Keep Left' in Afrikaans." He dropped us at the Birmingham Hotel, our home for the next six months.

The second person to welcome us to East London was Ann Kershaw. She popped in to the hotel for a coffee and said, "My mother and father would like to invite you both to Sunday luncheon to thank you for looking after me on my journey home." Well, her home was a delightful residence on the bank of the Nahoon River, and luncheon was more like a ten-course banquet of fish and meat cooked on the braai, the local name for barbecue, which pleased both Colin and me because we had been eating junk food since we left the boat. There was a sausage called boerewors, skewered meats like sosaties, kebabs, fish and rock lobster (kreef) – just wonderful. Following that first visit it was open house for Colin and me every weekend for the rest of our six-month stay.

Ann's mother had a family tree which traced her ancestry back to British royalty. Each time a child was born into her family their name was added to the tree, and a fresh parchment was presented to them at their christening. Ann's father Bob was a war hero, the first South African to receive the DSO in World War Two.

Bob Kershaw, a fighter pilot, and his squadron leader John Frost were flying Hawker Hurricanes for the South African Air Force when they were sent to Kenya in early 1941 as part of a campaign against the Italians in Abyssinia. During an attack on an airfield, John Frost's tank of glycol coolant was hit, forcing him to land quickly and to set his plane on fire to prevent its capture. Bob Kershaw landed beside him and picked him up. The cockpit in Bob's Hurricane was so small that John Frost had to sit on his lap, using the throttle and gear stick while Bob worked the foot pedals to get them up into the air. Bob was awarded the DSO and had his portrait painted, the picture appearing on a postage stamp. Bob returned to flying, adding a Distinguished Flying Cross to his DSO.

Having spent so many enjoyable days on the Nahoon River with Bob and the family, I wanted to give him and Tina something to thank them for their kind hospitality. There was little I could buy that they did not already have so I wrote him a special poem:

Kershaw's Lament

Ungainly seagull sitting there
With Mitchell's wings along your back
Stay rest awhile and listen here
To haunting thoughts we had to fear
Before attack.

I rode you once as just a boy
A prince his steed we galloped on
The changing hills of cloud to Troy
And never knew a greater joy
Than flying on.

Then heaven's blue was darkly scarred
With faces of the boys we knew
And other faces straining hard
As if to will this pious yard
Back to its blue.

We found the price too hard to pay
The loss of man, of friend, of foe
And grew our age before the day
Returning men who yearn to say
Why did we go.

Ungainly seagull sitting there
With Mitchell's wings along your back
Your restlessness I too can share
As lighter grows the load I bear
In looking back.

With grace and poise you take the air
And leave a problem world below
Why should we wingless creatures care
About the wonders you find there
Unless we know.

FER

When he finished reading it he was in tears, and he gave me a big emotional hug.

The college at which Colin coached, Selbourne, was the strongest cricketing school in East London. The boys there had received coaching from English cricketers for many years. My two schools, however, had received no specialised coaching, and in both cases I had to start from scratch. Cambridge was a co-educational English-speaking school with about 800 pupils. I restricted my activities to the school teams plus some reserves. After I had been coaching for about a month, one of the school's female teachers asked me if I was able to coach some of the girls. "If the cricket master is okay with it, there would be no problem with me," I told her. A form went up on the school notice board, and 96 girls put their name to it. I actually had a look at all 96 but only took on 20 of the best, those whom I felt would benefit most.

The essence of my batting philosophy was the simple fact that runs could only be scored if the batsman remained at the wicket. No one can score runs sitting in the pavilion. Therefore defence was of major importance. But cricketers under 14 also have to be encouraged to attack the bowling, to get the feel of playing shots and to develop their stroke-playing skills.

Coaches who were first-class bowlers make just as good, if not better, teachers of the basics of batting than former batsmen. The former batsman tends to teach his own style of play, whereas the bowlers look for weaknesses in all the styles of batting because they have to bowl against them. The same philosophy applies to teaching the basic principles of bowling where the batsman has the greater knowledge. This view does not apply at the higher level of the game.

121

Having watched coaches at work for 70 years, I definitely feel that more emphasis is given to batting than to bowling. We have possibly missed a few Fred Truemans or Shane Warnes because of this. I have always thought that we bowlers are nothing but cannon fodder for the batsmen, elsewise why do so many rules penalise the bowler?

Hoerskool Grens, my other school, was Afrikaans-speaking. "Speel vorentoe met die kolf," and "Speel terug met die kolf," I would shout at the young batsmen, usually adding the word 'jong'. Play forward and play back, youngster. They listened, and slowly their overall ability improved enough to play matches against Cambridge and to hold their own. To be able to play against Colin's Selbourne, I needed to combine my two schools, which we did on a number of occasions. We never won, but we did give them a run for their money.

At one of these matches I had a visit from an Afrikaans school inspector who complimented me on what I had achieved at Hoerskool Grens. He then gave me a lecture attempting to justify apartheid and the principle of separate development. "What you must understand," he said, "is that when we first arrived in the Cape, only a few Xhosa lived in the Eastern Cape of South Africa. The Zulu and other tribes moved down from central Africa to confront us. We fought a number of battles against these peoples and won the country by right of battle."

"No, you didn't," I said. "We won it by right of battle."

He did not speak to me anymore that day, prompting me to write this poem:

The White Indigene of South Africa

What do they know this prying world
I pay him well and treat him kind
What do they know this prying world
Of Schools, of Churches, Hospitals
I care not for the prying world
And know not why my creed be damned
Oh Lord I offer you this prayer
Show me a sign to help me face
I mean to help me know the wrong
What is this that has happened here?
My skin is black
Oh Lord give me my freedom back!

FER

Two years later I was contacted by the *Daily Mail*. They had heard that I wrote poems and wanted to include one in an article that featured verses by well-known people. I sent them this, and it duly appeared in print – between offerings by ex-Queen Dina of Jordan and Lord Sieff of Marks and Spencer. A few years later, John Snow brought out a collection of his poetry – and fast bowlers are supposed to be thick and insensitive.

25

Donald Woods

Another man who, like Bob Kershaw, had great charisma and courage was Donald Woods, the editor of East London's *Daily Dispatch*. Soon after I arrived in South Africa he asked me if I would write a weekly cricket column for his newspaper, which he would cast his eye over before publishing.

Donald was some man. His parents ran a trading post in the Transkei, a tribal reserve, and he spoke fluent Xhosa and Afrikaans as well as English. As a young law student at the University of Cape Town, he started to question the separatist views he had grown up with, becoming politically active, and at the age of 23 he stood unsuccessfully for parliament. He gave up the law to become a junior reporter for the *Daily Dispatch* and, at the age of 31, earlier in the year of my arrival in East London, he was appointed the newspaper's editor-in-chief, taking a strongly anti-apartheid position in his editorials. From the start he insisted on hiring black reporters, flouting the apartheid system by seating all his staff together. He had already had at least one run-in with the government by the time I arrived.

Coming from England which is, to all intents and purposes, a free country, you could not avoid falling foul of all the strange rules and regulations in the South African system. I did not like it at all – the whites at the front of the bus, the blacks at the back – and a lot of it was hypocritical and, in many cases, bizarre. The government did deals with the wealthy non-whites when it suited them. The Japanese were categorised as white but not the Chinese.

The hotel in East London accepted Indian and Coloured guests as long as they stayed in their rooms and did not go in the public places. The hotel manager decided to add a little glamour to the night club by putting an attractive girl alongside his usual barman. She was white, he was black, and soon enough government officials turned up to lay down the law. Either the barman could stock the bar and collect the empty glasses and the girl sell the drink, or the other way round, but they could not do the same job together.

Donald and I became close friends. Initially he liked me because he loved cricket and I was a cricketer, but we also shared a sense of humour. I admired him greatly, he had integrity and honesty, and he was a very good friend; he did not shirk friendship. You could not help but admire him but, if we had met on a bus anywhere, we would still have been mates.

His love of cricket was only surpassed by his love of chess. We decided to have a major challenge and play a chess tournament based on the first to 25 victories. At 24/24, before we played the decider, we discussed the victor's prize. It was agreed that in the future, whenever we met, the loser would go down on one knee, hold a forelock, if he had one, and declare, "Oh hail, Grandmaster." I lost that last game.

A year or two later I was playing for Somerset in Bristol when I received a telephone call from Donald. He was lecturing in the city, was going to be there for a few days and would I have dinner with him? We agreed to meet at seven o'clock.

"Don't be late," he said. "We don't want to waste good wine time."

On the dot of seven I arrived at the rendezvous, where he was waiting for me. After the back slapping was over, he said, "Well, where is my proper greeting?" I knew exactly what he wanted so I went down on one knee,

held my forelock, raised my left hand in salute and was just about to say, "Oh hail, Grandmaster" when three photographers appeared out of nowhere and caught me in this ridiculous position for the front page of the first editions.

We would discuss more cricket and chess than politics, but we did have conversations about apartheid. I remember him giving me a piece he had written in which he advocated partitioning the country, separating the Afrikaner heartlands from the English-speaking areas where the apartheid system would be abolished. He discussed the merits of it with me. I told him it would not work; too many of the main ports would be in the English-speaking areas.

During the period of my employ by the *Daily Dispatch*, there was a week where little had happened on the cricketing front so, stuck for something to fill my column, I wrote a story about a horse playing cricket at Lord's.

From Fred Rumsey comes a shaggy horse story

Some cricket fans from upcountry have written in asking for my favourite cricket story. Here it is:

The eve of the fifth Test between England and Australia at Lord's saw the English team having their customary net practice on the nursery ground.

As is usual a small crowd had gathered behind and around the netting enclosure. Trueman was bowling to Boycott—a bouncer. In an attempt to hook, Boycott slipped and became entangled with the stumps, receiving a nasty spike in the playing area.

Cowdrey, the captain of England, rushed into the net, only to find the wound inflicted on Boycott bad enough to hospitalise him for the duration of the Test.

BLOW

With the series level and one match to play, Boycott's unavailability was a sorry blow to England's chances of winning the match and the elusive Ashes.

As Boycott was gently manhandled from the net, a musing Cowdrey rejoined the other players, searching in his mind for a replacement. During the turmoil and drama of the Boycott incident, a grey dray horse had quietly detached himself from the back of the crowd and, in between the occasional munch of the lush green grass, sidled up to Colin Cowdrey and nozzled him in the back.

Colin's first reaction was to push the horse away, at which (for the purpose of this story) the horse said: "Hey!"

STARED

Cowdrey and all the other players stared in disbelief. "If you want a replacement for Boycott," the horse went on, "how about giving me a chance?"

Stunned and bemused by all that was happening, Cowdrey gave instructions for the horse to be removed.

With a startling whinny, the horse reared and, grabbing Dexter's bat in his seven-year-old teeth, he trotted slowly to the vacant net.

Once there, he adopted what is now known as the forward stance—hind legs apart, bat held with the forelegs.

Seeing there was nothing he could do, Cowdrey ordered his two fastest bowlers, Trueman and Statham, to bowl at the horse.

Kindness to animals prevented these two great bowlers from letting loose as is their wont. Trueman's first ball, at gentle medium pace, was dispatched by the horse over the gaping heads of the other players, vanishing into the gardens bordering St. Johns Wood Road.

PACE

Seeing this, Statham increased his pace a little, only to watch his ball follow the same arc, and land in the same garden.

The horse now, whinnying with obvious delight, settled down, while Trueman slowly walked his 30 paces away from the bowler's wicket.

Trueman turned and started into his famous rhythmic run. Like a lion closing on his kill, his powerful frame forced his muscles to a crescendo, and the eruption at the crease hurled the ball at nearly 100 m.p.h. in the direction of the horse.

The horse bent his hind legs and with a perfect hook, lifted the ball high over the grandstand.

The next ball from Statham, bowled with venom and accuracy from his full gangling run, was hit back past him with the elegance and ease of a Hammond or Hobbs.

TEST

Cowdrey had no other choice than to play the horse in the all-important final Test.

The world had by now heard of this phenomenon, and the ground was filled to capacity.

Television from all of Europe covered the match and all cameras were trained on the pavilion steps.

Cowdrey had won the toss and elected to bat. His opening partner was A. Horse.

The Australians took the field to thunderous applause.

Horse took strike, with Lindwall to bowl.

Lindwall, of the majestic run up, bowls to Horse.

With a flick of his forelegs, Horse sends the ball scorching the turf to hit the fence in front of the Warner Stand.

The next ball is cover-driven with such power that it returns half the distance after hitting the Mound Stand wall.

FURY

Lindwall bowls with fury, a short rising ball. Horse twists it off his nose with a delicate flick and lands it in the grandstand balcony.

Another bouncer this time, outside the off stump. With elegance supreme, Horse square-cuts first bounce through the Tavern door. Four balls, 16 runs. The crowd is in an uproar.

Lindwall bowls again. This time Horse delicately kneels on one hind leg and sweeps the ball to the boundary.

Last ball from Lindwall and, going for another classical cover drive, Horse edges the ball to third man.

Cowdrey starts running, calling Horse — who stays in his crease.

Third man gathers the ball quickly and throws to the bowler's end. Desperately Cowdrey tries to regain his territory, but is run out by a yard.

On his way to the pavilion he passes Horse. "Why didn't you run?" he inquires.

"Skipper," the horse replies, "if I could run, I wouldn't be here, I'd be at Epsom!"

125

When Donald vetted the piece, he asked why I had decided to write it.

"It seemed to me to be the thing to do at the time," I said.

"Pass that by me again."

So I did: "It seemed to me to be the thing to do at the time."

He thought for a moment, then said, "I'll publish it, and we'll both be damned." We actually got some wonderful compliments for being so refreshing.

The following winter, when I returned to South Africa with Coleen, we became a foursome – Donald and his wife Wendy, Coleen and me – and we all got on well together. Then, when I was back in England, we kept in touch, mostly by letter. He loved it that I was setting up a cricketers' union.

His anti-apartheid editorials landed him in more and more trouble with the South African security police. He became friendly with Stephen Biko, the leader of the Black Consciousness movement, and Wendy joined the Black Sash, a non-violent protest movement of white women.

In 1976, after the Soweto Uprising, when police killed hundreds of children protesting against being taught in Afrikaans, Stephen Biko was beaten to death in police custody. Donald went to the morgue with Stephen's wife Ntsiki and photographed the battered body. Soon afterwards he was placed under a five-year ban, stripped of his editorship and prevented from writing, travelling or speaking publicly. He was subjected to much harassment, his phone was tapped, and the final straw came when his six-year-old daughter was severely burned by an acid-laced t-shirt.

I was very concerned about them. At one point I tried to take up his case with politicians in England, but nothing came of my efforts.

Donald decided to leave South Africa. Having arranged for his wife Wendy and their children to visit Lesotho, he disguised himself as a priest and hitch-hiked 300 miles to the Telle River, which he planned to wade across to Lesotho. Unfortunately, following days of steady rain, the river had flooded, and he could not get across. Eventually, still in the robes of a priest, he persuaded the unsuspecting driver of a Lesotho Postal Service truck to give him a ride.

Some time after he arrived in England, he asked to see me. The secret service, who were covering his security, arranged for the meeting to take place. I was taken through a number of front doors and straight out the back, before I was dropped in a small mews court where Donald and Wendy were staying. After an emotional greeting, he related to me the story of his escape, telling me in detail about his plan to swim the flooded Telle River.

"At one point, while I was trying to get across the river, I asked myself, 'What the hell am I doing here?' And do you know what came into my mind? Those words of yours about that silly story of the horse. 'It seemed to me to be the thing to do at the time.'"

The story of his friendship with Stephen Biko was made into a film, 'Cry Freedom', by the director Richard Attenborough. Donald, who was played by Kevin Kline, and Wendy, by Penelope Wilton, worked closely with the cast and crew. When the film had its English premiere, at the Empire Cinema in Tottenham Court Road, Coleen and I went along with Donald and Wendy as a foursome.

In his last years Donald campaigned for a statue of Nelson Mandela to be erected outside the South African High Commission in Trafalgar Square. If it were my decision, I would erect one of Donald alongside it.

Donald Woods in later life

26

Christmas 1965

The Christmas break in South Africa is their long summer holiday. Colin and I were given the same break as our tutorial colleagues but, unlike them, we had no papers to prepare for the autumn term so we could run amok, which we chose to do in Johannesburg and Cape Town. There were a lot of English coaches in South Africa, and someone arranged for us to play a two-day game over the New Year against North-Eastern Transvaal in Benoni.

We stayed in a non-air-conditioned hotel during what must have been the hottest New Year on record. John Snow and I were the opening bowlers for the English Coaches XI and, in an attempt to undermine us for the following day's match, local Scottish supporters encouraged us to go 'first footing', visiting a number of residences offering coal, shortbread, salt, black bun and whisky. We were kept at this until the early hours and, when I did finally get to bed, it was impossible to sleep because of the heat.

The next day was even hotter, and it was with enormous delight I learned that our skipper had won the toss and elected to bat. I was the first to grab the masseur's table, followed quickly by John Snow, and after some sleep we were almost human by lunch time. When we did bowl later that first day, both of us were suffering from lung collapse by the third over. The temperature was over 100 degrees in the shade – what it was in the sun, I have no idea – and John and I were restricted to three-over spells. I cannot for the life of me remember the second day nor can I remember the result, but I can remember having a good time.

Opening the batting for the opposition was Eric Brotherton, who owned a citrus farm on the edge of the Kruger National Park. He suggested that I spend some time in the game reserve and some time at his farm. Colin had made other arrangements, but Dennis Amiss, the Warwickshire batsman, made himself available and together we hired a car for the trip.

Dennis sold me his old Voigtlander camera, and we set off into the park in search of the African 'Big Five': the lion, elephant, buffalo, leopard and rhino. Visitors can go years without seeing a leopard, but our luck was in when almost immediately we came upon one, basking himself in the sun. Then there were the buffalo and elephant.

On the second day a pride of lions was slowly crossing the road in front of us. I pulled into the middle of them, stopped and switched off the engine. I told Dennis to make sure he wound his window up, and I started to take photographs. The lions were not fussed at all by us or our car. One male sauntered over to Dennis's side of the vehicle, had a good sniff and an enormous yawn, showing his ample incisors, gave Dennis a long stare and sauntered away. It was at this moment that Dennis noticed that he had opened his window, not closed it.

Unfortunately we never saw the rhino.

"Not to worry," I said to Dennis. "We're seeing Colin in Cape Town!"

Forgive me for that, Colin, wherever you are. I couldn't resist it.

The Nuffield Schools Week was being played so Colin and I took the opportunity to watch our own Border Schools in a couple of matches and also to watch the South African Schools XI, the pick of the boys, play against Western Province in a one-day match at Newlands.

Otherwise we switched off for that week, meeting up with fellow travellers from the journey over, sampling the beaches either side of Cape Town and in my case tasting the wonderful variety of Cape wines available – in Colin's case, sampling gin and coke, which tastes the same whatever part of the world you are in. Meeting our fellow travellers did bring home to me the benefits that world travel brings to young, intelligent adults. Their attitudes and opinions are far more mature than those of their counterparts who never leave Britain.

On the stumps behind Colin is the Walter Lawrence Trophy, awarded for the fastest century of 1969, which he scored in his last Test innings.

Behind him are Fred Trueman and Tom Graveney.

Colin had two good eyes at this time and, although he was yet to play for England, that honour would come later in the year. His huge talent was obvious whenever he picked up a cricket bat; he was a big man with charisma to match, tremendous agility and great coordination. We spent a lot of time together, and he became my best friend in cricket. Later, when I was running the cricket festival in Barbados, his was always the first name I wrote down. I also took him on all the Test match tours I ran; I gave him a group of people to look after, and you could not have anyone better. People loved him. He had a great sense of humour – and a lovely singing voice, too.

He never really came to terms with losing an eye and not playing cricket, and as a consequence he drank too much. At one stage I was contacted by a brewery, who wanted to make him the landlord of one of their pubs, and I said no. Maybe I should not have interfered, but he was my friend and I saw it as the quickest way to his death. In the Caribbean he always stayed with me, and I never charged him for anything. I tried to help him without my giving him the feeling that I was doing him a favour. I stopped short of saying "Here's £500 a month" because I knew that would have upset him, but I found ways of employing him, sometimes unnecessarily.

He was so talented, everything came easily to him, and that made him lazy. No important engagement would worry him one iota. But he would not give up the drink, and that was because deep down he was a bit low – partly because he had lost his eye and his cricketing career but more because he did not have a companion. He liked women, but I never knew him to have a girl friend. I would love him to have married. If he had done so, he might still be alive now. He was always fun to be with, I never saw him bitter or miserable, but he had an inner loneliness. He was somebody who would love to have been loved.

He died of a heart attack in 1990 at the age of 48, coming out of a pub.

In South Africa we were being ribbed by our friends to hold a challenge match, Colin's XI versus Fred's XI, just for their amusement. The teams were organised by two companies, each of whom made donations to a local charity. Bob Kershaw's company, Grosvenor Ford, was one; the other, Cyril Lord Carpets, was managed by a Brit named Dennis Wood. The teams were made up of employees, with Colin captaining the Cyril Lord XI and me skippering Grosvenor Ford. Few of the players played cricket regularly so Colin and I agreed not to bowl at all. This put my side at an obvious disadvantage, bearing in mind that my prowess with the bat in first-class cricket was not much to write home about.

I won the toss and decided to bat. We were playing a limited-overs match so we needed to get on with it. I had hit hundreds at club level, but they were few and far between – and, more by luck than judgement, I scored a lifetime highest score of 190, enabling Grosvenor Ford to finish with an innings total of nearly 300. I was cock-a-hoop, over the moon, all the clichés to describe euphoria, and confident of victory.

Ninety minutes later, when the Cyril Lord XI passed our score, Colin was on 250 not out.

Although Colin was good fun to live with, I was missing Coleen. I would not have owned up to that fact so I turned to writing more poetry, much to Colin's disgust, and every airmail letter I sent to her carried a verse of a poem:

Dear Coleen

Heavenly sounds the name Coleen,
Yet sweeter is the mortal form it bears.
A smile as bright as young earth's start,
That warms a sad depressed heart.

Feelings as yet to be express'd
In words by poets, authors and their like,
Pierce my mind at musing hours
Bursting through like young spring flowers.

Deep below the shell of beauty
I sought and found the wonder of your soul.
Age-old fears fell all about me
And bared my heart for you to see.

With your being I am now join'd,
Not one but two hearts, not one but two minds.
Should yours be hate then also mine,
Should yours be love then also mine.

From first I view'd the shapely grace
Of girl and grew to daytime wondering.
I dared to dream that life would be
So good in giving you to me.

Though before us lovers parted
Airing the sorrow that was plainly theirs.
Let us learn from their repentance
Accepting all as a penance.

All love is touch'd by keen edge'd burrs
Of doubt, when little can the eye record
But keep my sated heart with care
I have no want to use it here.

The sun is down and darkness shrouds
This day of changing dreams and changing ways
Set only is the love I bear
In loneliness no one can share.

Before the body frees the mind
To search the jumbled vaults of hidden time
And falsely brings you near to me
I'll hold you close in memory.

FER

131

Cricket in South Africa and England

When I was at Coopers' Company School, there appeared to be no obvious path for aspiring young cricketers that would lead them to representative cricket. The teams existed, but how to get into them was extremely nebulous. Most of the selected sides consisted of public schoolboys, who had the big advantage of receiving professional coaching.

In South Africa, even though the big schools had coaching available, the system of selection was clearer and better than in the United Kingdom. Each province held a number of matches between the schools within its boundaries. From these matches a side was selected to represent the province in Nuffield Week, a tournament which was played during the Christmas holidays. The Week consisted of five days (Monday to Friday) of inter-provincial matches, culminating in a one-day match on Saturday between a selected South African Schools team and the host province. With the tournament in Cape Town that year, the Schools XI played Western Province, who were skippered by Peter van der Merwe, South Africa's captain.

East London was in the province of Border, which had two strong cricket-playing schools: Dale College in King William's Town and Queen's College in Queenstown. Both of these schools regularly had pupils selected to attend the Nuffield Week. One such, from Dale, was Hylton Ackerman, the captain of the South African Schools team, who had made his first-class debut two years earlier, at the age of 16, for Border. How many English schoolboys have made their first-class debuts at 16?

There were two other Border players in the Combined Schools XI: Bruce Groves and Tony Greig, from Queen's, both of whom made their first-class debuts for Border the next month. In the match Hylton Ackerman scored a useful 54, but the Schools were defeated by two wickets.

I am sure the boys learned more from that one-day match against Western Province than from all the other matches in the tournament, a fact borne out by the large number of Nuffield Schoolboys who went on to play first-class or, more importantly, Test cricket.

The only downside to the tournament was that it was restricted to white boys. This did not change till 1994 when it became the Coca-Cola Under-19 Week. In the Border Schools side that year was Makhaya Ntini, who would go on play in 101 Tests and to take 390 wickets, seven more than Sir Ian Botham. To this day they are doing an excellent job, though I would like a better finale than the current match between South African Schools and South African Colts.

I believe such a tournament in England, structured to suit our county system, would improve our search for young talent enormously, though I would prefer to see the selected side play a three- or four-day game against first-class opposition. There are bodies in this country who are quite capable of running such a show; I am sure that the Lord's Taverners would be prepared to get involved. If anyone is interested, contact me – as I have already part-prepared a suitable structure.

East London schools, made up of players from Selbourne College, Colin's school, and Cambridge and Grens, my two schools, challenged Dale College to a one-day game in King William's Town. Dale won the toss and batted first. The openers put on 115 runs before the first wicket fell, with the not-out batsman at that point on 80. Then Hylton Ackerman strode to the crease and dominated play for the next 90 minutes, scoring a hundred to the other batsman's 20 and enabling Dale to declare at 241 for one. We lost the match, but it was almost worth it to see the way Hylton controlled the outcome.

In February Colin and I were invited to play for Border in a friendly match against Eastern Province in Port Elizabeth. I cannot remember much about the game, except that Tony Greig from Queen's was playing for Border. When he came in to bat, he had to face his first ball from Peter Pollock, one of the quickest bowlers in the world at that time, and he hit it, off the back foot, straight over Peter's head. That shot gave me – and others – a funny feeling about Tony's future.

Two weeks later he was selected by Border to make his debut against Transvaal B. Tony's father Sandy, with some pressure from John Snow, asked to see me to discuss what life was like in the first-class cricket scene in England. I must have been quite convincing because later that year Tony signed professional terms for Sussex. The rest, as they say, is history.

> **Rumsey's lively spells ruffled the batsmen in both innings, and he finished with the commendable match figures of nine for 66, with Graeme Pollock (twice) and Eddie Barlow among his victims.**

*Since writing the book, I have found
a report of my match for Border in a
cutting from the Daily Dispatch.
It appears in full on page 252.
It seems that I did not have a bad game.*

We travelled home on the *Windsor Castle*, the largest of the ships on the Union-Castle Line. When we docked in Southampton, Coleen was waiting on the quayside. Before leaving for South Africa I had passed my very sporty red MGA 1600 twin-carburettor to her for safekeeping, but what was waiting for me when we reached the car park was a drab British racing green MGA 1600 twin-carburettor. Apparently a lorry had attached itself to the top of the bonnet of the car, causing considerable damage, and the repairing garage had suggested that a colour change to green would help to hide any imperfections that might be left after they had done their best. They would, wouldn't they?

We were hardly out of Southampton when Coleen raised the matter of our forthcoming marriage. "Are you still intending to marry me in seven days' time, or has six months of freedom caused a change of mind?"

"Yes, I intend to marry you," I said. "But I have thought a lot about our future. I do not hold with this new-fangled idea of equality in all things. Someone has to make the decisions for the both of us. It cannot all be by joint discussion."

"Yes," she interrupted. "I have decided to let that someone be you."

There was a strong emphasis on the word 'I', so I shut up and watched the beautiful Hampshire countryside as it was turning into spring.

We were married a week later in Bristol. Many of those present and others predicted not much more than a year of happy union but here we are: three children, five grandchildren, four dogs, four cats, 23 different homes and 53 years later.

We got some wonderful wedding presents, but the best of all came from Colin Milburn, who could not attend for cricket reasons. He gave us a kitchen utensil set made of alloy; there are no joints in any one of the six items, and we are still using them today. The board they hung on has long since disintegrated, but that was made of wood.

We held the reception at the Grand Hotel in Bristol, where attempts were made, by certain people, to establish the venue of our honeymoon. The intention was to create some embarrassing skulduggery. My cousin's husband, Eddie Grimstead, along with Peter Walker and Mervyn Kitchen, were the main culprits. What Eddie and his cronies did not find out was that, when the Grimsteads moved out of their room at the Grand, we were moving in.

We spent a few days at the Castle Hotel in Taunton before moving to a bungalow on the outskirts of town to prepare for the coming cricket season.

Wedding day

28

The summer of 1966

I thought my luck had changed when I received an invitation to play for the MCC against Surrey at Lord's. When I found out that three of my Somerset colleagues had also been selected, my euphoria evaporated. Of course, we were one of only two county teams not playing on the opening day of the championship season!

Our first championship match was against Hampshire at the Imperial Ground in Bristol. I remember this match particularly well because it was the first and only occasion that a batsman walked on my appeal for an lbw decision; the batsman was Roy Marshall. The ball swung in late, pitched middle and would have hit middle. I got as far as "How's" when he was off back to the pavilion, long before the umpire had raised his digit. Now there was a man who knew where his stumps were.

In my opinion the controversy over whether or not a batsman should walk when nicking the ball to the wicket-keeper is easily resolved. If the player knows that he has hit the ball and that it reached the keeper without bouncing, he walks. If he is genuinely doubtful about any aspect, he waits for the umpire's decision. Any other view must be regarded as cheating. If a batsman hits the ball into the hands of mid-off, he does not hang around, he walks. No difference at all when hitting it to the wicket-keeper. The saying 'It's not cricket' related to the honesty of the game. This has been somewhat tarnished in recent years by certain individuals who put personal gain above the spirit of the game. Those currently playing should be aware that they are the custodians of the spirit of 'It's not cricket'.

I was an established member of the Somerset side. Once the fear of being dropped from a team recedes, a more permanent confidence takes its place. Individual results become more predictable, according to the conditions. Once the stage is set by those conditions and the state of the wicket, professionalism kicks in and, akin to that of an actor playing Lear for the 50th time, the outcome becomes predictable.

My own performances were improving, and I believe that I bowled better during my last three seasons at Somerset than I did in the first three. But I felt that I had had my chance at Test level and that I would not see that arena again.

I took exactly 100 wickets in 1966, the 100th coming with the last ball of Somerset's season when we won for the 13th time in the championship, which is still a Somerset record. We finished in third place, equalling the county's best ever position.

Off the field I had my first taste of collective militant action.

The food served to the players and officials varied in quality from ground to ground. The best food was usually provided by the bigger Test match venues. In most cases these grounds provided hot sustenance of a high standard. At the other end of the scale were the caterers who believed that all food served on a cricket ground should be cold and in the form of a salad. At the bottom of that list came the caterers at the County Ground, Taunton. The food served there, like the environment in which it was served, the indoor cricket shed, was disgraceful. At luncheon the worst offender was the lettuce; it was wet, lank and mottled and, if that was not bad enough, the consumer had to share it with every known caterpillar, fly and bug imaginable. The potatoes were even worse: no flies or bugs but no taste either; they came in large cans, were ashen and had all the goodness boiled out of them. Tea followed the same pattern. If we got sandwiches the ends were turned up, almost meeting like the sails of ships. The only consumable item was the tea, and even that came in a large urn, stewed, weak and willing.

In discussions with all the players it was unanimously decided to boycott all the food served in the indoor school and send the twelfth man to the local fish-and-chipper, each player placing his order before taking the field for the morning session. After the first non-attendance the Secretary, Richard Robinson, was soon onto the situation. The players had elected me their spokesman and, after a brief discussion with Richard, he promised to do something about it. Although he did not say so, I believed that he was sympathetic to our cause. He was as good as his word, and the food improved immeasurably. In time the caterer was changed – and surprise, surprise, we were served hot food.

Not many weeks passed before I was taking the first steps in a mad idea I had to form a cricketers' union, but I will save that for a chapter all of its own.

I suppose the biggest event of the 1966 season took place on Saturday 30 July. We were playing Nottinghamshire at Weston-super-Mare and had been in the field for all of that first day. The afternoon noise from the beer tent started at a mumble, as it always did, rising to a crescendo when Geoff Hurst scored his third goal and England, led by my schoolboy friend Bobby Moore, beat West Germany 4-2 to win the World Cup.

In September I packed my seafaring trunk for a further visit to South Africa, this time accompanied by my new wife Coleen.

29

Back to South Africa

We boarded the *SA Oranje* for our cruise to Cape Town, stopping at the Canary Islands on the way. This time we were joined by Basil D'Oliveira on the voyage. He had made his debut for England during the summer and was returning home for a nationwide tour of the black and coloured communities.

It was another wonderful trip, with the water in the tropics again just like glass. I must admit that, with the pressure of playing professional cricket, plus the problems surrounding the formation of a trade union, I needed a switching-off period. And where better to get it than in the tropics, miles from land?

We spent a considerable amount of time with Basil during the 11-day trip, culminating with a slap-up dinner on the last evening before docking in Cape Town. Basil called it 'The Last Supper', making it clear to us that we would be unable to move in the same circles once we had disembarked. I objected strongly, but he was adamant and would not arrange to see us in Cape Town where we were spending a couple of days.

"This is not like England, and I don't want to cause you any trouble," were his parting words. I knew that East London was on his itinerary so I kept quiet, intending to do something about it later.

We continued around the Cape to our next port of call, Port Elizabeth. We were not staying long enough for a shore visit so we were taking the sun on the foredeck when we were buzzed by a single-prop Cessna. I thought nothing of it at the time until I was summoned to the bridge to take an air-to-ship call. It was Bob Kershaw, the pilot who had featured on the wartime stamp.

"I saw you sunning yourselves," he said. "I have come to shorten your journey and take you to your second home."

I had to seek Coleen's approval which was not forthcoming.

"No way am I travelling in that paper plane," she said.

So poor old Bob had a wasted journey and had to travel home on his own. A few days later we docked in East London, our home for the next six months.

Accommodation had been arranged for us at a block of apartments called Bowes-Lyon Court. The neighbours were chatty and friendly – that was until a certain Cape Coloured came to stay. I had obtained a copy of Basil D'Oliveira's itinerary and arranged with his tour organiser for him to spend a week with us. During and immediately after his stay we were shunned by the neighbours. Then one of them took me aside, after Basil had left, to give me 'a word of advice', as he put it.

"You mustn't have coloureds or blacks staying with you in this accommodation, it just isn't done," he said.

I angrily retorted, "Listen, Basil D'Oliveira has been a close friend of mine for three years now and I'm certainly not ..."

Before I got any further he interrupted me. "You're joking. That wasn't really Basil D'Oliveira, was it? Why didn't you tell us? We would love to have met him."

"How could I?" I replied. "No one was speaking to me!"

Coleen was declared pregnant after we had been in East London for about a month. This was going to be our first child, and she was having quite a rough time with it. She tried a number of 'old wives' remedies to alleviate severe indigestion, like sucking coke and coal, but nothing worked. As the days passed she became more and more irritated with me.

"Why don't you go out for a drink?" she asked one evening.

I declined, arguing the case that I wanted to look after her. After all, we were in a foreign country.

"I don't need looking after," she said. "I'm quite capable of looking after myself for an evening. You go out and enjoy yourself."

"No," I replied, "I am quite happy to be staying at home."

"Has it not occurred to you that I might want some time by myself?" she asked. "Go and enjoy a drink."

I took the hint, got changed and prepared myself for a few hours at the Buffalo Club, my local watering hole. I had said my goodbye and was heading for the front door when Coleen called out, "You, you're a typical male, aren't you? Going out to enjoy yourself, leaving me here to suffer all on my own!"

I continued to coach my usual two schools, Cambridge and Hoerskool Grens, but I received two additional requests. Whilst Basil was in East London, the Mayor put on a civic party to welcome him. The guest list included all organised cricketing officials, something I had never seen before. There were Border Province officials, officials from the local townships, coloured officials, coaches, virtually anyone involved in the management and promotion of cricket in the immediate area of East London.

One of the local townships approached me to establish my availability for a couple of nights' coaching per week. I agreed to do it, subject to my two schools agreeing. They both did, but there were unknown others who did not. After my first week's spell I received an anonymous call, suggesting that, if I refused to withdraw my services from the township, I would not be waking up one morning. Both Donald Woods and I felt that it was a crank call and that we would do nothing about it unless there were more threats; there were none. However, during the second week, I received a visit from the secret police, suggesting that it would be wiser to stop the coaching sessions. Their argument was based on the simple fact that, should I choose to continue, I could be deported. My immediate reaction to that was to suggest considerable anti-South African media coverage, should Coleen and I be forced to return to the UK.

"Are you threatening us?" one of the policemen asked.

"No," I replied. "I thought the boot was on the other foot."

They were both silent for a brief moment, then the older one said, "Look, we are suggesting this for your own good. We don't want anything to happen to you or your wife whilst you are here in East London" – which left me wondering where the threatening phone call had come from.

I completed my contract with the township without any further problems.

The second request came from a catholic school, De La Salle College. My duties there were to coach cricket for two hours on a Sunday morning: not to coach the pupils but to coach the brothers! I was asked to teach the basic rudiments of cricket to about fifteen brothers to enable them to pass this knowledge on to their students. They were an unusually rowdy lot, regularly playing pranks against each other. I had an occasion to admonish them when it got out of hand.

"Stop monkeying around in that net," I told them.

"That might be difficult for us," came back an Irish reply.

After a couple of weeks and with my permission, the brothers introduced two students into the group. One of them was particularly talented, and at the time I did not take particular note of the name. He learned quickly and had a natural aptitude for the game. I finally asked one of the brothers who he was.

"Ian Greig," he said. "Tony's brother."

Ian also ended up playing cricket for England after a spell at Cambridge University where he was a double blue, cricket and rugby.

Each session lasted about two hours, and as regular as clockwork two of the brothers were allocated to drink with me at the expiry. These drinking bouts could last anything up to three hours, depending upon which of the brothers were allocated. Bushmills, good Irish whiskey, was the favourite tipple. I must admit that they were then and still are the most enjoyable coaching sessions I ever ran.

I was able to arrange for the English coaches in South Africa to play a couple of matches against local opposition over the New Year period. As most were playing regularly at some level or other, we provided strong opponents. I had obtained local sponsorship to cover the costs, and these sponsors intended to use the occasion for a bit of local promotion.

I did not intend to play in the first match, against a Border XI, so I asked Phil Sharpe to skipper the side. Play started at 11.30, and by 12.30 Border had scored 30 runs for five wickets. I began to panic, visualising the innings

back: Rodney Cass, Albert Lightfoot, John Cotton, Fred Rumsey, Don Wilson,
Geoff Keith, David Steele   front: Dickie Bird, John Jameson, Phil Sharpe,
Mike Taylor, Ted Clark   lying: John Snow

Snow and Rumsey are particularly fast, although the latter is unfit and carrying a good deal of surplus weight.

However, I have seen him open up fully, spare tire and all, and even unfit as he is he would walk into the Springbok team tomorrow as Peter Pollock's opening partner.

He has a whiplash action and sends the ball down with real venom from a dizzy height.

Border fans will recall how Rumsey blasted through Eastern Province in a friendly match last year.

But if today is hot I don't know how many overs his 6ft. 4in. and 250 lbs. will take at top speed.

Effective

Snow I have yet to see, but he will probably be even more effective than Rumsey as he is fit and doesn't have quite as much weight to carry around.

He is England's leading fast bowler at the moment.

from Donald Woods' preview of
the match in the Daily Dispatch

being completed before the sponsors had begun their entertaining, so I sent a note out to Phil Sharpe asking him to take things easy for a while. I got my reply – "Bollocks"!

Bob Kershaw held a party for the England group, at which most over-indulged. Rodney Cass locked himself in the bathroom and fell asleep, I went to bed, only to be awakened by a giant spider crawling up my leg; it was as big as my hand and covered in hair. I yelled and Bob Kershaw rushed in, brushed it off the bed and threw it out of the window. "Harmless," he said with a wicked grin.

The Australians arrived in East London a couple of weeks later to enjoy another Bob Kershaw welcome, which was followed by the Mayor's soirée. None of the guests at the Town Hall came from the townships or from coloured cricket. I cheekily asked why they could attend the party for Basil but not for the Australians, only to receive the frowning glare that I had come to expect when asking such obviously crass questions.

At the end of March Coleen and I returned on the *Cape Town Castle*, a cruiser, to Southampton. I used the two-week journey to start my trip back into fitness by training in the gymnasium and running laps around the deck. There was a static bike in the gymnasium which I used quite often, and on one occasion I stupidly rode it without pumps on my feet. The resultant blister was not unknown to me so I burst it with the intention of cutting off the loose skin. I popped into the doctor's surgery to borrow some scissors. When the nurse saw the blister, she insisted that I saw the doctor which was not at all necessary. He cut off the loose skin, attached a plaster and charged me a full consultancy fee. When I paid the bill I added half a crown.

"What is that for?" asked the nurse.

"A tip," I said. "He obviously needs the money."

I beat a hasty retreat and headed for the bar. I was recounting what had happened when a fellow drinker told me about a certain very attractive lady who was travelling both out and back on the boat. She had struck up a mutual friendship with the doctor and, when she had fallen ill, he had treated her. A few days after her recovery she received quite a hefty bill, entitled 'To treatment rendered'. She found a typewriter and typed 'To services rendered', charged exactly the same amount and sent it back to the surgery. She heard no more.

Coleen was not at her best on the journey home. The baby looked as if it was going to be above average in weight at birth, judging by the size of the swelling. Consequently I tended to drink alone in the evenings or with the one or two pals I had met since sailing.

30

The summer of 1967

I played first-class cricket under a number of captains. Some were better than others. Reading the game is the most important part of captaincy. Of the England skippers of that time, Mike Smith could read a game better than Ted Dexter or Colin Cowdrey. Colin was the worst, mainly because he had doubts about himself. He would make a decision, then wonder if it was correct, and that is no way to be a leader. Unquestionably the best for that awareness on the field was Brian Close.

The best captain I played under was Ian Buxton at Derbyshire. He was a very talented man, he played football for Derby County, and he was also very humble. I was only playing in the Sunday League matches, and they were a real test of captaincy; it was a new form of the game, and there was so much less time to make decisions. At the toss some of the captains would always bat, some would always bowl, but Ian would work it out and he was always right.

Somehow, when Ian Buxton or Closey made a decision on the field, they would be two overs ahead of me. I would think, "Why are they making that change?" Then it would occur to me.

In 1967 Colin Atkinson was in his third and last summer as captain of Somerset. He was a decent cricketer – he scored 1,000 runs one year, and he bowled useful medium-pacers and occasionally leg-breaks – but there were more talented cricketers who could have been brought in. As a captain he did not read the game like Ian Buxton and Brian Close, but he was the best leader of men I played under.

For bonhomie and friendship, that Somerset side was the best I experienced in cricket. The dressing room was great; the humour, the crack, it was fun. We all took the piss out of each other. There was no tension. Bill Alley could be a bit snide, a bit Aussie from time to time, but I liked him a lot – and he was such a believer in perfection, he just went out and did his job every day.

Brian Langford was a nice fellow, with a lot of humour, very West Country. Then there were the humorists, Peter Robinson and Roy Palmer, and some nice fellows like Tony Clarkson and Graham Atkinson. And, of course, Chimp Clayton. In our different ways we were all winners in our approach to cricket. Roy Palmer was the least experienced at that time. He had less talent than his brother Kenny, but he believed in himself.

The hardest thing in first-class cricket is not coming to terms with failing; it is coming to terms with winning. As a bowler, when you know the conditions are in your favour and you have taken two or three wickets, you know you must end up with six or seven, and a lot of players cannot do that. They start trying too hard, and they lose their rhythm; they lose their line and length. Some people cannot make that transition. It is similar to tennis. The great players, once they get an opponent in a certain position, they take him apart and kill him. You have to have that instinct. You have to cash in when you are on top as a bowler. It is the same with batsmen. When they get in, they have to go on and make a big score. There is nothing worse than a batsman, when set, playing a stupid shot and getting out. The game does involve more than you as an individual batsman; you are the one who has the chance to put the team in a wining position.

When I joined Somerset in 1963, it was the first time the county attack had a pace bowler who could cause concern among the opposition. The Somerset batsmen had been on the reciving end of a number of bombardments, and suddenly they had their own strike force. It was a topic they often raised with the opposition batsmen early on in the game!

How fast was I? The only occasion when my speed was measured was when a journalist from Bristol came down to the nets at Taunton. He said he wanted

back: Geoff Clayton, Terry Barwell, Roy Palmer, Fred Rumsey,
Graham Burgess, Mervyn Kitchen, Peter Robinson
front: Roy Virgin, Brian Langford, Colin Atkinson (captain), Bill Alley, Ken Palmer

144

to know what it was like to face a fast bowler. I tried to dissuade him, but he put on all sorts of body armour and said he would take all responsibility. I was reluctant to do it, but I did bowl flat out at him, making sure not to hit him. He brought with him a photographer with a movie camera, who calculated my speed by the number of frames between my releasing the ball and the point at which it reached the other end. My quickest ball, he reckoned, was over 93 miles per hour.

Colin Atkinson, who at that time was deputy headmaster at Millfield, knew how to get the best out of each of us in our different ways. He understood that I enjoyed an evening out and a good drink, but we had an agreement that I would not do that if I was going to be bowling the next day. Bill was never expected to do the pre-season fitness training. There was no need for him to do it. He was 48 by the summer of 1967, and he was an extremely hard, tough man physically. He could not run far, but he fielded gully – he was a very good gully – and, if a spin bowler was on, he would go square on the off side.

If I had the opportunity to go back and change anything in my time in cricket, I would have a dietician sent to me when I started at Somerset, someone who would enable me to maintain my energy while keeping my weight down. I think that would have made a difference to me.

All through the period when I played Test cricket I had shin soreness. I would be all right when I was bowling but, as soon as I stopped, I would seize up and I would find it very difficult to move. Fortunately a lot of the time I was first slip so it did not matter. When I was out in the field, though, it was very painful. I would have liked to have wasted away about a stone of my weight but to have kept my physical strength. There was no advice on such things in the 1960s, but now it is commonplace.

Roy Palmer had the opposite problem. He was a beanpole with very little weight on him. He said to me one day, "I want to bowl as quick as you do. How do I put some weight on?"

"That's easy," I said. "You want to eat all the things I'm not allowed to eat. Condensed milk, fatty steaks. You'll see the difference within a fortnight."

Two weeks later, after following my advice, he had lost four pounds.

When we got back from South Africa Coleen returned to her parents' home to have her mother on hand during confinement, and I started pre-season training, although I had achieved quite a lot of fitness on the journey home.

The season started in April with a Gillette Cup match against Leicestershire at Taunton. We lost the toss, were asked to bat first and won comfortably. This was repeated in the next two rounds and, when we won the toss in the semi-final at Old Trafford, we also batted first and won. In the fifth year of the competition, and for the first time, Somerset had made it to the final at Lord's.

Left arm pace giant Fred Rumsey is Somerset's leading Gillette Cup bowler with 27 wickets for a remarkable 10.7 average. Here Rumsey is completely airborne as he bombs a delivery at Hampshire's Barry Reed.

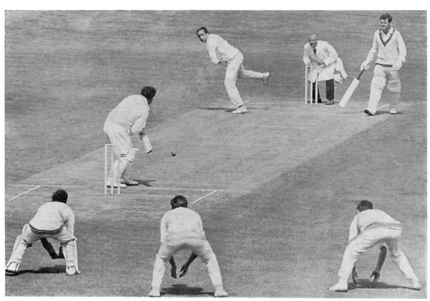

Here it is big hitting Colin Milburn who is forced on to the defensive as Rumsey hurls one down. Rumsey's ambitions are to get back into the England side and to see his recently launched County Cricketers Association raise the standard of living for the often poorly rewarded players.

A page from 'Up from Somerset for the Cup'

146

The atmosphere at the Lord's final

The idea behind the introduction of the Gillette Cup was to draw into the grounds people who were not prepared to wait three days for a result. You could see both teams batting and a result, all in a day. In that respect it was a great success. At a time when the crowds were dwindling at county championship matches, there were 15,000 at Old Trafford for our semi-final and 20,000 for the final at Lord's. In those days there was a rope around the boundary, and you could sit on the grass behind the rope, and that was filled as well as the ground. There was great excitement in Somerset, and on the day at Lord's there were Wurzels there, hayricks, barrels of cider. It was a wonderful occasion.

The county did not offer us anything extra for reaching the final so, with the help of John Davies, the *Daily Express*'s sports reporter in the south-west, I produced a booklet, 'Up from Somerset for the Cup', to celebrate our achievement in reaching the final. I sold 13 pages of advertising to local firms, and we made a profit of nearly £1,000. I set up a Somerset Players Welfare Fund to receive the money.

Unfortunately our performance at Lord's paled by comparison. We lost the toss and, for the first time that summer, we fielded first. Denness and Luckhurst, the Kent openers, both scored fifties and, although we bowled well to restrict them to a total of 193 in their 60 overs, we did not bat well and were all out for 161.

Although the competition was introduced with the idea that it would produce exciting cricket, it quickly came to be played quite negatively. If you were a bowler of my ilk, you did not bowl to get people out; you bowled to stop them scoring runs. If I bowled 12 overs and I could keep the batsmen to 20 runs, that was far more important than taking two wickets for 50 runs. The sensible fast bowlers all bowled just short of a length rather than pitching it up and looking to get an edge. Also you were not penalised if you went down the leg side. In my six years at Somerset, I played in 15 Gillette Cup matches, and I bowled 175 overs for 341 runs, a rate of 1.95 runs an over.

Away from the Gillette Cup Somerset did not have such a good season in 1967. There was no significant reason for that; these fluctuations happen in all sport. We did not win a championship match till June. We even managed to lose to Oxford University at The Parks – but that was more because the students had a post-match strategy that involved entertaining us particularly well in pubs and at parties.

Coleen and I moved into a flat in Taunton, owned by Somerset Cricket Club, and lived below Peter Robinson and his wife Elizabeth. I was playing at Leicester on 17 June, the day Warren Frederick, our first son, was born. He weighed in at 9lbs 3oz, a very bonny baby. When the landlord of the pub on the Leicester ground heard the news, he stuck me behind the bar and gave

At Warren's christening, with Peter Walker (left) and Mervyn Kitchen

the lads copious amounts of free beer as long as I served it. As at Oxford it did not aid our performance the next day. Despite a first-innings lead of 139 runs, we lost by two wickets.

The Gillette Cup final was held on Saturday 2 September. On the Monday the Cricketers' Association was formed. Then on Wednesday I was back at Taunton for Somerset's last match, against Lancashire.

At the end of the match, I got in my car to drive to Scarborough to play for the MCC against Yorkshire. It was a long pre-motorway journey, and I did not arrive till the early hours of the morning. I went straight to bed and slept the sleep of a babe. I awoke at about 11, with the match due to start at 11.30. I put a quick call in to the ground, established that we were in the field and told them I was on my way. I got dressed into my cricket clothes and, carrying my boots, I ran from the hotel down the hill into the ground. As I entered the ground, the umpires were taking the field. I dashed into the dressing room, put on my boots and ran after the rest of my team who were taking up their fielding positions. DC Morgan of Derbyshire was my captain, and he tossed the ball to me to bowl the first over. After the first ball was bowled, our keeper Roy Swetman said, "That ball should go into the Guinness Book of Records as the longest run-up ever recorded in the first-class game."

International Cricket Crusaders
standing: Colin Milburn, Len Coldwell, Harold Gimblett, Fred Rumsey, Mike Harris, Mervyn Kitchen, Hylton Ackerman, Peter Robinson, Brian Langford, Bill Frindall, Clive Lloyd   seated: Graham McKenzie, Garry Sobers, Fred Trueman, Basil D'Oliveira, John Edrich, Lance Gibbs
Also on tour were Tom Graveney, John Price and Jim Parks

That match brought to an end the first-class season but not the end of my summer's cricket, as I had agreed to manage a nine-day tour of Devon and Cornwall by the International Cricket Crusaders. Our team was the brainchild of Ross Salmon, a remarkable man. As a young naval pilot in World War Two he had won the Distinguished Service Cross for his bravery. Then, after answering a newspaper advertisement, he had become a ranch manager in the jungle of Columbia. A bad plane crash brought him home, where after a year in hospital he began a new life as television's 'jungle cowboy', riding horseback across Britain and writing a series of best-selling books. He moved to Devon to farm and became the scorer for BBC television's cricket coverage. He thought they were a little starved of top cricket in Cornwall and Devon so he came up with the idea of this tour. The money we raised all went to the local clubs that staged the matches.

I was to play as well as manage, although there was little managing to do; most of the hard work had already been completed by Ross. We put together a party of 20, 14 of whom had played Test cricket. The star of the week was Hylton Ackerman, who was like a run machine.

Everybody enjoyed it. The two people who really hit it off, as if they were bosom pals, were Clive Lloyd and Peter Robinson. I remember Lloydy saying to Robbo as we were leaving, "Hop in my bag, will you? I want to take you around with me." The two of them were very funny.

We lived with people; we didn't stay in hotels. Coleen and I stayed in Wadebridge with a charming couple in their sixties; neither of them had been outside of Wadebridge in the whole of their lives. I said, "What about Exeter? Plymouth?" No, never.

The Winchester Arms in Taunton had the excellent idea of converting an old BEA bus into a mobile bar. These buses were built with one level at the front and two levels at the rear, the lower level being used to carry the luggage of the passengers sitting above. The conversion filled the lower level with booze and the drinkers sat above. This bus followed us around Devon and Cornwall, providing refreshment at every venue.

On one occasion the match was abandoned because of rain, and we all adjourned to the bus for a little afternoon sustenance. Fred Trueman was preparing for his night club act at the time and kept us amused for most of the afternoon recounting anecdotes and telling jokes.

A wealthy businessman was on the bus that afternoon. He had attended a number of the matches, arriving in his chauffeur-driven Rolls Royce. We were due to play at Plymouth later in the week, and he asked if he could treat the players to dinner on that occasion. I told him such a decision would be their own but that I would certainly ask. Most of the team accepted, and he invited us to a grill-type chain restaurant. We were sitting at a series of long rectangular tables with the host sitting opposite me at one end.

"I understand that you know something about wines," he said to me. "Would you please order for the whole table and not worry about cost?"

I chose a middle-of-the-road red and white, so as not to dent his coffers too much. The white came, and the waiter poured it straight into the glass without giving me a chance to taste. I stopped him and tasted the wine, which unfortunately was corked. When told, the waiter picked up my glass, took a swig and declared that there was nothing wrong with it. I immediately asked to speak to the maitre d', but the manager came over.

Once the situation had been explained to him, he turned on me. "This is a problem we often get with so-called experts. This man," he said, pointing to the wine waiter, "is an expert. He surely knows better?"

Having delivered that rude bombshell, he walked away. I was livid but, before I could react, the host put his hand on my arm and rose from his chair. He approached the manager and, after a lot of finger wagging, a fresh bottle of white wine appeared at the table. This time it was perfect, as were the rest. When our host returned, I asked him what he had said to get such a quick reaction.

"I told the manager that I own this chain of restaurants and that he is fired."

THE CRICKETERS'
ASSOCIATION

Jim Parks, Jimmy Hill and me

31

A union for cricketers

The decision to form a union crept up on me very slowly. There was no inspirational flash of light, no sudden burst of understanding. It just seemed to me to be the thing to do at the time! The footballers had an active Players' Association, chaired by Jimmy Hill. So why shouldn't cricketers have one? It was as simple as that. Cricketers' remuneration was lower than any other professional sportsmen at the time. In my own case I was receiving £600 for the whole season and 100 guineas if I played in a Test match. The idea for a union had been mooted for years, but no one had attempted its formation. There was reluctance in the ranks of first-class cricketers to buck the establishment at any level, particularly 'Lord's'.

In the middle '60s there were a lot of changes being planned, in particular the introduction of one-day cricket. This would affect a cricketer's livelihood and, because there was no vehicle through which he could be given the chance to have his say, I thought that I would provide one. During the summer of 1966 I wrote a letter to all of the 17 Secretaries of the first-class county clubs and their senior professionals, outlining my proposal for a Players' Association.

The idea of the Association was not based on militancy, more on representation. The players needed to have a say in their own future, and the letter outlined that. Our pay at the time was way below the national average and only covered six months of the year. There was a great need for out-of-season employment opportunities, something only some form of employment exchange could provide. There was also a need for good injury insurance cover and for it not to be left to each player to find his own.

Whenever I was playing an away match I would arrange, with the permission of the home club, to have a meeting with the opposition players so I could provide more detail about the ideas I had for setting up such an organisation. All of the clubs were extremely helpful, and I held meetings in their dressing rooms through the summers of 1966 and 1967.

It was clear from the outset that I had a significant amount of support. A small number of players opted out, saying that they did not believe in unions, and there was a certain amount of cynicism about the idea, people saying "You can't do that", though not as much as I expected. The abolition of the amateur/professional distinction helped, in that it brought into the fold the university graduates who would previously have played as amateurs – or 'shamateurs', as they were called. Most of them had been paid to do non-existent jobs so that they could keep up the pretence of amateurism. The easiest dressing room of all was Yorkshire. They were all enthusiastic, from Brian Close downwards.

THE COUNTY CRICKETERS' ASSOCIATION

(A copy of this letter has been sent to the Secretary and Senior Professional)

Dear.................,

The idea of a County Cricketers' Association has been mooted many times in the past, but there would seem to be a very strong feeling in favour of its formation by present day cricketers, judging by the informal talks I have had this season with several counties.

This letter is a suggestion to all members of the staff as to how such an Association could benefit them, and also County Cricket.

Benefit to Players

1. The Association will provide a much needed organisation to which the Players can turn for advice and help on all matters concerning cricket.

2. The standard of living of the average county cricketer, is not keeping pace nationally due mainly to the poor financial position of most County Cricket Clubs. The Association will seek ways and means of elevating the standard of living without placing great burdens on the respective County resources, e.g.

   a. Negotiating with the B.B.C. (sound and TV) I.T.V. and the Press, nationally and locally, for fees and contracts.

   b. Negotiating with business houses, nationally and locally, for bulk advertising. (Certain sports firms may supply gear, and clothing, free of charge.

   c. Forming an out of season employment exchange, capable of placing those players in need of winter employment in suitable positions, and finding business houses who are prepared to train the younger cricketer, during the winter, for a career once cricketing days are over.

   d. Offering help in the organisation of a Player's Benefit/Testimonial Year.

   e. Generally becoming the County Cricketers' agent.

3. Liaison between Player and Committee particularly in times of dispute should the need arise.

Benefit to Cricket by:

1. Representing the collective view of County Cricketers it will be at all times working for the cause of County Cricket.

2. Endeavouring to impress on its members a code of conduct to be observed at all times.

3. Seeking to ascertain in what way the players themselves can best help the game.

4. Offering more security to the players and thereby making County Cricket a more attractive livelihood.

Formation of the Association

1. Each County Staff to elect one representative, who in turn will elect a governing Committee and Secretary from the seventeen representatives.

2. All County Players, including Captains, should be eligible for membership and elections as representatives.

3. Fees etc. would be decided upon by the representatives at the first meeting.

The points itemised are some of the suggestions I personally have to offer. The policy of the Association will be decided by the seventeen representatives, who in turn represent the County Cricketers. I do feel, however, that unless the Association is founded on integrity, the problems facing the Cricketer and Cricket will not be removed. The intention of the Association must be to bridge the gap between Player and administration by attacking the problems with them, and not to widen the gap by being intolerant and self-seeking.

If the idea is accepted by the Players, I feel that no time should be wasted in the endeavour to form the Association. In which case I would appreciate the name of your representative, enabling me to arrange an early meeting.

Yours sincerely,

(Fred. Rumsey)

The letter that began the PCA. I typed it onto a Gestetner stencil and ran off copies on foolscap paper in the office at the Somerset County Ground in Taunton.

I did not get round all the counties in 1966 so I continued the meetings in the summer of 1967. At that stage I was working on my own. People were supportive – Peter Walker, Fred Titmus, JT Murray and others – but nobody had said, "Do you need a hand?"

I was an isolated figure, going up against the governing body of cricket, the MCC Advisory Committee, which was not the brightest thing for a professional cricketer to do. Yet there were administrators in the counties who saw the merit of my proposal. In June Mike Turner, the Leicestershire Secretary, wrote a supportive article in the *Leicester Mercury* with the headline 'PLAYERS ASSOCIATION GOOD FOR THE GAME'.

My own county, Somerset, had a chairman called 'Bunty' Longrigg, a Bath solicitor who had been educated at Rugby and Cambridge. He had been captain of Somerset on either side of the war and was a man at ease in the cricketing establishment at Lord's. During one match at Bath he appeared in our dressing room.

"Skipper," he said to Colin Atkinson, "may I speak to Rumsey?"

"What are you doing tonight?" he asked me. "Would you care for a bit of dinner at my club? There is something I want to talk with you about."

I had a good idea what the subject was going to be when we sat down together. "I won't beat about the bush," he said. "I have been approached by certain of my friends at Lord's. They have requested of me that we at Somerset should curb your activities with this union you are planning to form."

"I see," I said. "So how did you reply?"

He was not a man who regularly used expletives but, in his best public school voice, he said loudly, "I told them to fx@# off. And, furthermore, I told them that the Somerset County Cricket Club and I will be giving you all the support we possibly can."

I was becoming more confident that my lone venture would come to fruition, and I had a major boost when the Warwickshire bowler Jack Bannister asked if he could get involved. When he did, he provided some much-needed administrative assistance.

It is not difficult for me to remember Jack with fondness. Up till his offer of help, I had been on my own. Now I had a close ally. We threw caution to the wind and worked hard to write a Memorandum & Articles of Association.

We came up with some weird and wonderful ideas, only to discard them in the cold light of day. We would argue on some ridiculous points, but our biggest argument was always about which of the two of us was the better bowler. However, like all good union officials, we were able to compromise.

I was the quickest, he was the straightest: which was no bad thing on his part, bearing in mind that he later became a bookmaker!

Once we were happy that a 'players' union' would have a chance of survival, we formed a plan of action. The Gillette Cup Final was scheduled for Saturday 2 September so, with no other county matches starting that day, we decided to call a meeting for the following Monday. John Davies of the *Daily Express* had a word with his paper, who agreed to sponsor the event and arranged for it to take place in the London Press Club. I asked Jimmy Hill and Cliff Lloyd, from the Professional Footballers' Association, Chairman and Secretary respectively, if they would address us. They agreed, and Jimmy's talk was to the point and very professional, expressing the need for player representation at the administrative level of all sports. He did show some surprise that we had only just got around to forming a union. If any of the delegates had doubts before his talk, they certainly did not after.

Jimmy Hill speaks to the first meeting of the Cricketers' Association, 4 September 1967

standing: Tony Jorden (Essex), Alan Oakman (Sussex), Ian Buxton (Derbyshire), Mike Smedley (Nottinghamshire), Terry Spencer (Leicestershire), Danny Livingstone (Hampshire), Don Shepherd (Glamorgan), Jack Bond (Lancashire), Jack Bannister (Warwickshire), Ken Taylor (Yorkshire), Cliff Lloyd (Professional Footballers' Association)

sitting: Jimmy Hill (Professional Footballers' Association), Arthur Milton (Gloucestershire), Mike Edwards (Surrey), Eric Russell (Middlesex), Jim Parks (Sussex), Fred Rumsey (Somerset), Roger Prideaux (Northamptonshire), David Sayer (Kent)

Doing for cricket what Jimmy Hill did for Soccer

MR. FREDERICK RUMSEY of Bristol is a highly skilled craftsman in a job which will probably throw him on the scrapheap when he is 35. He is hard up, unable to use his skill for the greater part of each year, and even when he is working is in constant danger of injury that may put him out of a job.

He is married, with a baby due any moment now, and his wife begins to wonder sometimes if he wouldn't be better off in some other business.

This is why, despite the outraged cries of elderly gentlemen at Lord's, the county cricketers of England

by WILLIAM CATER

Through John Davies we received extensive publicity in the Daily Express and Wales are going to get organised.

Fred Rumsey, of Somerset and England, is organising them. M o d e s t l y and cautiously he is attempting to do for them what Jimmy Hill did for Britain's footballers a few years ago.

Low-paid

" A county cricketer, a capped player, earns an average of £800 or £900 a year," Fred Rumsey told me yesterday. " Some of the younger players, married men with children, are getting only £400 to £500.

" What can you expect when a really top-class player like Freddie Trueman makes only £2,000 a year out of cricket ? "

Mr. Rumsey emphasises that the County Cricketers' Association which he has asked the M.C.C. to recognise is not a trade union. " A union works for its own body of members only. I hope the association will work for cricket as well as cricketers."

Like fruit-picking or snow-clearing, cricket is a seasonal job, and the season is short. While it is on, players work a seven-day week counting a day's travelling.

Odd jobs

" Two three-day matches a week, six hours cricket a day, but you're on the ground seven hours," said Rumsey. " And out of a four-month season a county player will be away from home for two months."

What happens when the season is over ? Once cricket-fancying employers offered jobs to their local county players during out-of-season months. But as industry gets tougher it has less time for part-timers.

" Cricketers have to take what jobs they can get, and it's often low-paid, unskilled work. Two lads f r o m Somerset were working on the railway as goods-yard porters last winter.

" That's why I want the association to set up its own out - of - season employment exchange."

There's a l o n g - t e r m uncertainty about cricket too. " One of our biggest bugbears is that we grow old not once but twice," said Rumsey, who at 31 is getting towards his first old age.

" Most players must consider retirement around 35. And then what good are you ? Some of us get jobs as representatives—for breweries, for grocery chains. Some become car salesmen. But you're starting in a new job at a time when everyone else in it has b e c o m e established.

Play safe

" Before I became a professional cricketer I was head of the advertising department of a glove manufacturer. If I'd stayed there I'd be getting three, four times what I'm earning now.

" I've seen some likely youngsters turn down a c h a n c e in professional cricket because it couldn't offer them the pay or prospects of other jobs. The game has suffered because of that.

" It suffers too because players feel insecure. Some of them play safe—to make sure their contracts are renewed at the end of the year. With more security I believe you'd get brighter cricket."

After seven years in the business Fred Rumsey knows most clubs just couldn't afford higher pay on their present takings. He hopes his association will appeal to industrialists and business men for money—to get things started.

Crowds

" Once we can offer players more, you'll get better cricket and that will get the bigger crowds in."

Relations between clubs and players aren't so bad, he says, as relations in the one-time " feudal " football business. But there's still room for more discussion between the two sides.

Players will be able to talk more effectively through their own association. Just like any other craftsmen in any other job.

Immediately after Jimmy's and Cliff's talks, the meeting went into private session to form the Association officially. Jim Parks chaired the meeting, which had representation from all 17 first-class counties, except Worcestershire who were on tour in Holland. Jim had made it clear at the offset that he would only chair this one meeting until a full-time chairman was elected, a role that went to Roger Prideaux. I felt that I could serve the Association best by taking on the day-to-day running so I took the title of General Secretary; this clearly described the role that I wished to play. Jack Bannister was appointed Treasurer. We then elected an executive committee which would run the day-to-day business, meeting once a month in London or more often if matters were pressing. The early meetings were held in a number of different venues, including the Cricketers' Club, both at their premises in Baker Street and when it occupied the cellar below Rothmans offices, and The Star, a pub used by the Middlesex cricketers after matches at Lord's. None of the officials received remuneration – there was hardly enough money coming in to sustain the administrative costs, let alone pay the officials.

I had suggested in the proposed Memorandum and Articles of Association that the Association should be called the County Cricketers' Association. The new committee did not like the word 'County' so we kicked it out and the Cricketers' Association was born. 'Professional' was added to the title later, with the body now known as the PCA, Professional Cricketers' Association. It celebrated its 50th anniversary on 4 September 2017.

During the winter of 1967/68 the Cricketers' Association held many debates about the possibility of appointing an Association President. Some illustrious names were proposed: Alec Bedser, Peter May, Denis Compton and Trevor Bailey, to name a few. Don Shepherd suggested that, if we wanted someone whose heart and soul was in the game of cricket, we should look no further than John Arlott, the broadcaster and writer. This was unanimously accepted, and I was given the task of putting the proposition to him.

John lived at the Old Sun in New Alresford, Hampshire, and was an ardent fan of that county. He told me that he had purchased the old public house to have the benefit of its cellars. He loved good wine and good cheese, and I was the recipient on this occasion. I put the offer of the Presidency during the first four bottles of claret and then celebrated his acceptance with the next two. He said it was the most wonderful offer he had ever received.

John held the post of President for many years, long after I had left the organisation. I only learned later that he had been waiting four years to join the Hampshire committee and, having accepted the Presidency of the Cricketers' Association, did not think it prudent to continue with what would have been a great honour for him.

Although I liked and admired him, we did fall out on one occasion. It had to do with the Basil D'Oliveira affair, as follows:

Basil was a South African who was classified as a Cape Coloured by the apartheid regime, and consequently he was ineligible to play first-class cricket in South Africa. He wrote to John Arlott in the late 1950s after hearing his radio commentaries, because his voice and the words he spoke convinced Basil that he was a nice and compassionate man. Basil wanted help to find an opportunity to play professional cricket in England, and John Arlott got him a summer contract with Middleton Cricket Club in the Central Lancashire League in 1960. John subsequently said that this was the achievement in his career of which he felt most proud. After topping the Central Lancashire League batting averages in his first season, Basil graduated to the first-class county circuit, joining Worcestershire in 1964. After acquiring British nationality he was selected to play for England, making his Test debut against the West Indies at Lord's in June 1966.

During the 1968 Ashes series, Basil scored 158 on his recall to the England side in the Fifth Test at The Oval, which seemed to make his selection for the winter tour to South Africa a certainty. However, when the side was announced, he was controversially omitted amidst allegations of South African political interference. John Arlott was incensed, condemning the selectors' decision in his press articles, and publicly stated that he would not commentate on any matches involving the South African team during their scheduled tour of England in 1970. John received support from many people over his uncompromising stand, including future England captain Mike Brearley, who called for the cessation of all South African tours, and the Reverend David Sheppard, who had been one of the first players to speak out against apartheid and who had refused to play against the 1960 South African touring side. However, John was subjected to some strong, not entirely unexpected, criticism from the English cricket establishment, particularly from the former England captain Peter May. Unfortunately, in his statements, John coupled his views with those of the Cricketers' Association, which he had no right to do because the Association's committee had not met to discuss the matter. I had cause to admonish him, and we fell out, even though my personal view was close to his.

When he retired in 1980 he spoke at a number of dinners around the country. I attended one at Trent Bridge and, during his speech, he broke off to say, "There is one man in this room to whom I want to apologise. I will not embarrass him by telling you who he is. He will know. I just want to say that I'm very sorry that I said what I did. I was wrong." He was in tears as he said it. He was a great man.

The first Annual General Meeting of the Cricketers' Association was held at Edgbaston on Friday 19 April 1968. We had fixed the membership fee at £1 for enrolment plus an annual subscription of five guineas. By this stage, we had recruited 170 out of the 220 possible members, and it was not long before we passed 200.

The appointments of John Arlott as President, Harold Goldblatt as auditor and Brendon Quirke as legal advisor were all ratified. We were finally, after nearly two years of slog, up and running legally.

The Cricketers' Association at its first annual meeting, Edgbaston, 19 April 1968
standing: Mike Edwards, Don Shepherd, Ken Taylor, Mike Smedley,
Ron Headley, Terry Spencer, Eric Russell, Jack Bond, Arthur Milton
sitting: Jack Bannister (Treasurer), Roger Prideaux (Chairman), Fred Rumsey (Secretary)

In closing this First Annual Report, your Committee would like to impress on all Members the need to promote and further the image of Cricket on and off the field, and to this end, EACH MEMBER HAS A VITAL ROLE TO PLAY. Cricket is going through a difficult period, and its eventual success can only come from within the game itself, mainly through the constant efforts OF ALL PLAYERS AT ALL TIMES TO BE SEEN TO BE ENJOYING THE GAME.

The closing paragraph of my first Annual Report

In the summer of 1968 all the talk was about launching a Sunday League competition for first-class cricket. My committee felt that cricketers, who were already working six days a week, could not be expected to give up their Sundays for the money that they were then being paid. Players were only contracted for six months of the year and, if they were going to lose their only day off to a new competition, there had to be some remuneration. There was also the extra travel involved, with some of the Sunday matches more than 100 miles away from the game that was being played on either side of it. Also the county beneficiaries would suffer because Sunday was the day when most of their activities took place.

Rothmans, the cigarette company, were sponsoring Sunday matches featuring their International Cavaliers XI, which were aired on BBC television on Sunday afternoons. Most of these games raised money for the county beneficiaries and, to satisfy BBC timings, had limited overs and shortened run-ups for bowlers. In May 1966 we played one at Taunton for Brian Langford's testimonial, and the Cavaliers XI included Garry Sobers, Bobby Simpson, Richie Benaud, Denis Compton, Colin Cowdrey and Roy Marshall.

The success of these matches led to the formation of the Sunday League, and it seemed obvious that Rothmans should be given the opportunity to sponsor the new league – but there was a hitch. The powers at Lord's, who controlled all national competitions, would not work with Bagenal Harvey, the agent and impresario who was representing Rothmans. Bagenal's contract with Rothmans had a few years to run, thereby leaving Rothmans out in the cold.

At this point two representatives of Bagenal's company, one a former England captain, met me. Their aim was to persuade the Cricketers' Association to refuse to take part in the new Sunday League and to support their Cavaliers matches instead, thereby protecting the money that they were raising for beneficiaries. My calculation, however, was that, if we negotiated the right deal for playing in the Sunday League, all cricketers, including the beneficiaries, would finish up being better off.

I had my concerns about Bagenal Harvey – in particular, how the money raised at the Rothmans' Cavaliers matches was distributed – so, rather than saying an outright no to his representatives, I told the two representatives that our committee would consider the matter if they would present me with an accounts sheet for one of their matches, itemising the money raised and where it went. But it never came.

As General Secretary of the Association I wanted to see £400 (about £7,000 in today's values) added to the basic salary of a capped player, in return for taking part in what was to become the John Player Sunday League. The authorities were not pleased with me; they thought I was asking for far too much.

In May 1968 I was playing for Somerset at Gravesend while discussions were taking place at Lord's, and I was forced to leave the field to take a phone call from Billy Griffith, Secretary of the MCC. He offered £200 on the basic salary, which I refused. "It's 400 pounds," I said. "25 pounds a match." I returned to the field, only to be summoned to the telephone again a few minutes later. "The committee have decided that we can increase our offer to 250 pounds."

"You're wasting my time," I said. "It's 400 pounds. Anything less, and you won't have any players." He accused me of holding them to ransom. What he did not realise was that I knew the fee they would be receiving from television for the rights to broadcast the games and also the amount that a sponsor would be prepared to pay. They could easily afford £400.

A third time I was called to the phone. "You might as well stay off," Bill Alley said as I left the field once more. This time, sounding very annoyed, Billy Griffith said that the committee had agreed to pay the full £400. In fact, when the league started, some counties – including Warwickshire – paid their players in excess of that figure. As Terry Bowles wrote recently, 'It was a pivotal milestone in the history of cricket in this country. For the very first time, professional cricketers had collectively fought their corner ... and won.'

The Association's prime concerns at that time were focused on employment outside the summer season, player insurance and the special registration period for players moving counties.

The Association was determined to reduce the special registration period to 12 months. At the time if a player wished to move counties, he could be forced to spend two years qualifying. We argued primarily on the basis that the laws of the land allowed any person to carry out their chosen profession without unreasonable restrictions. Barry Knight, my old Wanstead team-mate and now an England cricketer, had left Essex at the end of the summer of 1966, and he was banned from playing championship cricket for Leicestershire, his new county, for two years. He missed the summer of 1967, but we argued his case and his ban was overturned for the summer of 1968, when he played again for England. Ultimately these restrictions were removed completely. Players are now able to move freely once their contracts have ended.

Player insurance was a headache, and a great deal of work went into providing satisfactory cover for all things. It was not easy, and the job had not been completed by the time I left the Association.

During the winter, players were largely left to fend for themselves. Some survived and unfortunately some did not, so we set up an employment exchange programme so that we could place players in various positions during the off-season. A lot of assistance was given to us by the National Employment Exchange who provided us with access to their vast employment opportunities. It needed more than just jobs, however, and the idea of training programmes was discussed at length.

I wanted cricketers to feel comfortable within their own position in the game. I had been told that the rate of suicide in cricket was quite high, and I could understand that because sportsmen grow old twice: the first time when they find that they cannot play the game as well as they could and again in the normal run of things. I wanted the opportunity of good winter employment to be in place, enabling players to get into a routine which they could slip into full-time when their playing days were over. In my own experience I felt very emotional when I retired from the game, but my activities with the Lord's Taverners made my retirement much easier.

Over the fifty years of its existence the PCA has taken these ideas forward far beyond what we were dealing with in those first years. There is a Personal Development and Welfare Programme, which provides all players with a personalised support service, helping them to be not only better cricketers but also better people who are preparing for life after cricket. It also has a most successful Benevolent Fund which helps former and current cricketers through difficult times. This includes a Mind Matters initiative that deals with issues of mental health.

At the end of 1968 Roger Prideaux resigned as Chairman of the Cricketer's Association, and Jack Bannister was elected to the post. Then in 1969, when I joined Derbyshire County Cricket Club as an administrator, I resigned from the Association, and Jack became the Secretary, a post he held for 19 years. Jack's election as President in 1994 was the icing on the cake as he was unique in the fact that he held all four of the Association's major posts. Suffice for me to say, I knew Jack Bannister through trying times and found him up to the mark on all occasions. He truly was a man of integrity.

I regard the PCA with a great deal of warmth. I know what it took to form the Association and hoped it would reach the heights it has. We really were a bunch of amateurs in the early days. We held our meetings in public houses and clubs, finding our feet in the wilderness of employer/employee relationships.

At the time of writing, cricket is going through a difficult period. Attendances are beginning to drop in the five-day game, and fewer people are playing at club level. The lack of terrestrial television does not help, nor do the ludicrous ideas emanating from the ECB. It is now that the PCA must be strong, making sure that they fully represent the players' view in every aspect of the game. After all, that is why they have been elected. I do not believe that the game requires major changes. certainly not Fred Karno-style one-day games played in clown suits. If the ECB, who appear to have lost their way, really want to promote the game, get it back on terrestrial television before it is too late.

PUBLIC RELATIONS

At the reopening, after refurbishment, of the Crown and Sceptre in Taunton.
To add to the sense of occasion I got Everton Weekes (left) to come along with me.

32

Fund raising for Somerset

In July 1967, while I was preparing for the inaugural meeting of the Cricketers' Association, I prepared a report and business plan for the Somerset committee, arguing the merits of employing a fund-raiser, to generate income for the club during the off-season. I also suggested that there was a need for good public relations.

It was obvious to me that sponsorship money was there for the taking, yet nobody was doing the asking. The people running county cricket could not see beyond the end of their noses; not one of the counties had created such a post. Yet sponsorship was the only way the game was going to survive; it was not going to survive on gate receipts.

I demonstrated how easy it was to raise money when I produced 'Up for the Cup', the booklet to accompany Somerset's appearance in the Gillette Cup final. So, after a few months' deliberation, the Somerset committee agreed to employ me – on the understanding that I raised my own fee and that any money I raised in excess of that would go to the club. That suited me, so I got down to the task of being the first Public Relations Officer/Fund Raiser in the first-class game.

With this and with the work I was doing for the Cricketers' Association, the winter passed very quickly. By April I had successfully covered my fee and provided additional funds for the Somerset County Cricket Club coffers. I had sold advertising on the ground, found match sponsors, lunch and tea sponsors, ball sponsors. In fact, anything that was capable of being

RUMSEY IS SOMERSET 'Mr IDEAS'

SOMERSET have appointed Fred Rumsey, their 31-year-old fast bowler, as public relations officer.

Rumsey recently elected general secretary of the Cricketers Association — a players' trade union — will be responsible for promotional activities, Press relations, and fund raising.

Rumsey said last night: "The County and I feel that relationships between ourselves and club sides are not good enough. The same applies to other counties.

MAIN JOBS

"One of my main jobs will be to improve this state of affairs."

Somerset secretary Richard Robinson said: "I'm certain there are an enormous number of people interested in helping the club through social functions and other fund-raising activities.

"Now we have an agent who can give them assistance with publicity and ideas."

Rumsey will continue to play for Somerset, whom he joined from Worcester in 1963.

sponsored, I got sponsored. Following on from the success of the Gillette Cup booklet, I introduced a new magazine called *The Somerset Dragon*, which provided a series of titbits about the club and players.

Because I had been an advertising purchaser at Fownes, I knew when and how to approach companies and, of course, it helped that I was a cricketer myself – an England cricketer, too. In later years, when I was in property, I would go to an important meeting in London, lasting an hour and a half, and for an hour and a quarter of it I would be talking cricket. Then I would do the deal. All the time it was like that. I was spoiled really because everybody wanted to talk cricket.

RUMSEY PULLS IN THE MONEY
By Eric Hill

Things are shaping up promisingly for Somerset's new cricket season, especially from a financial point of view

Already their new PRO Fred Rumsey has brought in more than £1,500 of advertising revenue, and more than 800 members have joined the club as vice-presidents for 1968.

*

A major reorganisation of the administration of English cricket took place in 1968, resulting in the end of MCC's long reign as the controlling body of the game, although that organisation still retains the responsibility for the laws. When Viscount Cobham was President of MCC in 1954 he described the then Conservative government as a bunch of communists compared to the MCC committee – many a true word is spoken in jest!

The government established a Sports Council that was responsible for giving grants to various sports, and it insisted that, if cricket wanted to benefit, it could not be run by MCC, a private members' club. As a result the MCC created the Cricket Council, which was made up of the Test and County Cricket Board (an amalgamation of the Advisory County Cricket Committee and the Board of Control of Test Matches), the National Cricket Association (representing clubs, schools, umpires, armed services and women's cricket) and the MCC. However, there was no real change of personnel. The secretariat of the TCCB was the same group that administered the MCC.

In July 1968 I was invited to become a member of the TCCB's new Public Relations and Promotions Sub-Committee. They were not meetings that I enjoyed. There seemed to be a constant battle between the old regime, the MCC, and the newer, more progressive approach provided by Raman Subba Row, the sub-committee's chairman. On one occasion Raman suggested that we should give some thought to the Gillette Cup sponsorship which was coming up for renewal, only to be told by Gubby Allen that the matter had already been dealt with. Raman was furious; he made it very clear to Gubby and Billy Griffith, who was also present, that it was our committee who would deal with all sponsorship negotiations in the future, not the MCC.

I had a similar battle with them when I argued that the TCCB secretariat should be appointed by the TCCB, not by the MCC. Along with my role in setting up the Cricketers' Association, it was soon clear to me that I was not somebody they wanted there. Billy Griffith accused me of being 'a young upstart coming into the game, believing you can change everything overnight'. He was not wrong there!

It took six years to separate the two secretariats, and even then the new TCCB Secretary, Donald Carr, moved over from being MCC's Assistant Secretary. Raman went on to chair Surrey County Cricket Club and the TCCB. He was a man of vision; it was a pity there were not more like him.

I began to feel more like a square peg in a round hole every time I attended a meeting at Lord's. Finally, after two or three years, I decided to call it a day and resigned my position.

When I finished playing, Kenny Barrington and the MCC Secretary, Jack Bailey, insisted that I become an MCC member. I let them put me down, and I regretted it. I tried to resign three times, and they would not let me. Successive secretaries refused my request. In the end I stopped paying my membership fee; it was the only way I could get out. I don't admire them. They think they own the game, and they are not good when they go abroad.

I remember a time in Barbados when I was walking to the Kensington Oval with Peter Short of the West Indies Cricket Board. We got to the gate, and the gateman was having a set-to with an Englishman.

I said to the Englishman, "Is there a problem?"

He said, "Yes. This fellow won't let me in here."

"Have you got a ticket?"

"Yes, I'm an MCC member."

"Well, that doesn't necessarily qualify you for entrance to the ground here."

"Why not? We run cricket, don't we?"

"That's beside the point."

He said, "Who are you anyway?"

So I told him, and he said, "Oh."

I said, "More importantly, this is the President of the West Indies Cricket Board, Mr Peter Short."

"Ah, you're Short, are you?"

Peter said, "Yes."

He said, "What's this business that I cannot come in here?"

Peter said, "I have presented myself at the Grace Gates at London as President of the West Indies Cricket Board, and they have refused to let me in because I haven't got a ticket. Why should we be any different?"

The fellow grunted and popped off.

I said, "Thank you, Peter. He's the last person I want you to put in your pavilion."

33

Last summer at Somerset

During the summer of 1968 I was, to say the least, very busy. I had numerous duties as General Secretary of the Cricketer's Association, plenty to occupy my mind as Public Relations and Fund Raising Officer for Somerset and a lot of pressure opening the bowling for the county. However, all these responsibilities paled into insignificance on 12 July with the arrival of our second child and only daughter, Claire Johanne. Being the father of two young children certainly eclipsed the responsibility of everything else I had on my plate, although it might be hard to convince Coleen of that.

The summer of 1968 was the first when overseas cricketers could join county sides without undergoing a period of residential qualification. In that first year only Yorkshire and Derbyshire refused to sign one. Some of the players, especially some of the best Engand players, did not like the wages being paid to the newcomers, but how could you expect Garry Sobers, the world's greatest cricketer, to play for the same as a capped player at Nottinghamshire?

The Australian Greg Chappell was advised – I think by Don Bradman – to obtain experience of English conditions. He wrote to Somerset, and the county were delighted to offer him a two-year contract.

From the time I picked him up at the airport, I knew that I would like this personable young man. He had an aura of quiet confidence and openness. I think Coleen liked him even more than I did – particularly when he popped round to the flat each week to pick up her wash and take it to the local laundrette.

I was amused by one incident concerning Greg and Cec Pepper, the Australian umpire. We were playing Yorkshire at Scarborough in August 1968, and in the second innings Greg was given out caught behind by Cec. He was fuming when he returned to the pavilion. "I was nowhere near it," he said. At the next break we both went to the umpire's room to have a word with Cec.

"I was nowhere near that ball," said Greg.

"I know," replied Cec. "But there are 10,000 Yorkshiremen out there and just us two Australians – you were out!"

After the match we travelled from Scarborough to Hove, without motorways, arriving at four o'clock in the morning. We lost the toss and took to the field at 11.30am. One of the Somerset committee men, who had had a good night's sleep, complained to the club that we all looked jaded and lethargic – it is no wonder I formed a union! Just to stir matters up a bit, I told John Snow that he should avoid bowling bouncers at Greg because he would hook him out of sight. Not heeding me one bit, Snowball gave him a torrid time which resulted in Greg receiving a nasty blow to the head, putting him in hospital. A few of us went to see him after the match, and he had obviously improved because he was ranting and raving about the cause.

"What idiot told John Snow that I could hook?" he said. I said nothing.

Our paths did not cross often after we both left Somerset but there was one occasion, in 1980, when the true character of the man rose to the fore. I had become very close to David Gower – in fact, he referred to me as Dad. At the age of 23 and after he had played 18 Test matches, David was dropped by England during a visit by the West Indies. He missed four Tests and went through a very bad patch, losing confidence and drive. There was even talk of him withdrawing from the game altogether. David's manager Jon Holmes contacted me, knowing my relationship with David, to establish if I could help.

We decided that David needed to talk to a batsman whom he admired in the hope that his confidence could be rebuilt. Greg Chappell was one such person, but he was the enemy. He was in the country at the time and, despite my explaining that what I wanted him to do could backfire on him, he accepted immediately. A dinner was arranged at an Italian restaurant in Nottingham, attended by Greg Chappell, David Gower, Jon Holmes and me. I can say without a shadow of doubt that I was privy to the most intelligent cricket conversation I had ever heard.

"Early on in my innings I play with the inside half of my bat," said Greg.

"I suppose that this gives you the confidence that you are playing close to your pad," suggested David.

"Yes, and by only playing to mid-off and mid-on in the early overs, I am minimising the possibility of edging to the keeper or the slips," continued Greg.

The conversation went back and forth on the many topics related to batting techniques. An overawed Jon Holmes and I said very little; we just sat and listened. The occasion worked, and David regained his desire and confidence, going on to greater things. I just increased my admiration for Greg Chappell.

Having successfully fulfilled my role as Somerset's fund-raising public relations officer during the winter of 1967/68, I fully expected the club to

175

engage me on a full-time basis for 1968/69. I wrote a business plan along with a job description and applied for the position. To me the answer was simple: "Yes, it is a good idea" or "No, we do not want you". But I got neither.

Whilst Somerset was making their decision, or in their case not, I was advised to follow the classified columns of the *Daily Telegraph* and there it was: 'Derbyshire County Cricket Club seek to employ a fund raising public relations officer with special emphasis on their forthcoming Centenary Celebrations in 1970.'

I understand that there were hundreds of applicants – no one would tell me exactly how many. The job's attraction was self-evident, and after three interviews I was short-listed. Although the Somerset committee were aware of my interest in the Derbyshire position, they made no attempt to answer my application or reply to my proposals.

The Chairman of Derbyshire's interviewing committee Guy Turner was an extremely detailed and efficient businessman. He brought into the meetings a professionalism the game sadly lacked, and it warmed the cockles of my heart.

I had only seen such an approach once before. It was at Worcestershire when I had a little financial problem. Sir George Dowty, President of the club and head of the Dowty Aircraft Group, called me to his office in Cheltenham. "This debt you owe," he began. I thought that he was going to write it off for me, but no such luck. "You will not be getting a penny from me. You solve your own problem. However, my secretary, accountant and lawyers are all available to you to help with the solution." Very clever, I thought, as I learned another lesson.

Guy Turner asked me if there was anything particular I would require if I was the successful candidate. Without hesitation I replied, "All the fund raising under my banner." I had seen what trouble can be caused when supporters' clubs insist on administering the funds they raise. The tail wags the dog with multiple disagreements. Although my point was accepted, it never happened. The Derbyshire County Cricket Club's Supporters Association refused to release the reins of their football lottery which was linked with the bigger one at Warwickshire. It was a perfect example of how damaging petty politics can be. Unfortunately a lot of this type of thinking existed on the general committees of cricket clubs.

I was offered the job and was asked to start at the end of the 1968 season. At the same time Surrey, influenced by Raman Subba Row, were establishing a similar post. Slowly cricket was starting to grasp the opportunities that lay around it.

There was still a season to finish with Somerset and a couple of games to play at the Scarborough Festival. My last match for Somerset was against Gloucestershire in Bristol. Following that game the county made it clear that they wanted me to stay with them, but there was still no mention of my proposal. I told them it was too late and that I had accepted Derbyshire's offer and would be joining them immediately.

I enjoyed my six years with Somerset and only came away with one beef. I hated it when the groundsman started up his roller every time I went in to bat at number 11.

The two matches at Scarborough were both for England XIs, the first against a Rest of the World XI, the second against an England Under-25 XI. In both games I opened the bowling with Fred Trueman. He announced his retirement that autumn so we went out together.

34

To Derbyshire

Somerset were not difficult about my move to Derbyshire. It was understandable that they did not want me to play championship cricket, but they had no objection to one-day matches so it looked as if the move was going to be smooth. Douglas Carr, the Secretary of Derbyshire, applied for permission for me to be specially registered for one-day cricket.

It was necessary for the last county played for and the county of birth to give their approval. Somerset had already approved so it only needed Essex to do so. However, despite Worcestershire and Somerset having both sought approval from Essex, it transpired that Stepney was in Middlesex and, when they were approached for approval, they refused, arguing that they wanted me to play for them. A distraught Douglas Carr telephoned Lord's to speak to the Middlesex Secretary who could hardly contain himself when he informed Douglas that he was the victim of a mammoth leg pull. So it was that my life with Derbyshire began.

I was still General Secretary of the Cricketer's Association which involved quite a lot of activity. It was not necessary for me to represent Derbyshire – Ian Buxton carried out that role – but I was beginning to find conflict between my executive role with the Association and my ex-officio role on the Derbyshire committee, also with my membership of the TCCB Public Relations and Promotions Sub-Committee. A number of matters were arising which, although not in direct conflict with the Cricketer's Association, were certainly borderline.

FRED RUMSEY, the new Public Relations Officer to Derbyshire Cricket Club, goes over some details with Major Douglas Carr (right), the club secretary.

Rumsey—cricket super salesman

CRICKET'S Victorian, cobwebbed image is at last about to be put to the sword. Leading the crusade is the formidable, heavyweight figure of Fred Rumsey.

By VERNON ADDISON

Fred, whose trusty left hand made the sparks fly as a fast bowler for Worcester, Somerset, and England, is now bringing off-the-field fireworks to the game as the Public Relations Officer of Derbyshire.

It would be truer to call him a business manager and he goes straight into attack, saying:

"We have a good product to sell but we are not selling it. Cricket has been like a firm that has a good product but doesn't market it properly."

Although he has only been in the job a few months he has made his mark with ideas tumbling out as fast as batsmen on his old county's notorious Bath wicket.

Sponsored matches . . . sponsored meals . . . advertising round the boundary . . . prepacked membership on sale in pubs and shops . . . a 200 club . . . portable souvenir shop . . . breaking the county up into nine regional councils. . . .

WEAPONS

These are the main weapons of his revolution—he prefers to call it a complete reorganisation—which aims at doubling the membership; bringing the game to the public and making everyone in the county feel he can play a part.

The 33-year-old Rumsey then expanded on his ideas. . . .

● ADVERTISING. Derbyshire have eight boards, measuring 24ft by 2ft 4in, which will be transported to their five home venues for every first-team game.

They will go round the boundary, rather like adverts round soccer grounds, but will not obstruct anyone's view. Cost to the advertiser, £250 for a season. Some have already been booked and there are vacancies.

● SPONSORED MATCHES. Games are being "sold" at £250 for three days, with the exception of a few better supported matches, when the rates will be higher.

Explains Rumsey: "Firms can use these for goodwill promotions to the public with their products on display in tents; for launching sales and advertising campaigns; or for goodwill to their customers, inviting them along to the match.

● SPONSORED MEALS. These are available at £25 a day for lunches and teas for an entire match at £25. This covers the cost of meals for players and umpires and the names of all sponsors will be announced over the loudspeaker system.

Even match balls can be sponsored—and business firms have already taken advantage of all these different ways of promoting their goods—but, of course, there are still vacancies, too.

● MEMBERSHIP. "Many people still think that you have to be nominated," continued Rumsey. "We want to cut out having to fill in a form and send it to headquarters at Derby.

"We plan membership booklets and everything you need in specially prepared packages to be bought over the counter at hotels, shops, etc, and even for junior members, perhaps, in schools."

● A MOBILE CARAVAN will be on duty in the public enclosure at every match. It will contain a shop, selling car badges, cuff-links, ashtrays, ties, brooches, etc, and also have a PRO on duty to give help.

"Many supporters who would like to become members are put off by having to get past doormen to the secretary's office. We are going to the people," said Rumsey.

● REGIONAL COUNCILS. These nine bodies will cover the entire county with its own officials and one representative from HQ.

"This means," continued the non-stop enthusiastic Fred, "that the smallest groan and moan can get back to the county officials.

"It also means that a promising player from the most obscure side can come to our notice. Many people want to recommend players but don't know how to go about it. These regional councils will also run their own social events.

Six councils already have set up their committees,

● A SOCIAL CLUB, an exclusive "200 club" which has proved successful with some soccer clubs, draws and joint membership for a man and his wife at £4 4s—"ordinary membership at £2 15s must be the best value in sport"—are all other aspects of the job which are getting Rumsey's attention.

TROUBLE

Rumsey sums up the trouble with cricket as the gap between the man in the street and the county clubs, and the lack of business promotion.

"Cricket isn't just somewhere to sit on a hard seat and then clear off."

Surrey are the only other county with a PRO, but Rumsey, who lives in a farmhouse at Shirley, near Ashbourne. with his wife and baby son and daughter, is emphatic that they will all follow Derbyshire's methods.

"With business-minded administrations cricket will be able to compete successfully with all other sports in the future."

Rumsey is such an enthusiast about the game that he admits he would go "door to door, cap in hand," to sell it.

I don't think there is any danger of his doing that, for he looks like becoming cricket's first tycoon.

He hopes that if work permits he will be able to play in the new one-day Sunday League. As work at present is a seven-day-a-week business I am not so confident about his playing hopes.

I decided it was necessary to withdraw from the union as I was not prepared to give up my new career. I wrote a letter of resignation explaining my position and the fact that I could not serve two conflicting masters. I received a charming reply from Jack Bannister, on behalf of the committee, thanking me for all I had achieved on behalf of the Association and offering me the post of Honorary Life Founder Member, a role I willingly and eagerly accepted. Forty years later, the appointment was ratified.

At Derby I appointed a personal assistant/secretary, tucked us both away in an outbuilding at the back of the Secretary's office and prepared the programmes for the 1969 season and the 1970 Centenary celebrations. I needed to learn more about the history of Derbyshire so I studied what old books and general literature I could get my hands on.

I found some very interesting facts. For example, Derby County Football Club was once the football section and played on what is now the cricket ground. Brian Clough, who was a very good cricketer and manager of the football club, had the idea of bringing them back together again. He approached me with a suggestion that he should run the cricket club alongside the football club: "What would your club think if I came in and sorted them out?"

"They'd go berserk, Brian." I said. "You're just the person we need, but they wouldn't let you in."

I liked Brian Clough and often played charity cricket with him. He had a very generous nature but could be wicked at times. During a match at Nottingham Forest, when he was manager there, one of his players was seriously concussed. The club's physiotherapist told Brian that the player concerned did not know who he was and asked what he should do. "Tell him he's Pele and put him back in the game," said Brian.

Brian Clough, a Lord's Taverner

The 1969 cricket season was soon upon us and, my own one-day cricket apart, I had duties at all Derbyshire home matches. These ranged from selling raffle tickets to making public address announcements – my jobs were endless. I sold a number of mobile advertising boards during the winter; these were in two sections, each about ten feet long, and needed to be bolted together. It was necessary to display them on all home grounds to meet the contract. To move them around I got the club to buy me a caravan which could double as a mobile office. I used to stick the advertising hoardings though the caravan's back window and transport them from ground to ground. It was no pleasure for a motorist to meet the car, caravan and me on the picturesque back lanes of the Derbyshire countryside.

Part of the success of the Sunday League was the fact that BBC 2 covered one entire match from 2pm to the close every Sunday. Derbyshire's first home match, at the Derby County Ground, was chosen for televising, but unfortunately it was a particularly bleak day. During the morning I set out the advertising boards in positions which would maximise good television coverage. Kennings, a Chesterfield car company, had reluctantly purchased two boards, not fully believing that the idea had value. I sited them on either side of the sight screen, directly opposite the camera position.

When the BBC2 producer arrived, he sought to admonish me. "Those two Kennings boards are filling my frame," he said. "You must move them further away from the sight screen."

"I'll do it when it stops raining," I replied.

Well, the rain lingered, the ground was wet, and play did not get under way till after five o'clock. So for most of the afternoon the BBC were broadcasting a frozen frame of the ground with the words 'No play yet' – and dominating the screen for a good three hours were the two Kennings signs. The following morning I discovered that George Kenning thought I was the greatest thing since sliced bread.

I was a regular member of Derbyshire's Sunday side. The atmosphere in the dressing room was quite a shock after six years at Somerset. There wasn't the humour; it was all downside, as if it was a chore to play. I thought to myself, "What have I come here for?" With public relations you can't be dour; you have to get out and talk with enthusiasm to people. But the more I met people up there, the more I realised it was part of their culture, like in Yorkshire. They were so used to being downtrodden, they viewed everything in that way. Heaven help anybody who turned up wearing a cravat.

The committee had had the foresight to create my position, but they were no different from most of the county committees at that time, with too many people around the table who did not understand the game. There was a meeting in 1972 when they were discussing contracts for the next season, and they were about to fire the wrong person.

"Excuse me, sir," I said. "I would like to make a comment. Is that permissible?"

"Of course it is," the chairman said. "You're an ex-officio member."

"Well, I feel that the committee should know that the person they're firing is not the person they think they're firing."

We had two slow bowlers, one called Swarbrook, a slow left-armer, and one called Swindell, an off-spinner, and they were going to fire Swarbrook, thinking he was Swindell. I put them right, but the next meeting they started on again about Swarbrook. "He's been with the club a long time; he's getting on now. It's better if we let him go."

He had made his debut for the county at 16 and had gone prematurely bald, so they thought he was much older than he was.

"He's only 22," I said. "He's still very young."

"Oh, oh, well, he doesn't look very young."

That was the sort of nonsense you had to suffer – and they were making decisions about people's livelihoods.

With Harold Rhodes, Alan Ward and me in the one-day team for 1969, we had the fastest attack in the country, though the league's restriction of run-ups to 15 yards did not help us. There was no such restriction in the Gillette Cup where we had considerable success.

In the first round we were drawn to play against my old club Somerset. The game was held at the County Ground, Taunton, where we won the toss and asked Somerset to bat. They scored 144 all out, which we knocked off,

Derbyshire's one-day side 1969
standing: David Smith, Peter Gibbs, Mike Page, Alan Ward,
Fred Rumsey, Peter Eyre, John Harvey, Fred Allen (masseur)
sitting: Bob Taylor, Ian Buxton, Derek Morgan (captain), Harold Rhodes, Ian Hall

winning by three wickets. I will modestly own up to being man of the match, with three for 19 off nine overs.

In the second round we faced another old club of mine, Worcestershire. We were at home this time, at the County Ground in Derby. Worcestershire elected to bat, but they managed only 156 for six in their 60 overs, and we won by four wickets.

The quarter-final found us in Wales at Sophia Gardens, Cardiff, for a tie against Glamorgan. The home side decided to bat and were all out for 117 in the 55th over. Tony Lewis, the Glamorgan captain, scored 60 of their runs and, with the young Alan Ward and me in the side, he was heard to say that for the first time in his career he was happy to be at the end facing Harold Rhodes. We won by nine wickets, and Harold – with four for 18 off 12 overs – was man of the match.

The semi-final was at Queen's Park, Chesterfield, against Sussex. Derbyshire won the toss and decided to bat. On a slow wicket we scored a laboured 136 all out, at the end of which David Smith, one of our opening bats, said, "If they get 50 runs off our attack on that wicket, they are super human!" In fact, Sussex were bowled out in the 36th over for 49, then the lowest total ever made in a one-day game. Alan Ward took two for 11 in 8 overs, I took two for 13 in 9, Harold took nought for 4 in 7, and Peter Eyre, our fourth quick bowler, took six for 18, winning the man of the match award. Such was the strength of our bowling that year that we won four matches to reach the final of the Gillette Cup without any of our batsmen hitting a fifty.

The final was to be played against Yorkshire at Lord's on 6 September. As at Somerset, on behalf of the players, I created a souvenir brochure to celebrate the achievement. A number of noteworthies were asked to contribute articles, including one Michael Parkinson. Michael was a staunch Yorkshire supporter, but that did not stop him from supporting a Derbyshire magazine.

Our paths had crossed when I was playing for Somerset – both when he was reporting for the *Yorkshire Post* and again, later, when we attended a cricket club dinner in Salisbury. I had to give a speech toasting the club, and he was replying on behalf of the guests. I sat on one side of the Bishop of Salisbury, and Coleen on the other. On the table in front of us was a candelabra. When we finished the meal, Coleen got out a cigarette and reached for the candelabra. Before she could finish, the Bishop was on his feet: "Ladies and gentlemen, the loyal toast." He then said, "You can now smoke."

They had a tombola, and in the centre of it was this double Chianti bottle where the two necks crossed over, with wicker all around the bottom. It looked very attractive. "I like that," Coleen said. So Parkinson said, "We'll get that then." He turned to me – "Come on, let's get it" – and we kept buying tickets till we got it. In doing so, we ended up with a good dozen bottles of alcohol as well as various chocolates and sweets.

"What are we going to do with this lot?" I asked Parky.

"Let's drink them," he said.

"I live just down the road," one of the guests said. "We can drink them at my place." He handed round all the bottles, and off we went.

We got halfway down the road, and Parky asked him, "How far is it?"

"You can see it," he said. "It's where that tarpaulin is hanging over the wall."

Ten yards further on, Parky turned to me. "Bet you I'm in the garden before you are," and off he ran. I ran behind him, about five yards behind, and, when he got to the wall, he vaulted it. What neither of us knew was that the tarpaulin was there because the owner had dug a hole to get down to some pipes in his garden – and the hole was full of water and muck. Parkinson had got this light suit on, and he came up bedraggled. A total mess.

The bloke's wife said they owned the local launderette, with a dry-cleaning machine, and she headed off with his suit. Meanwhile Parkinson sat in their front room in his pants. Somebody brought him a big sweater – he didn't bother with trousers – and we sat there, drinking wine and laughing, while his suit was dry-cleaned.

When I approached him to contribute a piece for Derbyshire's brochure for the Gillette Cup final, he asked me what he should write about. "Anything," I said – and he sent in the story about the evening in Salisbury and the hole in the garden. Only the blighter changed all the details.

Michael Parkinson Sunday Times

When Fred was still playing for Somerset we found ourselves as guests at a cricket dinner and afterwards decided to round off the evening at Fred's home. When we got to his house he demonstrated his athletic prowess and power over the demon drink by vaulting over a low wall surrounding his garden. We who watched this antic with mild amusement were soon horror stricken as Rumsey disappeared behind the wall and we heard, about ten seconds later, a dull thud. It was like dropping a stone down a well and hearing it reach the bottom. We raced to the wall and peered into the blackness below, where we could just make out the spreadeagled figure of Fred Rumsey. At great personal risk we rescued him from the abyss. Fortunately he was alright and later as he counted his bruises he explained that the accident was due to a lapse of memory on his part in that he had forgotten he had a sunken garden. That I rescued Fred Rumsey that evening and that he now goes out to try and defeat my beloved Yorkshire is proof enough of my service to Derbyshire cricket. I want you to know I wouldn't do it for Lancashire.

At the Gillette Final at Lord's Derek Morgan won the toss and put Yorkshire in to bat. I suppose he thought that with three 90 mph bowlers in his team, he stood a good chance of bowling Yorkshire out quite cheaply. They scored 219 for eight, not a big score in 60-over matches, but more than enough to beat Derbyshire who were all out for 150. Barrie Leadbeater received the man of the match from Colin Cowdrey for his score of 76. I was reasonably happy with my performance through the five matches, taking 11 wickets for 118 runs at an average of 10.72 with an economy rate of 2.28 runs per over.

The Derbyshire committee decided to organise a get-together for their London members after the match had finished. It was held in the pavilion and attended by some of the senior Derbyshire players and by Donald Carr, a former England and Derbyshire player, who worked as an assistant secretary for MCC at Lord's. As Derbyshire's Public Relations Officer I was expected to receive the guests and hang around until the last member had left. Donald stayed with me all the way and joined me in the dressing room whilst I changed out of my cricket gear. He had the foresight to bring a bottle of wine with him, and we put the world to rights as I changed.

Bottle consumed, we made our way out of the pavilion and said our goodbyes on the back steps, he going through a garden gate to his residence, which was in the grounds of Lord's. I headed for the Grace Gates, only to find it locked and barred and not a soul in sight. I went back to Donald's garden gate, but that was now locked. Mobile phones did not exist at this time and I could not gain access to any building, to find a phone, other than the back entrance of the Tavern. Fortunately I knew my way around the Tavern even in the dark and headed for the main bar. I opened the door and entered the room. It was pitch black, and even the lights from outside did not help.

Suddenly all hell broke loose. At least three bodies jumped on me, wrestling me to the ground, demanding to know who I was and what I was doing there.

"I was playing in the match," I said.

By this time the lights had been switched on.

"Playing in the match? Who are you then?"

"Fred Rumsey," I said.

"Fred Rumsey?" one of them said. "I know Fred Rumsey. You don't look a bit like him."

Eventually it was sorted out, and there were handshakes all round. A few drinks later I was on my way to the Clarendon Court Hotel where, hopefully, a pregnant Coleen would still be waiting for me.

*

I did win one trophy for Derbyshire, though it was in the television studio, not on the cricket field – a regional inter-county quiz that was broadcast by the BBC from Birmingham.

Our team of three got through to the semi-finals which we won on the final question when I was able to name the seven wonders of the ancient world. In the final we also won on the final question, this time with my naming six formations of cloud.

When I was young, I learned these things, and they have just stayed in my mind. I can name them now, even after two strokes.

Somewhere I still have my silver trophy of a sculpted carnation.

*

Derbyshire in final of TV county quiz

DERBYSHIRE won their semi-final in the B.B.C.1 Midlands "Contact" inter-county quiz programme "Out for the Count" last night by beating Northamptonshire.

Derbyshire were losing by six rounds to seven when the last round came up, but then won the contest by a knock-out. This was because Fred Rumsey, Derbyshire County Cricket Club's fund raising consultant, was able to name correctly the Seven Wonders of the World.

The other members of the Derbyshire team were Miss Tricia Thorns, Derby Playhouse actress, and Mr. Paul Nunn, editor of the "Rock Climbing Guide to the Peak District."

It was in late 1969 that I became a member of the Lord's Taverners. Up until that time I was unable to meet the requirements of membership which put a block on practising first-class cricketers unless appointed honorary members. One-day cricket did not count so I became Taverner number 799. I had already raised funds for the Taverners' cause with an event in Taunton, an all-night party starting with supper and ending with breakfast. I had also turned out in cricket matches, the first being the game in 1961 at Worcester with David Frost. I was proposed and seconded by Kenny Barrington and Neil Durden-Smith, both active Taverner supporters, but other than to attend their events there was little I could do for the charity in my early days as a member.

The Derbyshire committee, like Yorkshire, opposed the introduction of overseas players and, in fact, were the penultimate county to give in to the policy. They did so during the winter of 1969/70 when at my suggestion they signed Chris Wilkins, with whom I had played for Border in a friendly with Eastern Province. He was an attacking batsman, an excellent fielder and, after he came to England, a lively bowler as well – in fact, a true all-rounder.

He took a while to adapt to English conditions but, once he did, he had an outstanding season, adding much-needed power to our batting. In his last innings of the summer, for a Rest of the World XI at Scarborough, he hit the fastest first-class hundred of the year. Ford Motor Company was sponsoring first-class cricket at that time and awarded him a 3.5 litre Capri.

As a general run-around Ford had given each county a 1600cc Capri with the club's logo on the doors. As their Public Relations Officer, I had first call on Derbyshire's car. Chris's car was not delivered until the beginning of the 1971 season so Coleen and I decided to meet him on arrival with his prize. He was arriving in Southampton, by mail ship, in early April, at some ungodly hour in the morning so we decided to stay overnight just outside Southampton.

Coleen drove the 1600cc Capri and I chauffeured the 3.5 litre, both arriving in the hotel car park at the same time. When booking in as Mr & Mrs Rumsey and giving the details of the two cars, I was getting knowing looks from the desk clerk. He asked me what beverage we wanted in the morning, so in a loud voice I called across the reception hall to Coleen, "What do you drink in the mornings?"

I suffered for that, I can tell you.

35

Centenary celebrations

Coleen's pregnancy culminated in the birth of our third child and second son, Matthew, on 31 January 1970. According to Matthew it is the greatest event of my lifetime. He was born in Ashbourne, West Derbyshire and as I am sure you know:

> Derbyshire born, Derbyshire bred
> Strong int arm and quick int 'ead

I prefer an alternative:

> Strong int arm and thick int 'ead

Need I say more!

He was named Matthew William Gothard Rumsey, William being his grandfather's name and Gothard being his godfather's name: Eddie Gothard, the Treasurer of Derbyshire County Cricket Club. A county hockey player, he made his debut in first-class cricket at the age of 42 when he was appointed captain of Derbyshire in 1947. He led the county to fifth and sixth places respectively, and he took a hat-trick against Middlesex, but he always maintained that his greatest achievement was to clean bowl Don Bradman.

A great deal of positive activity had been created as part of the Derbyshire centenary celebrations. During the latter part of the previous year, regional committees – co-ordinated by my office – had been formed throughout the county with special briefs to organise functions and raise funds for the club.

I approached Royal Crown Derby who produced a wonderfully designed casket for auction. Webb Corbett, the glass manufacturers, followed suit with a magnificent chalice, sand-blasted with a rose and crown. From both companies I purchased further items, in limited editions, all of which sold out.

I wanted to auction the casket and chalice at Chatsworth House, so I arranged to see the Duke of Devonshire. I liked the Duke; he was a plain speaker who could read any situation well. Our meeting was in his library which was lined with bookcases all round. When the door was closed, it was impossible to see where you had come in.

"You smoke, don't you?" he said, throwing a Royal Crown Derby bonbon dish at me for use as an ash tray. "What do you want from me?"

There I was, an East End boy drinking wine with a duke, but without hesitation I launched into my list of requests. "I would like to hold a major fete in the grounds of Chatsworth, linked with a charity cricket match."

"That's okay as long as you clean up afterwards," he replied. "I'll get the Comptroller to get some dates for you."

"I'd also like you to host a couple of lunches for local businesses here at Chatsworth."

"That's no problem. You can have the State Room, which seats up to a hundred, or, if you prefer, my private suite, where we can seat 25."

As soon as he mentioned the private suite, I thought, "That's me." Two consecutive Mondays. He agreed. "In fact," he said, "we will have the Duchess along as well."

I invited top companies to each of the lunches, and every one of them accepted. In every case it was the chairman or managing director, not just a director, who booked to attend.

When I woke up on the morning of the first luncheon I was horrified. The ground was covered in thick snow. At about eight o'clock I got a phone call at home. "It's the Comptroller here." I said, "Sorry?"

"The Comptroller at Chatsworth. The Duke has asked me to call you."

I said, "Are you cancelling?"

"Oh no, we never cancel. Don't worry about that. The Duke has asked me to ring you to ask if you would like the water on." I was thinking that he was talking about the toilets. I had visions that the plumbing had failed because of the bad weather. "You know the water?"

I said, "I'm not quite sure."

"The fountain in the garden. We have the highest natural fountain in England. It can be seen from the luncheon room."

"Oh yes," I said, "That will be lovely."

It was stunning. If you can imagine virgin snow everywhere – nobody had walked on it – and right in the middle was this fountain which was creating prisms. It was a magnificent sight.

At the luncheon Eddie Gothard and I presented the case for the club, then the Duke spoke. The Duchess also spoke at the second lunch. Every single company there made a donation to the club's centenary celebrations. One in particular – Blue Circle, a cement company – sponsored a lot. They had an office in London, overlooking Buckingham Palace, and their chairman invited me down.

The MCC played against Derbyshire in a 40-over match at Chesterfield on 5 July. It not only celebrated the club's centenary but also commemorated the centenary of the meeting of the two sides at Lord's, on 21 and 22 July 1870. The MCC team was skippered by Donald Carr and consisted mostly of retired Derbyshire players, including Les Jackson and Cliff Gladwin. Thanks to Ian Hall and Ian Buxton, the club won by 58 runs.

Derbyshire v MCC, Chesterfield, 5 July 1970

Without doubt the biggest and best event of the centenary year was the fete in the grounds of Chatsworth House. Derbyshire played an eleven captained by the entertainer Leslie Crowther and including Reg Simpson, Les Jackson, the footballer Alan Durban and the actor Peter Hughes, whose son Simon played for Middlesex and now commentates on the game.

If the cricket did not tickle your fancy, there were many other attractions to enjoy. There were numerous stalls and games; a sea-casting fisherman was on the river, casting his line over 100 yards into floating truck tyres; and the Rolls Royce enthusiasts club turned up with 73 Rolls Royces, ranging in vintage from 1907 to 1970, the latter being the most recently completed model.

We had set a high target for fund-raising during the centenary year because we wanted to develop a sports centre on the Derby ground. We fell short of the sum required for that but were still quite satisfied with the final outcome.

The centenary was only part of the equation. We also felt that by extending the image of the club we would generate more interest. To that end it was necessary for me, as Public Relations Officer, to be available for functions thoughout the county. During February I attended thirty; there was one day when I judged children's fancy dress in the morning, opened a cricket pavilion at lunch time and made a speech at a cricket club in the evening.

On one occasion I was speaking at the Centenary Anniversary Dinner of a Derby cricket club. Coleen was helping me to get ready for the event.

"What jokes should I tell this evening?" I asked.

"It doesn't really matter," she retorted. "If it's a centenary dinner, all yours qualify!"

Having admonished her for her sarcastic humour I asked if my being away every night concerned her. "No," she said. "But, if anything unusual happens, make sure that you give me a ring."

The dinner went well, and I was half way through my speech, replying on behalf of the guests, when a note was passed to me: 'Would you wind up as soon as you can? The stripper has arrived.'

I had received such notes before. "Your zipper is undone – sit down before you embarrass yourself," was a regular one – but I followed instructions and, after some polite applause, was led to a seat in the front row and handed a bottle of wine and a glass.

I had already had a lot to drink and found focusing a little difficult. When the stripper began her performance I was not sure if there was one or two of her and started to close and open one eye to get a more positive view. She got the wrong impression from this action, and suddenly she was sitting on my knee, draping chiffon all over me. In a momentary lull, remembering what Coleen had said, I was able to break free and headed for the telephone.

"Coleen, this almost naked girl was on my knee, draping chiffon all over me. What should I do?" Quick as a flash she replied, "If you think you can do anything, come home."

Derbyshire performed quite well in the John Player League in 1970, finishing in third place. There was a presentation dinner in London where medals were given to the first three places. Although cricket is a popular sport, very few trophies are associated with it. During my 15 years of involvement I received six medals: three man-of-the-match gold awards (one Gillette Cup, two Benson & Hedges), two Gillette Cup runners-up medals and this third-place bronze for the John Player League.

You will notice that all these were for one-day cricket. Before their introduction we got, as a cockney would say, 'naff all'. I suppose something was awarded if your county won the championship; I wouldn't know as I never rose to those dizzy heights.

I was awarded two county caps: one by Somerset and one by Derbyshire, the Derbyshire one being for one-day cricket only; I believe it to be the first of its kind. The England policy of providing a cap is somewhat disappointing. Unlike soccer, when selected for England the first cap you receive is the only cap you receive – unless it fades, becomes threadbare or is lost. Mark you, a tie, two sweaters and a blazer were also provided with that first England cap. Recently all surviving Test cricketers received a braided cap with a tassel, their name and Test number embroidered on it. At the time of writing only 689 players have worn the three lions since 1877, a very small masonry indeed.

The summer of 1970 featured my final first-class cricket match. With Harold Rhodes having retired, Peter Eyre not fit and Alan Ward selected for England, I played for the only time for Derbyshire in the championship – ironically against Somerset at Bath. I managed to scramble two wickets, the ultimate one being Maurice Hill, who had moved to Somerset from Nottinghamshire.

People sometimes ask me who was the best batsman I bowled to, and it is a difficult question; batting is about what happens on the day. Three of the best I saw were Dick Richardson, Peter Marner and Maurice Hill. On their day they could take any bowling apart; they had all the shots. All three had the talent to become regular Test batsmen, but they only showed the form required on rare occasions. When they did fully perform, it was worth the watching.

Other batsmen had less talent but more application. Kenny Barrington was one. He was not a great player, but he had unbelievable application. He played in four of my five Tests, and he scored 256, 137, 163 and 91.

Garry Sobers, Colin Cowdrey and Tom Graveney were all great batsmen. Up to a point Ted Dexter was; he could take the bowling apart, but you always had a chance against him, he rarely got a big hundred. Mike Smith was a bad starter, which affected his reputation, but, if he got in, he was as good as any of them.

All things considered, the best batsman I ever bowled against – the one with the greatest talent *and* the greatest application – was Barry Richards.

36

Langley Mill

I have often been asked about the standard of cricket at different levels – in particular, the difference between first-class and club cricket. I had an excellent experience in the early 1970s which explains the difference, but you must accept my pomposity in its telling.

The only cricket I was playing at the time was in the one-day matches for Derbyshire, and most of these were in the John Player League on a Sunday. If a match was rained off, it meant that I did not play for at least two weeks. Net practice is okay, but there is no substitute for a competitive game.

Ian Buxton recommended that I found some games somewhere, and a Derbyshire stalwart John Brown suggested that I play for his club, Langley Mill. I did not want a fee for playing but the club insisted – so, for player's consumption only, I said I would put the money behind the bar at The Thorn Tree, a pub they used for post-match drinking.

The matches were played on Saturdays so, one hour before the first game was due to start, I presented myself at the ground for pre-match practice and warm-up, only to find it closed. After climbing a fence I reached the pavilion – that, too, was closed. I waited 15 minutes before the pavilion attendant came to open up. I changed into my whites and waited another 15 minutes before another player and the opposition arrived. Twenty minutes before the start, the captain Barry Marsh and most of the team arrived. They sauntered around the dressing room, chatting about everything but the forthcoming game. Barry changed into his whites, found the opposition captain and went out to make the toss, which he lost. With ten minutes to go and with the umpires hanging around in front of the pavilion, I discovered that my opening bowling partner had not arrived.

The umpires took to the field with most of our team in tow. I was halfway through the first over when my partner appeared on the pitch with his shirt hanging out and boot laces undone. He was just about fully attired when I finished my over. These were 45-over league matches, and I found myself bowling 23 of them. This I did not mind because I was there to get the exercise.

The game continued. Our wicket-keeper appealed for a catch which bounced a metre in front of him, gully appealed for an lbw when the ball would not have hit a row of palings and, throughout the afternoon, fielders once placed could not seem to find the same position a second time.

We won the match and returned to a very cheerful dressing room. I was asked if I had enjoyed my first game. "No," I said, "and it is not my intention to repeat the experience and play again."

There was a hushed silence before Barry Marsh asked why.

"For over ten years I have been associated with and played first-class cricket. As a professional I am aware of the need to prepare my body and mind for activity. It is important to warm up before commencing strenuous exercise. Apart from getting the stiffness out of the limbs, it is also necessary to co-ordinate eye and hand. Not being mentally prepared leads to a lot of early mistakes. I am sorry to say that, as a team, you were a shambles before the match and in some instances on the pitch. A good side does not have to cheat or to appeal from fielding positions that have no idea of the line of the ball and, when the captain or bowler places a fielder, they do not want him to wander around aimlessly."

Another silence followed my outburst until the captain asked, "Would you stay if we make the changes you suggest?"

"Yes," I said. "As long as every team member arrives one hour before the start, changes and warms up. If you as captain give anyone permission to be late, that is acceptable as long as it is not too often."

Even the keeper agreed and, during the season, they were disciplined beyond measure, which was why they went on in future years to win the league. By approaching the game in a professional manner, club players can reach their full potential and, in some cases, go on to higher planes.

I particularly enjoyed the public relations aspect of my appointment with Derbyshire. It was never necessary to seek a lot of publicity, county cricket generates its own; it was more important to make sure that what was reaching the media was in the club's best interest. To this end the more journalistic friends I had, the better. I wrote articles and columns for local papers and fed radio and television with as many releases as I could muster. At this time the Head of Sport for ATV and Central Television was Billy Wright, the former England football captain, and I would appear on his evening programme if there was a cricket story. Billy was one of the nicest media men I ever met; when he died in 1994, it affected me much more than I expected.

Even though the centenary celebrations had come and gone, I still had a lot to do. Fund-raising was a very important part of my remit, and it was necessary to maintain a flow of new ideas. In 1972 I introduced sponsored matches, usually for the more important games.

A group called FPA Finnegan agreed to sponsor a visit to Chesterfield by the Australians and to take a marquee on the ground for entertainment. It was at the end of May, and the weather was a little unsettled. On the morning of the first day it bucketed down, and the day's play was called off by 9am. I telephoned Ron Palfreyman, the chairman of FPA Finnegan, with whom I was quite friendly.

"There are people coming from all over England," he said. "We cannot cancel. Will the caterer go ahead irrespective of the weather?"

"Yes, I have already checked with him," I replied.

"Good, and I expect you to be on duty," he said in closing.

I had taken the precaution of installing a raised wooden floor in the marquee, just in case of bad weather, and it was working. By 1pm the rain was still persisting, but the tent was full and throbbing. The later it became, the louder it got. I could not believe the enjoyment being had on a rain-soaked deserted cricket ground. The party continued for six hours until the chairman decided to invite everyone to dinner at a local hostelry.

Days two and three were entirely different. The weather improved, and Ron Palfreyman's guests were treated to a feast of cricket with 641 runs scored in the two days, including three centuries, two by the Australians, Bruce Francis and Doug Walters, and one by Chris Wilkins. The match was drawn, but Ron Palfreyman was delighted and sponsored again the following year.

In 1972 I managed to persuade Fred Trueman to come out of retirement and play for Derbyshire in the Sunday League. He played six matches in all, but I got the feeling that he was not really happy. We opened the bowling together in a match against Yorkshire at Bradford. He received a warm welcome from his old fans, but journalist Mike Carey, writing in the *Guardian*, suggested 'with Rumsey and Trueman opening the bowling at Bradford it was less like the John Player League more like All Our Yesterdays.'

Most years county cricket clubs grant a benefit or testimonial to one of their players. This enables the player to boost his income during that year by running a series of fund-raising events. In 1974 Derbyshire decided to award itself a benefit year, which meant that I had to find more ways to augment the coffers. When I started planning for it in 1973, Dave Allen, the Irish comedian, was appearing at The Talk of the Midlands, an old cinema converted into a theatre/restaurant/nightclub, so I asked one of the owners, Julian Beck, whom I knew quite well, if he would support the club by donating an evening at his premises for us to put on a show. He agreed on condition that we paid for the food, but he offered the bar profits for the night as a donation to the club. He suggested a date in 1974 when Dave Allen was again performing.

"Would Dave consider being our top act if we paid his fee?" I asked.

"I don't know. He's in his dressing room. Go and ask him."

I knocked on the dressing room door, and a familiar Irish voice bade me enter and be seated. I explained what we had planned for 1974 and wondered if, for his normal fee, he would consider performing.

"No," he said, "I don't intend to do that."

There was a moment of silence, and I rose to leave.

"Where are you going?"

"I thought our negotiations were complete."

"I said no to your proposition, I didn't say I wouldn't do it."

Confused, I sat back down and waited for him to continue.

"I will do your special evening, but it will be completely free of charge – as long as I can join your celebrations after the act."

"Agreed," I said with a great deal of relief and pleasure.

It was the beginning of a close friendship which lasted almost to the day he died in 2005.

37

Property development

After a couple of seasons Derbyshire and I came to an agreement whereby they employed my public relations company to take over the duties I had previously performed as an employee. I branched out into other activities almost immediately and employed a former Somerset cricketer, Mike Barnwell, to handle the day-to-day business at the cricket club.

I was approached by a Nottingham builder, Eddie Meek, to create and promote a golf tournament at a course in East Leake, South Nottinghamshire. I hired the course and clubhouse for two days and invited 40 golfers from the top of the British rankings. It was a two-day tournament with a pro/am on the first day and just the professionals on the second, with the professionals' scores over the two days deciding the champion. To make the pro/am more interesting I added a few celebrities, including the Bedser twins, Kenny Lynch, Graham Hill and Max Bygraves. Standing on the first tee Max threw some grass in the air, to check the wind, then turned to his caddie and said, "Give me my cashmere sweater!"

At 7.30 on the first morning the mist reduced the visibility to 30 metres, causing me acute stress. By start time it had reached 100 metres, and I could relax. The tournament was won by the Irish golfer Eamonn Darcy.

Eddie Meek was very happy with the tournament and asked if I could structure a new company for him. He was looking to split with his partner and to take Parmeco Ltd, the sponsoring company of the golf tournament, along with some other associated building companies, into a new group.

Eddie wanted Parmeco to be operative as soon as possible. I set about the task, finding office accommodation in Derby, a staff to man it and a number of property negotiators to cover the length and breadth of the UK. When I had finished, I had a meeting with Eddie to sign off.

"You've done a good job," he said, "but where's the group managing director?"

"That's you," I replied.

"Oh no, I plan to be executive chairman. But, to save you setting up more interviews, I do have someone in mind."

"Thank goodness," I said. "Who is it?"

"You," he said.

"I know nothing about the property business. I would be like a fish out of water. Anyway, I have my own business to run."

"I'll soon have you up to speed in the property business, and I would only need you three days a week. I would suggest, however, that you merge all activities with your Parmeco duties and operate everything from the new offices in Derby, with the assistance of a personal secretary. I will give you 10% of the business. Name your price."

I did, and he accepted.

It was all very confusing at first because Parmeco was developing in the specialised market of petrol filling stations. With the introduction of self service, there were major changes to the forecourts, with more pumps under wide canopies. We were only interested in developing sites that could produce a minimum sell of 500,000 gallons a year. Our negotiators would find a potential site and prepare a feasibility study, counting all the cars that passed. They would then check for the nearest filling stations and how many houses there were in the catchment. Armed with all this information, it was possible to calculate the potential gallonage. We then looked for the nearest petrol distribution centre and offered the station, as if constructed, to that oil company. Although we were talking about high turnovers, the oil companies would not even look at a study unless the site could operate with Green Shield stamps.

We had one or two lawyers working with us, but the one I became closest to was Brian Evans, who was based in Nottingham. We were both Sagittarians, with similar likes and dislikes, and, 45 years on, our friendship is still strong. He was an excellent lawyer, quick to spot the silly games that sellers tried to play when they returned contracts.

An added bonus to any petrol filling station was the introduction of a Little Chef restaurant. Trust House Forte owned Little Chef, and we were able to negotiate with them a construction contract to build units of various sizes all over the country. With our own gang of four and using local tradesmen, we could complete a site within 12 weeks.

Mike Barnwell left my employ to join the RAF so I required someone to look after my interests at Derbyshire. I settled on a non-cricketer called Peter Miln, a man of many and varied ideas and talents. One of his first fund-raising events was to hold a midnight matinee of the film 'Last Tango in Paris'. The occasion started with an 11pm champagne party, which was very much to Coleen's and my liking, so much so that we ended up sleeping through three-quarters of the film.

Eventually my company ceased its activities with Derbyshire Cricket Club. I opened a restaurant in Derby called the Bistro Belge specialising in Belgian cuisine, and I made Peter Miln the chef/manager.

Parmeco suffered from a down-flow in property values, and they went into administration. Barclays merchant bank asked me to sell the Parmeco properties that were under its control but the clearing bank, concerned about their customers who were creditors of Parmeco, would not use me because I was unqualified. The fact that I understood Parmeco's operation better than anyone was beside the point.

I had a similar debate with a qualified chartered surveyor. He asked why I only used him for residential valuations and sales, and I told him that he did not understand the filling station business. He scoffed at that so I got him to value a flooded and run-down station that we had purchased in Birmingham. I gave him the plans for redevelopment and asked him to value both the purchase price of the site and its selling price after development. He came back with the two prices: purchase at £17,000, sell at £40,000. His jaw dropped when I told him that we had paid £30,000 and had already sold it, when developed, to Mobil Oil for £120,000. We had valued the site on its gallonage throughput, which he had not considered.

The liquidator had received an offer on a filling station site in Nottingham. I advised them that it was too low, but it appeared that they were going to accept it anyway. I spoke to a friend, Peter Short, who owned a property company in Chesterfield, to see if he would be interested in entering into a joint development project with me; he would put up the money, and I would carry out the development. So I was now back into the property business, this time with a 50% interest.

After a few more developments Peter offered to sell his interest in the firm to me. I was reluctant to lose him, but I was sympathetic to his reason for leaving. We visited our accountants with a prepared verbal agreement covering the split. They were astounded that no aspect of our agreement was in writing and even more amazed when, within minutes, Peter and I had settled our parting with a shaking of hands. I was then, and I am still, a believer that a person's word is their bond – although the older I get, the more disappointed I become when finding that fewer people think this way.

I was now total owner of my own development company and began to look for construction sites. This was before I had set up my own building arm,

Dave Allen
on the JCB

so it was necessary to use sub-contractors or building companies to carry out the work. One such company approached me with a proposition to develop a small site in South Derbyshire. The local authority wanted to acquire the site in exhange for the construction of four senior citizen bungalows on a separate piece of land. I accepted the offer, only to find out that the building of the bungalows required the demolition of a row of cottages and that there was local opposition to this.

I came to the conclusion that, whatever we did, we would be criticised for knocking down the cottages. The answer was to maximise our own publicity and create some local goodwill, so I asked Dave Allen to come and help. First, he visited some of the elderly people who were going to live in the bungalows; then he mounted the JCB to start the destruction of the existing properties. Apart from his nearly turning the machine over, it was an excellent exercise and there were no complaints.

38

Growing potatoes

When we first moved to Derbyshire we lived in a rented cottage in a delightful little village called Shirley; it was very rural and served the farming industry. We were there for three years before we had to move on. I was very busy at the time and had failed to arrange for suitable alternative accommodation. It was my intention to live in a hotel until I could find something suitable.

When the local vicar heard of my plan, he was horrified. "You cannot take your lovely wife and three young children to a hotel," he said. "You should be ashamed of yourself for being so laxed. I intend to take over the arrangements for your move and find something suitable, whatever you may think."

And find something suitable he did: the Curate's House in Ashbourne. Ashbourne was without a curate at the time so it was made available to us for a couple of years. The two oldest children began their education with the Parents' National Education Union, a home-schooling scheme, and I continued to build my businesses.

I tried to make myself available to the family as much as I could, but I must admit the drink after work at the Greyhound in Friargate was pure pleasure. One evening I received a phone call at the pub. The landlord, applying his usual customer protection, told the caller that he would check if I was there; it was Coleen. I took the call which I thought could be urgent.

"You have received a wine delivery," she said. "If you are not home by nine o'clock, I shall open a bottle and pour it down the sink. I will then continue that exercise until you return." I arrived home on the stroke of nine. Because it was red wine I knew there was little chance of her carrying out the threat, but I could not be totally sure.

I was often late home and suffered for it. On one occasion I asked where my dinner was and was told that it was in the dog. On another, when I had taken the plate out of the oven, she took it from me with oven gloves and threw it through the open window. On a third occasion, when I lifted off the plate covering my meal, all I found was a strip of paper with the word 'Bollox' written on it. Her spelling never was one of her greatest attributes!

We were doing well in the business and decided to purchase a modern lodge house with seven acres on the fringe of Ashbourne. The land was split into two paddocks, one of which – three acres in size – we turned into the 'Grow Patch'. We employed a full-time gardener, George Renshaw, who came with a reference that was almost beyond belief and eventually left with one just as glowing. His responsibilities were to look after the lawns, plant and maintain the garden and help me with the Grow Patch.

Ted Moult, the farmer and broadcaster, gave me some advice. "Plough and disc the field first, then make sure that potato is your first crop. This will work the soil even more and make it easier to till in the future. I will provide the seed potatoes," he ventured.

It was getting late in the season when we ploughed and disced and, after fencing off a corner for a kitchen garden, we eventually planted the remaining acreage with Ted's spuds from the back of a tractor. There was a severe late frost that year, killing the early growth, but ours were not out of the ground by then so we were not affected. When we harvested we had a much larger crop than most growers, and the price for a hundredweight had more than doubled. We removed the cars from our double garage, filled it with potatoes and successfully sold them to a local hotel.

During the late autumn of that year I was asked to speak at the Lincolnshire County Cricket Club dinner. I was placed next to the president, who was very chatty. He asked me what my hobbies were, and I gave him chapter and verse about my 'Grow Patch' and the garden. I asked him if he liked gardening, and he said he enjoyed growing vegetables and flowers.

"How many acres have you got?" I asked.

"A few thousand," he replied. I found out later that he was one of the biggest bulb growers in the region. I felt stupid, having bashed his ear for about 15 minutes about my three acres.

A few weeks later a big lorry, full of sacks, came up my drive. "Are you Fred Rumsey?" asked the driver.

I confirmed that I was but that I had not ordered any produce.

"I don't know about that," said the driver. "I was asked to deliver these bulbs to you at no charge."

We unloaded them and filled the garage again; there were thousands. I guessed from whom they had come, and I was delighted. Not so George – he was the one who was going to have to plant them. We wintered over with spring cabbage in the patch and then planted peas for the summer. Even though we staggered the planting, they caught us by surprise by all maturing in one week. We sold them to my pal John Smith, who managed the Pennine Hotel in Derby, and he made a type of pease pudding out of them, something he never ceases to remind me of.

My venture into trout farming was less successful. Our farming neighbour Jeff Joules was not a sporting man and offered me, free of charge, the fishing rights on his land, where he had two large ponds. I contacted the local water authority to remove the coarse fish from the larger of the ponds. This they did with a fine net, depositing them in a local reservoir. I purchased some young trout and waited for them to grow so that I could indulge in a little fly-fishing. I waited years, only to find out that some of the pike had avoided the water authority's nets and had been eating all my young tender trout.

*

I was approached by the directors of Johnson and Nephew, a wire-pulling company in Ambergate. They were due to celebrate their centenary but were at loggerheads with their employees over it. The workforce did not want the company to waste money on a celebratory meal; they would rather have that money put into their pay packets.

Having given the matter considerable thought, I suggested that the celebration should be aimed at the workers' families and, in particular, their children. The board liked this, and I came up with the idea of a football match between the company's own team and the cast of a popular Saturday morning children's TV show called Tiswas – 'Today is Saturday, Watch and Smile'. I arranged for Ed 'Stewpot' Stewart, a keen Lord's Taverner who presented 'Junior Choice' on Radio 1, to captain the company's team – and, to ensure good viewing, I took the precaution of importing a mobile stand from Derbyshire's Ilkeston ground.

On the day the Tiswas team, including the creator Peter Tomlinson, Bob Carolgees (Spit the Dog) and the charismatic Chris Tarrant, turned up in a London bus, prepared to do battle. The publicity created by me and by the Tiswas programme resulted in thousands of people turning out who, apart from filling the stand, were six deep around the pitch. Unfortunately most of the board members could not find a satisfactory viewing position, but they were not fussed. They did not receive one complaint from their workforce.

I was also pleased because I got a bonus.

LORD'S TAVERNERS

A Lord's Taverners match at Edgbaston

sitting: Reg Simpson, Fred Trueman, Rachael Heyhoe Flint, Fred Rumsey,
Bob Bevan, Neil Durden-Smith, Willie Rushton

Among those standing are Bob Cowper, Colin Milburn, John Price, Ed Stewart,
Bill Tidy, Jimmy Ellis (Z Cars), Bill Simpson (Dr Finlay) and Mike Smith

Anita Harris (left) bowls the game's first ball, and Willie Rushton (right) bats

39

Lord's Taverners

The Lord's Taverners is a charitable club, founded in 1950 by a group of actors and people associated with cricket. Its objective from the start was to raise funds to ensure that the underprivileged and disabled are given plenty of opportunities to benefit from sport.

In 1974 the Lord's Taverners Secretary, Captain Tony Swainson, invited me to stand for the Council, the governing body of the club. I was duly elected and served for six years. We were approaching our 25th anniversary, and it soon became apparent to me that little had altered in those years. An element of the council was particularly conservative, whereas a number of newer members, including me, wanted to move with the times.

Membership was a bone of contention. At the time the criterion for membership was 'an artist with a love for cricket or a cricketer with a love for art'. The new brigade wanted this extended to bring into the club more business acumen and promotional flair, and we got our way.

Matches were being organised where only a handful of celebrities were on display, particularly when they were situated north of Watford. One Sunday I was picked to play in a match close to Manchester and, at kick-off time, only three members of the Taverners took to the field: the cartoonist Bill Tidy, the former Yorkshire captain Billy Sutcliffe and me. The remainder of the team was made up of local cricketers and members of the club we were playing. There had been a full eleven on Wednesday, but eight of them had cried off. To me the answer was simple: pick more than eleven and, if they all turn up, play the lot. This solution was not appreciated by the diehards, but it did become the norm.

The annual income fluctuated considerably, and this created problems for the organisations we supported, such as the National Playing Fields Association – so we evened out our payments by building up capital in a reserve fund. In 1976 we began providing special minibuses to schools and organisations that help disabled and disadvantaged youngsters, a scheme that has been a great success, with more than 1,150 of these buses being donated in the past 42 years.

Up to this point membership had been open only to men so we created the Lady Taverners in recognition of the assistance the ladies gave to the club at cricket matches and functions like the annual ball. Coleen was one of the first, along with other wives of cricket-playing members. They were given free honorary membership of the organisation, to which I had no objection – though I was a little put out when they were invited to become members of the Lord's Taverners itself and were allowed to carry across their honorary status while I was still paying for my membership!

Captain Tony Swainson RN was the perfect person for the job of administrating a charitable club. He was creative, likeable, honest, blunt and pleasantly rude, even to royalty. He would often ring me to discuss some weird and wonderful idea for furthering the cause of the Taverners and never took offence if my opinions did not gel with his. One idea, suggested by Ben Brocklehurst, a former Somerset captain and owner of *The Cricketer* magazine, involved creating a new membership level called the Friends of the Lord's Taverners, to be controlled by regional committees.

Tony asked me to be part of a small committee of Ben, himself and me to develop the idea, out of which I set up a trial region in the East Midlands. With so much going on in my life at the time – at one stage I was a director of over forty companies – I decided to include this Taverners work as part of my small group activity, with my staff becoming responsible for my private life, my business life and the Lord's Taverners. But neither I nor my staff ever received any money from the charity, not even expenses. Everything we did, we did freely for the charity.

Forty years on, there are far too many people being paid by the organisation. Back in the 1970s it was only Tony Swainson, two secretaries and a part-time accountant. All the rest was done without charge.

Although there were many fund-raising functions – dinners, lunches and a ball – the most important Taverner activity to my mind was the series of cricket matches played up and down the kingdom. We played in every part of the British Isles and then spread to Europe, the Americas, Africa and Asia.

Even though the prime function of a Taverners match was to raise funds, it was important that the spectators enjoyed the occasion. We noticed that, however good the weather was, the crowd would start to leave the ground at around four o'clock, usually before tea. So, to ensure that the public had a good opportunity to see all the celebrities, the Taverners would field first. It was important to create credibility so, as long as the opposition early order could bat a little, we would begin with our England opening bowlers, which for some years would be John Price, John Snow, Butch White and me. Then Bill Tidy, Ted Moult, Willie Rushton, Robert Powell, John Alderton and others were allowed to apply their various mystical bowling techniques. The same applied to the batting; each Taverner team would include at least two first-class batsmen and, because we only batted eleven, we bowlers would stay in reserve just in case. Having said that, John Price opened the batting in Corfu and scored a hundred. He claims it as an international ton and is very proud of it.

For the most part we bowled within ourselves, and there was a convention that the umpires would not give lbws. But there was one match – at Sutton in Surrey – when the opposition asked us to bowl flat out: "Our batsmen want to know what it's like." I got three wickets in the first over, and they took me off.

Harry Secombe's house overlooked the ground at Sutton, and he used to play for us. One year I gave him my England sweater. He thought I'd given him the world. He couldn't put it down and wore it all evening. He was a people lifter. He was always on about it in the dressing room: "I'm the champion people lifter." He would pick me to lift because I was the biggest, and he'd heave me over his shoulder. I tried to lift him, but he was so round, it was difficult.

Managing the mix of cricketers and celebrities was an art. Back in the 1960s I had played once for an Old England XI, sponsored by Gallaher the cigarette company, and their policy was to pick ten cricketers and one celebrity. In the match Ian Carmichael, the actor, was the celebrity. We batted first and he sat in the dressing room, away from everybody, never attempting to make any conversation, right the way up to teatime.

At tea I went over to him and said, "Don't you like being with us?"

He said, "You don't know how frightening this is. You're all Test players."

"But that shouldn't make any difference to you. It's no different from the first night of a show."

"Not quite," he said. "I am so overawed by the whole thing."

No one sought payment or expenses when turning out for the Taverners. Most of those I played with were givers, not takers. This created a certain bonhomie, which made the playing far more enjoyable. I joined the Taverners to put something back into the game, to pay for the enjoyment I had got out of it when playing professionally, only to find that I got more pleasure playing for the Taverners than I did playing first-class cricket.

Giving time to the charity is one thing, but on one occasion David Frost took this to the extreme. For a match in the east of England which I was managing, David arrived earlier than most and asked me if I could arrange an extra four places at lunch, for which he would pay. I told him that it was not a problem and that no payment was necessary. Luncheon had commenced when four people, in uniform, entered the tent. David went over to greet and seat them and returned to his chair next to me.

"Are they your four guests?" I asked.

"Yes," he replied.

"But they're aircrew," I said, surprised.

"Yes, they've flown me from New York and are flying me straight back after the game!" He had chartered a plane and flown over especially for the match.

At a Taverners match at Lichfield

Lord Lichfield, Lord Stafford, David Frost, Fred Rumsey and Willie Rushton

The match featured many of the cast of Crossroads who, in the weeks beforehand, kept mentioning the game on the programme. As a result we had a crowd of 10,000, which did not please Derbyshire. They were playing Leicestershire at the County Ground, close by, and only attracted 2,000.

We played a match in The Hague, Holland, at the same time as a top bridge tournament which featured Omar Sharif, the Egyptian actor. He appeared to enjoy the bonhomie of the Taverners and agreed to turn out in our next European match, on the old football stadium in Monaco.

Bob Cowper, the Aussie all-rounder, who was living in Monaco at the time, captained the Monaco team, and I led the Taverners side – though, in truth, both sides were made up of Taverners and their friends. Bob was batting when I decided to bring Omar into the attack. Our wicket-keeper was the ever-enthusiastic JPR Williams, of Welsh rugby fame. Bob had scored a few runs and, facing Omar, he walked down the wicket, deliberately missed the ball and was stumped. At tea I asked Bob why he had chosen to get out at that point.

"Too good an opportunity to miss," he said. "I can dine out on stumped JPR Williams bowled Omar Sharif for months."

"Not if I have my say," I countered.

"What do you mean?"

"JPR took the ball in front of the wickets so, in fact, it was a no ball."

Upon receipt of a decent bottle of red, I said no more.

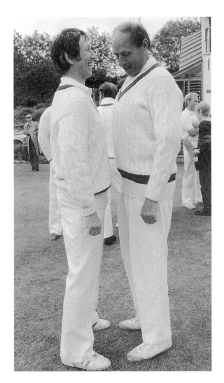

left: JPR Williams and me at Bath
above: Godfrey Evans

Wisden described Godfrey Evans as 'arguably the best wicket-keeper the game has ever seen'. I would certainly not disagree. He kept to me on a number of occasions in charity matches. In fact, I played in his last ever match, at Canterbury; he was 70 years old, and he was still standing up to the wicket. He used to call me 'Master', an endearing term, and together we would see off a few bottles of whatever. Later in his life he made some excellent home-made wine, which we both thoroughly enjoyed, sometimes to excess. He was over the limit at one of my promotions, and it was with a great deal of reluctance that I had to call him to task and withdraw him from the action. He apologised profusely and promised that it would never happen again. It never did.

In 1999 Coleen and I were at the Taunton Races when the loudspeaker asked me to report to the steward's office. It was to take a call from a hospital in Northampton, letting me know that Godfrey was in a critical condition and that he had been asking for me. The doctors were planning to inject a pain killer that would render him unconscious but, if I left Taunton immediately, they would hold off until I arrived. It was a hair-raising trip, culminating with us running down the corridors of the hospital.

I entered his room, he smiled and said, "Hello, Master." Then the doctor inserted the needle, and we never spoke again. He died soon after.

I was asked to distribute his ashes over the playing area of the Canterbury cricket ground. Some I gently poured behind the stumps on the cricket square and some around the base of the famous lime tree inside the boundary. Whilst doing so, a gust of wind blew some of the ashes onto my shoes. I did not brush the ash off; I decided to take it to his memorial service to be held later at Canterbury Cathedral. A touch, I think Godfrey would have enjoyed.

Willie Rushton, who co-founded *Private Eye*, was an extremely generous and likeable individual who, with Bill Tidy, provided much of the dressing-room humour. Willie loved playing for the Taverners and was a regular up to the time of his death at the age of 59. He was a huge Surrey supporter and, when he died, I arranged for his ashes to be buried just outside the gate where the players enter onto the Oval turf.

Nicholas Parsons was another who gave a lot of his time to the Taverners. He was travelling by train to a match in the north when a fellow traveller in his compartment said, "Excuse me, but didn't you used to be Nicholas Parsons?"

Eric Morecambe's love for sport and his dedication to charity led him into the ranks of the Lord's Taverners, and it was at one of their many dinner functions that our paths first crossed. I had been a fan of his for years, but what I did not know was that he had never heard of me!

At Taverners matches Coleen used to run the Polaroid club, an enclosure where people could pay to have their photograph taken with a celebrity. Jack Robertson, the Middlesex and England batsman, used to take the pictures. If Eric went in, the place would be inundated with people queuing up for photographs; I have known him stay in there for the whole of one innings.

At that time Eric was one of the best after-dinner speakers making the rounds – in his case it was mostly for fun and charity. The fact that his presentation was short, to the point and funny gave rise to little criticism. In one such speech he accused me of alcoholic over-indulgence and holding up a ship launch because I would not let go of the bottle. I was also accused of being a legend in my own lunch time.

I liked Eric a lot, and I also liked to be known as the man who was a friend of Eric Morecambe. Whenever he visited me in Derbyshire, I would throw a little soirée to introduce him to my local friends and acquaintances. On one such occasion we had spent the whole day fly-fishing on the Wye and the Derwent, arriving back after the party had started. True to form, Eric wasted no time and immediately set about entertaining the gathering with his usual wit and charm. At about 11.30pm, a tired-looking Eric took me to one side and asked me to call an end to the proceedings. Knowing that we were off fishing again at the break of dawn and respecting his wishes, I did so.

In the photograph enclosure Noele Gordon of Crossroads and Eric Morecambe sit on either side of a spectator while Jack Robertson photographs them

Coleen began to batten down the hatches, and Eric called for a final night cap. Brian Evans and one of his friends were spending the night, and the five of us relaxed with what I incorrectly thought was going to be our last drink. From that moment on, Eric re-enacted the whole day's fishing, finding humour in situations that had simply passed me by. For two and a half hours he had us laughing until our sides were fit to burst. There was no stealing from past scripts or repetition of catch phrases, just humour based on the day's events. When he finally finished, possibly out of exhaustion, a wide grin spread across his face.

"You know," he said, "I got more pleasure out of that, making you my friends laugh, than I get out of many of the professional appearances I make."

At one Taverners match at Lord's, Eric asked Fred Trueman and me to accompany him on a goodwill tour of the sponsors' boxes in the Tavern stand. From the time we entered the first box until the moment we got back to the pavilion, Fred had held forth with opinions on almost every subject associated with cricket. Most of them included humour and, when we were halfway round, Eric stopped and said to Fred, "You must put all this into a book."

"I couldn't do that," replied Fred. "I use most of it in my after-dinner speeches."

"How many books do you expect to ruddy well sell?" countered Eric.

Both Eric and I were aware that Fred was going through a difficult financial period, and I am sure that led to Eric's next comment.

"I'll tell you what. You put down your thoughts, and I will comment on them. And he," he said, pointing at me, "will write and compile the book."

I was just about to object when Eric gave me a look. "Oh yes, you will, sunshine," he said.

After a short hesitation I said, "Okay, I'll do it – as long as Willie Rushton agrees to illustrate."

I wasted no time in contacting Willie, who was one of the best caricaturists in the business. I felt the book needed caricatures rather than cartoons. Willie's first reaction to my request was to say, "Aha, The Thoughts of Trueman Now". He had visions of thousands of people standing in front of the pavilion at Lord's, waving a little green book.

Before I got started, I suffered a mild heart attack, putting me out of action for about six months. I was convalescing in Spain when I decided to start on the book. My plan was to interview Fred with a tape recorder, type up his replies, then pass the manuscript on to Eric for his comments and to Willie for his drawings. I got up early each morning to make a list of over 600 heads relating to cricket.

I spent a few days in Yorkshire with Fred. A friend was going to type it all up, but unfortunately Fred's speech needed a lot of sorting out. I had to rewrite all his comments, thinking in Yorkshire speech as if I were Fred. This slowed down the process – so, to speed things up, I went to visit Eric, spending two Saturday afternoons at his home in Harpenden. I don't think that I could have managed a third, as I was nearly collapsed with laughter both times. Some of Eric's replies were unprintable, but the main gist was excellent – and his tapes required no editing from me.

Willie's caricatures were tremendous – my favourite was his one of Clive Lloyd – and the publisher's designer did a wonderful job in laying it all out.

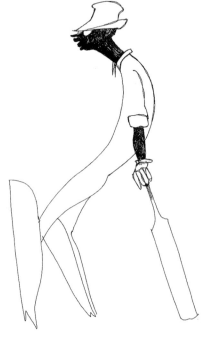

Clive Lloyd

212

THE THOUGHTS OF
TRUEMAN NOW
by Fred Trueman

with Eric Morecambe, William Rushton & Fred Rumsey

The Thoughts of Trueman Now went on the market in 1978 and was high in the non-fiction best-seller list for quite a while, alongside *The Country Diary of an Edwardian Lady* and a cookery book by Clement Freud.

The publishers wanted me to write a second volume with Brian Clough, *The Thoughts of Clough Now*, and Brian was keen. But he had a contract with another publisher, and it never went ahead. Instead, I started work with Lawrie McMenemy, the Southampton football manager. I finished the interviews – *Thanks for the McMenemy* was the title – but I never got as far as typing them up. I still have the tapes if anybody is interested. I also have six taped interviews with Test match captains – Ted Dexter, John Goddard, Peter van der Merwe, the Nawab of Pataudi, Greg Chappell and John Reid – in which each of them talks about his best match as captain.

*

I hold the Lord's Taverners responsible for my becoming obsessed with golf. They invited me to join them on a seven-day cricket tour to Sarasota in Florida. Two matches were to be played, one on Tuesday and one on Thursday, but what they did not tell me was that sandwiched between those two matches they had arranged a special golf tournament. I could not cry off because all the pairings had been made in advance. Whilst grinning and bearing it, I played the worst golf imaginable, and this was not helped by the numerous alligators wanting to partner me throughout the round.

As is the wont of most golf tournaments, an auction was held during the post-golf meal, so I kept my eye open for the possibility of a bargain. Dave Stockton, the winning American Ryder Cup captain in 1991, had donated one of his tournament golf bags which had reached and was sticking at $50. I entered the bidding and purchased it for $75. Why, I still do not know. A local suggested that I should fill it with clubs, because they are cheaper in the USA than in Britain, and he knew the owner of a store next door to that night's party. The fellow opened up his store, and I filled the bag with tailor-made clubs.

"What do you plan to do with those?" Coleen asked. "I've been a cricket widow for the last thirty years. If you think I will now become a golf widow, you still have a lot to learn."

So we took up golf together. For the first few years we could not keep our hands off the clubs and played wherever and whenever we could. We both got down to a handicap of 16 but stayed around that number.

Coleen and I enjoyed our limited involvement with golf, particularly the pleasure of what golfers call 'the crack'. It is a humour that is similar to that in cricket, and it was usually provided by Tony and Cob Butlin, Frank 'Stormy' Pepperell and Scott Whitmore.

Although Scott was by far the youngest of our group, he was constantly honing his wit, usually at the expense of his playing partner. I was playing with him one afternoon following a hospital visit in which I had had a camera investigate my inner bowel. By the 16th hole I was beginning to feel the effects of the morning activity – so, as Scott rushed off to the 17th tee, I asked him to slow down.

"What's the matter?" he asked. "You've been dragging your heels all afternoon."

"I had a small operation at the hospital this morning," I replied.

"Oh, on what?"

"I don't want to tell you."

"You may as well, now that you have aroused my interest."

"Okay, it was on my backside."

There was a slight pause. "It's no wonder you've not been talking much today," he said.

The two sports most revered for their honesty were cricket and golf but not any more; even those two pinnacles of integrity have succumbed to modern living. We know of the gambling in cricket and the humbling of the phrase 'It is not cricket', but golf has dropped even lower. I was playing in a charity tournament when the winning team were having their handicaps checked with their home clubs. When given one name, a secretary said that was not possible as he was having a drink with the member in the bar at that moment!

Playing charity golf is a must for former cricketers, and on one occasion my team was playing behind a team led by Brian Close. Brian could play golf either left- or right-handed to the very low handicap of three. We waited whilst he played his second shot, which finished up in the middle of a large lake. It was not long before the club followed the ball, and in even less time his golf bag and trolley followed the club into the water. As we teed off, an angry Brian stormed past us en route to the clubhouse.

My ball landed close to where Brian had played his final shot into the lake and, as I settled over it, Brian returned from his hasty departure.

"Are you going to finish your round?" I asked.

He glared at me. "No, my flaming car keys are in the bag."

*

As the result of money raised by a successful motor racing promotion at the Albert Hall, the Taverners formed a motor-racing sub-committee, to which I was appointed. This led to the Lord's Taverners becoming involved in the Formula Ford 2000 Championship. At each meeting a Taverners celebrity presented the winner with a magnum of champagne, sometimes doing a victory circuit with them. I took on the task of organising the Taverners' role in this.

On one occasion we had a visit from James Hunt, the former world champion who was fun to be around. He had the role of driving fans around the track in a 12-seater transit. Tim Brooke-Taylor and I agreed to sit with him in the front, then regretted it. He got faster and faster, and by the third corner he was on two wheels with my door at 45 degrees to the track.

The meetings raised good money, but I was not too impressed by the attitudes of those working in the motor-racing scene; too many of them were in the sport for what they could get out of it for themselves. But the director of Oulton Park was the very amiable Rex Foster. We hit it off from the first time we met. I don't think that he was over-enamoured by the people at his head office but, like me, accepted the situation as inescapable. He had a son called Drew who, along with Geoff Moss as his junior partner, ran a travel company called Caribbean Connection. Rex asked me if I would give Drew some advice on how he could introduce cricket into his programme.

A meeting with Drew was arranged for the following Wednesday in his Chester office. It was apparent that, before I could give Drew any hard and fast advice, I would need to see the product.

"Is Friday too soon?" asked Drew.

"No," I replied, and by 4pm Friday in the summer of 1978 we were touching down at Grantley Adams International Airport in Seawell, Barbados.

TO THE CARIBBEAN AND BEYOND

Fred Rumsey, Colin Milburn, Trevor Bailey, Denis Compton and Charlie Griffith, with (front) Owen Estwick, the Secretary of the Barbados Cricket League

40

Barbados cricket festival

Drew and I stayed on the west coast of Barbados, close to Holetown, at a private estate owned by Peter Moores of Littlewoods fame. The house, called Landfall, was in the Alan Bay complex on the Sandy Lane beach, and we were looked after by a butler, cook, housemaid, laundrymaid and gardener. We did some of our work on the beach close to the edge of the garden and, every 15 minutes or so, in all his regalia and carrying a silver salver, the butler would appear with two fresh glasses of cold rum punch: what a way to work!

I wanted to hear the views of local cricket personalities to establish the credibility of the idea that was forming in my mind. The first person I approached was Tony Cozier, who was already a legend in West Indies cricket broadcasting. Tony was as enthusiastic about cricket as he was about his field-hockey goalkeeping and, as a great promoter of all that was West Indies, he believed that my idea, at worst, would promote his beloved island.

My idea was simple. I would invite a number of former Test match and professional cricketers to play in and skipper teams, filled by amateur players of any level, from both the UK and Barbados, in a tournament that would be held in Barbados every November. This would give Drew Foster a flagship event to promote to his cricket-loving clients in the UK, as well as offering an opportunity to the Barbadian players to exhibit their talents to the visiting cricketers. Peter Short, who was President of the Barbados Cricket Association, thought the idea to be sound but, knowing the West Indian attitude to new ideas of this nature, gave the tournament two years of success, three at the most – something I reminded Peter of after the 10th, 20th and 30th festivals!

My promotions company was to organise the cricket, and Drew's Caribbean Connection was to arrange the travel. In the early years the competition was played on a two-league basis, according to John Player League rules, with the winners of the Buccaneer League playing the winners of the Caribbean League for the British Airways Trophy. The highlight of the tournament was a one-day game at the Wanderers Ground between the Fred Rumsey XI, the pick of the festival, and the Barbados Cricket Association XI. The event was called The Pro/Am Cricket Festival, with the idea that club players of any standard could play with and against top cricketers from Barbados and England. The invitations went out to club cricketers, umpires, scorers and spectators alike, anyone who enjoyed cricket and would like to sample the pleasures that Barbados had to offer. A friend once told me that, if paradise is the end of the line, then Barbados is the penultimate stop.

For the first festival in 1978 I decided to have eight teams, each of which would have at least two local Bajan players. Invitations to captain the sides were sent out to Denis Compton, Trevor Bailey, Reg Simpson, Colin Milburn, Brian Close, Wes Hall and Charlie Griffith (who shared a team), the Barbados Cricket League and me. By late July the sales were poor, and I was worried. Then Trevor Bailey discussed the tournament with Peter Baxter during a *Test Match Special* broadcast, the switchboard at the BBC was flooded with calls, and in no time our numbers had risen close to a hundred.

For that first festival Coleen and I stayed at Bluff House, which was also part of Peter Moores' Alan Bay Complex; we had Jane Asher as a neighbour with Jon Pertwee just across the road.

Altogether, including umpires, scorers and supporters, there were about 150 people at the first festival. Among the local players were Keith Boyce, Desmond Haynes, Richard Edwards and Franklyn Stephenson. A touch of humour was provided by Tim Brooke-Taylor, of The Goodies fame. The Barbados Cricket League won the first British Airways Trophy, beating Denis Compton's XI in the final, and Oliver Reed drowned his sorrows by buying all of Denis's team all their drinks all night! My own XI finished last in eighth position. To a man my team asked to play under someone else in the future – a request firmly refused!

Oliver Reed and Denis Compton, with festival regulars
John Flood and his wife Fern, who scored the matches

*A typical festival team – featuring (all standing) Colin Milburn,
Brian Close and Franklyn Stephenson*

I made the mistake that first year of playing too much cricket, and it was not long before I reduced the overs-per-side down to 35 and eventually we played Twenty20. It was too hot in the afternoon sun and, with no policy for rationing rum, the players were finding 40 overs a little too much! I had already introduced restricted run-ups, which proved worthwhile because nearly every young cricketer in Barbados had a fast bowler's run-up.

For a small island, with a population of around 250,000, Barbados had an uncanny ability to produce and nurture fast bowlers. During that winter of 1978/79, Joel Garner and Wayne Daniel were playing in the Packer World Series in Australia while Vanburn Holder, Sylvester Clarke and Malcolm Marshall were with the West Indies in India. Had Barbados had a Shell Shield match in the Caribbean, they would still have been able to open their attack with young fast bowlers such as Hartley Alleyne, Ezra Moseley and Franklyn Stephenson, all of whom were kicking their heels in the Caribbean sun.

I first came across Franklyn during that first Pro/Am Festival. He was a young man of 19, full of fun, and he loved the tournament. He kept turning up in different teams: Colin Milburn's XI, Greensleeves XI, St James Beach Hotels XI, then my XI against the Barbados Cricket Association. Cricket was much more than a game to him, it was simply his whole life!

It was another three years before he made his debut for Barbados. Action follows Franklyn wherever he plays and, in that match against the Leeward Islands, he was sent in as nightwatchman on the first evening and was out the next day for 165. The following winter he joined Lawrence Rowe on the rebel West Indies tour to South Africa and was barred for life from all levels of cricket in the West Indies. After great success in English county cricket, he retired from the game in 1997. Now he runs a coaching school for both golf and cricket in Barbados. He always contacts me when he is in England.

The second festival was also an overwhelming success. 183 tourists travelled from the UK, and at least 50 joined us from Barbados. The tournament included 12 sides that year and, added to the previous year's list of captains, we had four former West Indies Test players: Richard Edwards, David Holford, Keith Boyce and Norman Marshall, brother of the former Hampshire batsman Roy.

Quickly the Pro/Am Cricket Festival became a fixture in the Barbados cricket calendar. It was enjoyed by tourists as well as local players, some of whom saw the festival as a stepping stone to cricket in England. Due to contacts made during the festival Ezra Moseley, Hartley Alleyne, Neal Phillips and Franklyn Stephenson came to England, to play county or league cricket, and they all enjoyed the transition they made.

Drew Foster and I decided on a change. Instead of two companies arranging and organising the festival, we formed a new international sports and group travel company called Gateways Abroad to do both jobs. We were attracting a lot more local sponsorship which, when added to the British Airways support, covered most of the costs of the event in Barbados.

For the third year, 1980, I elevated Denis Compton and Trevor Bailey to the rank of manager, which was more suited to their respective ages of 62 and 56. This gave me the opportunity to introduce two extra Test players, and I invited Don Wilson and David Gower.

Having David Gower on board for the third festival gave me some parental satisfaction. We had been friends since early in his career and, for some forgotten reason, I had become his Dad. The fact that I was David's Dad, Ian Botham's Uncle and Geoff Miller was Son of Fred led to some confusion with my own children and even my wife – although no great issue was ever made of the matter!

The British Airways Pro/Am Cricket Festival

BARBADOS — NOVEMBER 1980

Team Sheet

THE BUCCANEERS GROUP — Manager: Denis Compton

Fred Rumsey XI	Don Wilson XI (Riverdale Hall)	David Gower XI	David Holford XI	Barbados Cricket League XI
†Fred Rumsey	†Don Wilson	†David Gower	†David Holford	This team to be selected by the League in Barbados.
Duncan Carter	Ezra Moseley	Franklyn Stephenson	Hartley Alleyne	
*Roger Freeland	*M. Baker	Sam Wilkinson	Stuart Bell	
K. Barnett	A. Beal G. Clark	Nigel Caplin	P. Beddington	**Note:**
Alan Edwards	T. Bell J. Cocker	*Tony Cozier	D. Boots	A number of Barbados Players will be joining us. They are sometimes shown as A Bajan.
Alan Payne	H. Foster	Steve Edwards	*J. Clegg	
Sherman Marshall	D. Gubbins	I. Johnson	T. Dandridge	
Mike Smith	A. Stevenson	Dr. D. Kelleher	J. Harrison	
Ray Smith	J. Swan	P. Oliver	J. Toon	
Tweety Whitney	S. Tose	G. Parsons	J. Warburton	
R. Wood		Charles Thompson	A Bajan	

THE CARIBS GROUP — Manager: Trevor Bailey

Colin Milburn XI	Reg Simpson XI	Brian Close XI	Richard Edwards XI	John Snow XI (Baccas)
†Colin Milburn	†Reg Simpson	†Brian Close	†Richard Edwards	†John Snow
Rickie Clarke	Stephen Farmer	Neil Phillips	Calvin Hope	Emerson Trotman
~~Shane Julien~~ COLLIS KING	Roy Allyene	Steve Hinkson	P. Dickerson	Philip Alston
John Capps	G. Allcoat	John Flood	Alan Fantham	Rod Berkley
Martin Field	H. Blucher	Mike Hibbert	I. Hills	Peter Brown
Jim Foote	*Jim Fookes	A. Kieft	*C. P. Knight	Richard Cavendish
J. Gorman	H. St. J. Heggs	Bob Meikle	T. Lewis	Tony Cotter
*D. Knight	C. Hull	A. Petter	Jeff Nash	*David Hopkinson
A. Stevens	Steve Nash	M. Potter	F. Robins	Ted LeGresley
Mike Walton	Phil Rowley	J. Williamson	Laurie Shaw	Peter Lockwood
~~A Bajan~~ CHARLIE GRIFFITH	A Bajan	*A Bajan	A Bajan	Clive Smith

† Captain   * Wicket Keeper

David Gower was born on the 1st April, and he once told me that you cannot April fool an April 1st baby – a very silly thing to say. One year I asked him what his birthday plans were, saying that I hoped he had included me in the arrangements. I already knew that he was planning to have a boy's night out, in London, with his pal Chris Cowdrey, and my request caused him some consternation. Finally he suggested that Coleen and I should join him and his then girlfriend Vicki for dinner at home with a few local friends. What he did not know was that I had already primed his local mates about the dinner, telling them to refuse his invitation when he rang. Neither did he know that I had invited Chris Cowdrey and his lady Christel to attend the party and stay the night; they had also refused David's invitation to attend. David was to play squash with one of his friends in the early afternoon under the assumption that the only guests for dinner were the two old fogies, Coleen and me. Whilst he was out, Chris Cowdrey arrived and parked his car in the garage, staying there with the party food which had been prepared earlier. We put Vicki's car in front of the doors in case David wanted to enter the garage on his return.

When David did return, he came straight into the kitchen, looking as miserable as sin. In a resigned voice he said, "I suppose we may as well have a drink." At that prearranged moment the telephone rang. It was Chris from the garage, wishing David a happy birthday, then asking to speak to me. With reluctance David handed over the phone and, if it were possible, looked even more miserable. I had a one-way conversation on the telephone whilst Chris and Christel were making their way through the house. When they entered the kitchen the incredulous look on David's face made the whole charade worthwhile. Whilst the hugging was taking place, the front door-bell rang, and all David's local friends poured into the house.

*

The third festival was won by the Brian Close XI. Even in this holiday cricket Brian was intensely competitive. The English batsmen, professionals apart, struggled on the Barbados wickets against the local bowlers – so, to keep the more prolific Bajan batsmen from the crease, Brian instructed his fielders to drop all catches whilst the less free-scoring English batsmen were out in the middle. Even though he had captained England, it was necessary for me to have a quiet word in his ear.

Closey loved a challenge. On one occasion we were being entertained at the home of the British Airways manager where there was a swimming pool. Not content to dive into the pool, Closey put a chair by the poolside, ran up and jumped over it into the pool. Then he put a chair on top of the chair and repeated the performance. Then out came a table, which he dived over, and for his final tour de force he put a chair on a chair on the table. By this time, with all his splashing, there was water everywhere and, when he ran in, he slipped and the whole lot – table, chairs and Closey – all finished up in the water.

41

Fred Rumsey Travel

A further innovation took place in 1981. Up to that time organised tours to overseas Test matches had been the domain of the Cricketers Club of London, *The Cricketer* magazine and the MCC. Gateways Abroad Limited, our new sporting travel company, entered the business, going a step further by inviting former Test cricketers to host the clients. Our first venture in February and March 1981 took tourist groups to the West Indies to support England's tour there.

A major problem arose when the England team reached Guyana for the Second Test. One of England's players, Robin Jackman, was married to a South African and, because he had coached and played there, it was construed that he had links with apartheid. The Guyanese government revoked his visa and issued him with a deportation order. This led to the Test match being cancelled, with the remainder of the tour hanging in the balance. With our supporters and the England party stranded, Drew Foster and his sidekick Geoff Moss had the wherewithal to arrange for a BWIA 707 to land, pick up all our clients and anyone else who was not happy with the situation and fly them all to Barbados.

With less than a fortnight to go to the third Test in Barbados, no decision about the tour was forthcoming. I contacted Peter Short, the Barbados President of Cricket, pleading with him to make a positive decision for all our sakes, pointing out that tourism was the most important income to that island. Fortunately he already held that view and, within a few days, confirmed that the tour could proceed.

A year later he was on an Air Guyana flight, on which Forbes Burnham, the Guyanese President, and his entourage had taken over the first-class cabin. Peter sent him a note, explaining who he was and could he have a brief audience. The reply was immediate: "I will send an aide shortly." Peter spent the waiting time making some notes on what he should say. He was finally ushered to a seat next to the President but, before he could utter a single sentence, Forbes Burnham said, "I believe I owe you an apology, Mr Short. Didn't I mess up your cricket arrangements in Guyana last year? I hope you will understand that it was too good an opportunity to miss." At that point Peter mentally tore up his notes.

By far the favourite venue for my Test match tours was Barbados, where 400 plus a school group of 25 booked their passage. I split the party into roughly 10 subsidiary groups and allocated one celebrity cricketer to each 40 or so tourists. I had hired a house on the Sandy Lane golf course, called Coralita, for the sole purpose of entertaining the 400 guests. By splitting them into manageable groups we were able to hold ten cocktail parties during the 14-day stay. Each cocktail party was attended by all ten former players and one or two of the current Test team. Although the parties were only supposed to last an hour, we often awoke to find bodies sleeping around the swimming pool.

Among a group that Don Wilson was looking after was an Irish contingent, one of whom was sadly drowned whilst they were at the beach bar in the early evening. Once the coroner had reached his verdict, it was necessary for us to arrange transport home as soon as possible so I contacted an undertaker to take care of the body and to transport it to the airport after the hearing. Don Wilson attended the hearing, which concluded death by misadventure, and was waiting with the body outside the Coroner's Court when a hearse arrived. The driver said he was there to pick up a body, which was then loaded onto the hearse, and he departed. Don was making his way to the car park when another hearse arrived, this time presenting documents for the collection of the body. The new driver, having heard that the body had already been collected, immediately accused his brother of stealing it in order to collect the sizeable commission which goes with shipping bodies by air.

We informed the police, and a hunt for the rogue hearse was put in place. It was finally found hidden in a garage on the east coast of the island.

I arranged for the body to leave Barbados within 24 hours and asked the genuine undertaker to pick it up from the police. He contacted me to say that the police would not release the body because it was evidence in a criminal act and that I would need a court order to obtain its release. By now my nerve ends were glowing but, when I contacted a judge, he was sympathetic and arranged an immediate court order, instructing the police to free the body. When the body finally reached the airport security, they came up with a further problem. Because the coffin was flying to Ireland it was necessary to create a visible access to confirm that it only held a body – something I immediately agreed to, and a window was cut in the top.

Apart from the 425 supporters we had in Barbados, we were also handling the official England party. On the 14th March we were having dinner, following one of the cocktail parties, when I received a call from Bernard Thomas, the England team physiotherapist. He informed me that Kenny Barrington, who was managing the tour, had just died, and it would be necessary for me to arrange for the body and Kenny's wife Ann to return to England as soon as possible. He asked me to ring him about nine in the morning to make the final arrangements. I phoned at the requested time, only to be answered by a very grumpy and agitated Bernard. When he realised it was me, his tone softened a little, and he explained the reason for his irritation. At about 8.30 he had been woken by a knock on his bedroom door. He opened the door to find a certain England player asking him if he could have Kenny's room in Antigua, now that it was not required. Bernard saw red but refrained from hitting him. He closed the door but, within ten minutes, another knock revealed a former Test player, from the same county as the first, with exactly the same request!

The news had quite an effect on me. Kenny was a very close friend, who was always telling me to take things easy. His death was a tremendous shock, and it upset most of the England team, who found that coping with cricket the following day was a real chore. They lost the Test by 298 runs. Michael Holding's six balls to Boycott will be forever etched into my memory.

*

With the enormous success of the tours to the West Indies behind us, we prepared a number of group visits to India and Sri Lanka for the winter of 1981/82. We were still organising the official England party, and this time the press decided to climb aboard. I must say that, in all my years in travel, I never came across a more difficult, petulant group than the British cricket press. Apart from constantly moaning about their own arrangements, they interfered with mine and even on one occasion commandeered transport from an airport that had been organised for a supporters' group, leaving that group stranded.

We had arranged tours to Sri Lanka to watch two four-day matches against the island, one in Colombo, the other in Kandy, when in July 1981, after we had prepared our brochure, they were awarded Test match status. We had quickly to revamp the tour to include a five-day inaugural Test match and two one-day internationals.

Shortly before Christmas I was in England when I had a call from David Gower who was with the England team

in Delhi. He said that he wanted to see me – so, with my tour group having a few problems, I decided to fly out. I was due to leave on Air India on 23rd December, but the flight was overbooked. I believe they did this deliberately at festive times, forcing passengers to wait overnight, then putting them on the next day's flight, displacing even more passengers and repeating this until there were enough people waiting to fill an extra jumbo! I didn't fly out till early on Christmas Eve, but I arrived in time for dinner with David in Delhi and to sort out the various tour problems, some of which had been caused by the press group.

David explained to me that he had been asked to join a rebel tour to South Africa; he wanted to know my view as to whether or not he should accept. The gist of my reply concerned his future and the possibility of the England captaincy. In short, I told him that he should turn it down and, when I had finished, he said, "Yes, that is the conclusion I had reached." I felt like a sounding board. I caught the next flight back to England and arrived home just before the Queen's Speech on Christmas Day.

Ian Botham decided not to accept the invitation for similar reasons. All three of us, however, were to be proved wrong. Although the rebels were banned for a short period and labelled 'the dirty dozen' in parliament, they were soon back in the fold. In fact, both Graham Gooch, who led the rebels, and John Emburey went on to captain England. So much for the cricket authorities' ethics!

I had a business falling out with Drew Foster and, although we parted on good terms, it became necessary for me to form my own travel company, and

Fred Rumsey Travel was born. Property and development was still my main source of income, but the introduction of travel to the public relations arm kept me very busy indeed.

For the winter of 1982/83, when England were in Australia, I organised four tours, each of three weeks or so. My chosen hosts were Colin Milburn, Trevor Bailey and Don Wilson, the best of the many good people I had employed in Barbados, and I hosted the tour to Melbourne and Sydney that took in Christmas and the New Year.

On Christmas Day my party took over a restaurant in Melbourne. Then for a New Year thrash I hired the roof of the Sebal Town House in Sydney. I always tried to create a more enjoyable occasion by inviting other celebrities and, despite saying that he could not come, at about 11pm, shortly before the famous Sydney Bridge firework display, Michael Parkinson turned up with a large group of friends, including Fred Trueman and Tim Rice. I was doing well in business, but not on the scale of some in that world. At a Boxing Day party Robert Sangster, the Australian horse-breeder and football-pool owner, had told Tim Rice that he earned about £500 an hour. "Do you realise that, Parky?" said an incredulous Tim. "He earns £500 per hour." "So how much do you earn?" asked Michael. "About 450," replied a resigned Tim.

For the Barbados cricket festival in November 1983 Denis Compton, Colin Milburn and Don Wilson were unavailable so we added Godfrey Evans, who enjoyed his visits to Godfrey's Bar, and David Gower, at the time vice-captain of England. To Tim Brooke-Taylor, who alone had been carrying the celebrity aspect on his broad shoulders, we added a whole team of Lord's Taverners, including Robin Askwith, Gareth Davies, Richard Kershaw, Richard O'Sullivan, Ted Moult and Nicholas Parsons.

Headquarters was Tall Trees in Holetown, a beautiful beach-side residence adjacent to Smugglers Cove. The property holds fond memories for Coleen and me, not least because it was the venue of the first wedding we had on tour. The happy groom, cricket photographer Graham Morris, married his long-term partner, Diana, in an idyllic garden ceremony, with the Caribbean Sea lapping the shore only a few metres away.

'David Gower's team were the dominant force in the 1983 festival. They emerged with a 100 per cent record and thoroughly deserved to lift the BWIA Tri Star trophy.' So wrote Alan Birkinshaw, a sports journalist from Southend, whom I had hired to spread news of our festival to a wider audience. As a result of his efforts we obtained clients from Australia, United States and other parts of the Caribbean. The Lord's Taverners did a marvellous job, particularly Gareth Davies, who showed that his talents with bat and ball were almost equal to his rugby prowess for Wales and the British Lions.

The wedding reception of Graham and Diana Morris

Graham and Diana are between best man David Gower and me.
Also in the picture are Trevor and Greta Bailey, Reg Simpson,
Nicholas Parsons, Gareth Davies and, lying on the floor, Ted Moult.

David Gower and Gareth Davies

After the festival Coleen and I booked a ten-day cruise into the Grenadines, inviting David Gower and his girlfriend Vicki, Robin Askwith and Leonie Mellinger to join us. On the first evening Robin, who had achieved fame with his 'Confessions' films, said out of the blue to David and me, "You two may well be known in Barbados for your cricket prowess but, away from there, my films will make me better known than any cricketer."

All trip, to our great amusement, people kept coming up to David. I remember walking into a bank with him and hearing whispers all round the room: "It's David Gower; it's David Gower." "Mr Gower, what are you doing on our island?" the teller asked. Then, when David said he wanted to cash some money, the teller asked him, "Have you any means of identification?"

There were even people who came up to me – "Thank you so much, Mr Rumsey, for the wonderful job you are doing in Barbados" – but not once to Robin, at least not till the final evening when an attractive young lady approached him with an autograph book in her hand. His face lit up with this recognition at last. When she reached our group, she gave Robin a wonderful smile and said, "May I have your autograph, Mr Jagger?"

At the start of the 1984 festival, the Barbados Advocate printed an article with a picture caption that read as follows:

> *From left to right are Godfrey Evans, Tim Brooke-Taylor, Nick Cook, Fred Rumsey, Bill Athey, Ian Gould and Trevor Bailey, all of whom, with the exception of Rumsey, have represented England's national cricket side.*

(right) Tim Brooke-Taylor proves the point.

42

Off to Bangkok

During the sixth festival Gareth Davies discussed with me the possibility of my arranging a tour to Barbados for a group of Cardiff rugby players. I thought that the idea sounded great so I contacted the Barbados Rugby

Union and together we created the template of a tour that would include Barbados and St Lucia. The visit was arranged for the following July, giving the Cardiff players a chance to prepare for their forthcoming season. At this stage it was just a group of players wanting a fun-and-rum trip to the sunny Caribbean.

When the Cardiff club discovered the players' intentions they decided to make the tour official, increase the numbers and pay much of the cost. It was at this point that my troubles started. Apparently Cardiff had toured the banned South Africa, a point made very clear by a Cardiff journalist in print. This information filtered through to the United Nations, who made representations to the Barbados government. I received a phone call from the Barbados High Commissioner in London, informing me that the Barbados Cabinet would not welcome Cardiff Rugby Club to its shores. "So you are banning them," I said. "I did not say that," said a wary Commissioner. "I said they would not be welcome." As I was entrenched in the Barbados tourist industry, I took the hint, cancelled the tour and started looking for an alternative venue.

A friend told me that rugby was played in the middle of the Bangkok race course. I contacted the sports editor of a Bangkok newspaper, who to my surprise turned out to be a fanatical supporter of Welsh rugby and immediately offered his services as tour organiser. So I set up the travel arrangements. Again the issue of Cardiff's tour of South Africa was raised, but it only reached the Thai government two days before the start of the tour, and the Crown Prince, who was also the foreign secretary, decided it was too late to cancel the trip.

Coleen became the first woman ever to travel on a Cardiff rugby club coach, a 'crime' for which she stood trial when the team enacted a court tribunal. The captain, Terry Holmes, sat as judge, wearing a bath towel cut to create the ringlets of a lawyer's wig. Prosecution and defence lawyers were appointed, they made Coleen's case appear like murder, and she was found guilty. The punishment was for her to take her clothes off, down to her bra and panties, or drink a pint of bitter without stopping. Upon appeal the size of the glass was reduced by half. Knowing that she was not capable of gulping, I suggested that she took her clothes off. She answered me with a fearful glare, half-spilling the drink over me in revenge.

The trip was a great success. Cardiff won their two matches, which were well attended, and the whole group were excellent ambassadors for Wales. Barbados lost out on what would have been a prosperous and prestigious tour, but they did make amends with me when, for promotional purposes, $5,000 found its way into my Barbados bank account.

43

Shell Caribbean Cup

Cricket West Indies, formerly known as the West Indies Cricket Board, owe a debt of gratitude to the Royal Dutch Shell Company which can never be repaid. One of the main reasons for the West Indies cricket team's rise to power in the 1960s was the support given to them by the company in the form of the Shell Shield. This was the first annual, four-day, first-class tournament to be held in the Caribbean. It involved all of the board's members – Barbados, Guyana, Jamaica, Trinidad and Tobago, Leeward Islands and Windward Islands, the latter two initially playing as the Combined Islands. The first matches were played in January 1966.

For 21 years these sides fought for the coveted Shell Shield, and I am certain that had it not been for an administrative error on Shell's part they would be doing so today. In 1987, when the West Indies Cricket Board contacted the Barbados offices of Shell with a request to renew the sponsorship of the Shell Shield, the company was going through an administrative change at senior level, and the request was overlooked. This opened the door for Red Stripe to became the new sponsors of Caribbean Cricket.

In early 1988 I was contacted by John Taylor, the Wales and British Lions flanker, advising me that Shell, having lost the sponsorship of the cricket, were extremely worried about their image in the Caribbean. John had met the Barbados company's new general manager, Peter Lane, at a cocktail party in London, and John had suggested that he should contact me for advice. Not long after that, Shell asked me to come up with some new ideas for their Caribbean sponsorship. I prepared a feasibility study and business plan for three worthwhile alternatives, and in the summer of 1988 I travelled to Barbados to present them to Peter Lane and his staff.

The first idea involved the sponsorship of tourism throughout the Caribbean; the second was aimed at young people, providing assistance with the development of arts and crafts in the region. The third was the introduction of a major knock-out football tournament involving all the members of the Caribbean Football Union. It was this last presentation which received the overwhelming support of Peter Lane and his team, and the Shell Caribbean Cup was born.

It was my belief that the tournament should be owned and organised by Shell, with invitations to participate issued to countries within the Football Union, not organised by the Union and sponsored by Shell. This enabled Shell to have control of the event and to minimise any cultural difficulties. I was asked to organise and administer the first tournament on condition that I would personally oversee all the arrangements. This I agreed to, but I added my own condition, that the appointment was only for the first event, to be held in 1989.

I set about writing the rules, regulations and the form the competition would take, adapting FIFA's World Cup to suit the Caribbean. I formed a company in Barbados, Caribbean Sport Limited, and, at the request of Peter Short, one-time President of the West Indies Cricket Board and a good friend, I headed it up with Alison Camacho, the wife of Steve Camacho who was Secretary of the WICB at the time. Duncan Carter and Ricky Clarke, both extremely fine cricketers, were added to the staff. For Duncan who played for Barbados, the post led to a successful political career. Ricky already worked with me as a member of my travel business and, as travel arrangements were a major factor in the tournament, he was to become extremely valuable.

A management committee was set up representing all the countries in the Caribbean Football Union plus senior officials of Shell in the Caribbean. This committee was chaired by Peter Lane, General Manager of Shell Antilles and Guianas Ltd. They in turn appointed an organising committee, chaired by Jack Warner, who was President of the Caribbean Football Union. Jack was the Caribbean's representative on FIFA and later became involved in some of that organisation's troubles, but I must confess that in my dealings with him I found him to be extremely able, helpful and charming. He was a man who did an enormous amount to promote the game in his region.

The competition consisted of two stages: a preliminary competition, which would be played in three zones, followed by a finals competition in Barbados. In 1989 there were 17 countries in the Caribbean Football Union. With the hosts Barbados receiving a bye and Guyana under suspension by FIFA at the time, the zonal competition was reduced to 15 teams.

Zone A	Zone B	Zone C
Aruba	British Virgin Islands	Antigua/Barbuda
French Guiana	Martinique	Dominica
Grenada	Netherlands Antilles	Guadeloupe
St Kitts/Nevis	St Maarten	Jamaica
Trinidad/Tobago	St Vincent	St Lucia

The zonal competition was to be played on a league basis between April and June. The six finalists would be the three zonal winners, the two best runners-up and Barbados.

The pre-finals arrangements in Barbados caused me some concern. I was not getting on well with the President of the Barbados Football Association, a man called George Lascaris. He appeared to resent the fact that a non-Caribbean man had been chosen to run the most important football event in the region and on a number of occasions made my job unnecessarily difficult. He tried to get Barbados seeded into a group that did not include Trinidad/Tobago. I explained that it might work for the World Cup but, with only six teams qualifying, it would not be fair practice. Although knowing my view, he still chose to confront me during the live draw on television, suggesting that the two teams should be kept apart until the final. They were drawn in the same group, and it was the match of the tournament, but it would have still been unfair to the other four teams had the draw been rigged.

I asked CBC, the local Barbados television station, if they would like to buy the rights to cover the finals competition. They replied that they wanted free access to all matches or they were not interested. I refused point blank and considered that that was an end to the matter. That evening on their news programme they accused me of denying the Barbados public the chance of watching the most important football tournament ever played in the Caribbean, an accusation that incensed me.

My best friend in Barbados, Livy Greaves, phoned me in a fury. "I understand that you offered CBC the chance to buy the rights to your football tournament," he stated.

"I did," I replied, "but they turned it down."

"Get yourself to my house," he ordered. "We are off to see my cousin."

Livy's cousin was Philip Greaves, the Deputy Prime Minister of Barbados. He listened carefully to my version of the events and said that he would speak to me again later. This he did, telling me that he was not satisfied with the way CBC had dealt with the matter. "I have told them to broadcast a retraction along with an apology," he said. "I also made it clear that the apology should be made at the same time as the accusation was aired and not in the early hours of the morning!"

This they did with a great deal of reluctance, and to say things were frosty between us would be a gross understatement.

I still had a television problem to solve. I had purchased a half-hour slot on satellite for each day of the finals. I would therefore need 30 minutes of action immediately after each match, and the only company capable of providing such a service was, you've guessed it, CBC! In this instance I was paying, and my terms were immediately accepted. I appointed a former BBC employee, who had returned home to Barbados to retire, as co-ordinator and left all television arrangements to him.

During half time in the first match I sought out my co-ordinator to check how things were going. He checked with the director, only to discover that, after filming for 45 minutes, they had not switched on the video. Fortunately there was little of note in the first half, and we were able to get all the action, including the goals, from the second half.

The publicity Shell received in the run-up to finals week was enormous. Every day the media throughout the Caribbean carried stories of their local teams, especially in Barbados. The week before the event, when the publicity was at its height, there was so much coverage on radio, television and in the press that it prompted Livy Greaves' son, who was the head of Texaco on the island, to threaten me with extinction for the trouble I had caused him.

So much excitement was generated in that inaugural season that the future of the tournament looked very bright indeed. Grenada, St Vincent, Guadeloupe, Trinidad/Tobago and Netherlands Antilles all qualified from the zonal matches and, with Barbados, they made up the six teams in the final.

The finals week provided a feast of football. The standard of the players surpassed my expectations and indeed a number of them, including Dwight Yorke, went on to play professionally in Europe and the USA. Apart from an issue over national anthems – Guadeloupe did not want La Marseillaise played before their matches – the cultural disagreements that I feared at the outset did not transpire. The match of the tournament was, without doubt, the one between Barbados and Trinidad/Tobago. A packed stadium, it had never held so many people before, saw Trinidad/Tobago narrowly beat Barbados, going on to beat Grenada in the final and become the first winners of the Shell Caribbean Cup.

True to my word, I withdrew my company and left the next year's organisation to Alison Comacho. Sadly the 1990 tournament, held in Trinidad, was not completed. First, it was suspended when there was an attempted coup d'etat. Then, when Tropical Storm Arthur hit the island, it was abandoned.

The Cup continued till 2017, when the Caribbean nations decided to join a wider competition across the whole of North and Central America.

44

33 years of the Festival

One of the reasons why the festival ran with so few hitches was the local people who worked hard to ensure its smooth running. In the early days Calvin Hope provided a lot of support, along with Tony and Jillian Cozier, Richard Edwards and Peter Short, but the main man and the one without whom the festival would have struggled was Ricky Clarke. A talented club cricketer, he had the flair and enthusiasm for the many tasks I set him. He would find the local players, arrange the grounds, handle all the transport, deal with the media and still find the time to socialise with the tourists at the many parties that were arranged each year.

By November 1998 the festival had reached its 21st year. The event had become a fixture in the Barbados cricket calendar and in the life of Mike Walton who attended for the 21st time! Peter Short graciously accepted my 21st anniversary jibe and agreed to present the trophies at the presentation evening. To celebrate our coming of age, Tony Marshall and the Barbados Cricket Association invited us to include an England XI to play against a Barbados XI in a series of three one-day matches for the Wes Hall Trophy. We lost the series, but it was a load of fun on and off the field! My England twelve were David Capel, Chris Broad, Bill Athey, David Sales, Keith Medlycott, Paul Jarvis, Devon Malcolm, Jason Gallian, Rob Bailey, Glen Chapple, Chris Read and Craig White.

Mike Walton, our most regular player, receives a trophy from Garry Sobers

My eldest son, Warren, took over the festival in 1999, the 22nd year, and ran it along similar lines for another 11 years. His welcome in the 2010 booklet carried the following kind words: 'It feels like the last 33 years have flown by since the creation of this fantastic cricket festival, which has gone from strength to strength. Of course there was a man with a plan and without him none of this would have ever been possible. So we have to say a huge thank you to my dad Fred and offer him our congratulations on reaching the 33rd year.'

Warren was not to know at the time that the 33rd festival in 2010 would be the last of its kind. Although the 34th was advertised, insufficient numbers made it impossible to continue the arrangements as planned. However, those who booked had a pleasant two weeks on the west coast of Barbados, saying goodbye to a very dear old friend!

More than a gross of first-class cricketers played in the festival over the 33 years, of which 101 were Test or one-day international players. It became a training ground for aspiring Barbados talent and a very special event for numerous English club players. Even a young Jonny Bairstow honed his cover drive on the beach, in Holetown, with his father David.

David Bairstow, with his boy Jonny

Of all the hosts I employed over the years, David Bairstow and Colin Milburn were the very best. They both understood completely what was required, they related so easily to everybody, and they seemed always to being enjoying it.

All the club cricketers arrived home with a feast of anecdotes for those who did not travel. Of all the client throwaway lines, the following one was my favourite: "We were in the Bamboo Beach Bar on the West Coast of Barbados when I suggested to Denis Compton that Sobers didn't bat very well today and Oliver Reed agreed!" Mike Walton attended 31 of the 33 years and is still going strong, even though the festival no longer exists.

Throughout the festival period I spent a total of six and a half years of my life living in Barbados. It became a second home to me. I love the people, I love the culture, I love the humour and I love the country. I am an Englishman at heart but Bajan by adoption. There is one major drawback – I might not have made their national side!

IN CONCLUSION

Receiving a Lifetime Achievement Award
from Freddie Flintoff at the PCA Awards Dinner in 2017,
which celebrated the 50th anniversary of our first meeting

45

Last reflections

The war years apart, the structure of English cricket in my youth was basically afternoon and the occasional all-day game at club level and three-day and five-day games at first-class level. Club cricket has not changed in this respect, but the first-class game began a whole series of changes, starting with the introduction of the Gillette Cup in 1963.

I preferred the first-class cricket of my youth. I could see the need for the financial return that one-day cricket provided, but I do not hold with the view that the Gillette Cup was the saviour of the first-class game. As time progressed and the overs reduced, the game has ended up with Twenty20, where the bowler might just as well be replaced by a bowling machine providing fodder for the batsmen to hit to cow-shot corner. The real art of cricket is the battle between bowler and batsman, both adapting to the prevailing conditions with one surviving.

There appears to be a misguided belief by the current organisers of first-class cricket that the greater income they can achieve, the greater the job they have done for the game. Wrong. By selling out to Sky Television in 2006, with their limited coverage in England and Wales, they have certainly obtained more income, but at what cost? According to an ECB survey in 2014, participation in the sport had dropped by 64,000 in that one year, and cricket is now hardly mentioned on terrestrial television, the greatest medium of our time. There is no doubt in my mind that, unless greater care is taken, cricket in England and Wales is in danger of becoming a second-class sport.

My father played cricket and, during the four years before his call-up, instilled a love for the game into my being. I was a lucky child, born with excellent eye-and-hand coordination, and any ball sport appeared natural to me. I have read about players, spectators and writers becoming attracted to cricket because of a certain event or player. I was born into it. So too was my sister Jean. She became so skilled at scoring that she invented her own colour code system. She continued scoring up to her 83rd year, the year in which she died. My mother also had her cricket duties in preparing teas every weekend for my father's team, my team or my sister's team.

This family involvement with cricket did not continue with Coleen and my family. Only Warren showed any real interest, but even he had a greater love of rugby. Matthew preferred soccer but did play a little cricket in his youth. Claire had no interest except in looking after the many infants brought to Taverner matches by the players.

During the Taverner years my whole family would attend the cricket matches, making themselves helpful in many ways to the benefit of that excellent cause. I thoroughly enjoyed the club atmosphere of those matches in the '70s, '80s and '90s – something, I guess, that is extremely hard to maintain.

Warren married Philippa and produced three daughters, Charlotte, Emma and Harriet, with only Harriet showing a little interest in the game. Charlotte is an excellent gymnast and represented England in her youth, Emma is into art and drama and Harriet has a beautiful singing voice. Matthew married Kasia, and they too have a daughter; they live in Spain so I doubt if she has ever heard of the word 'cricket'! My last hope was with Claire, whose partner Brent is half-Jamaican. Their son, Jacob, showed some interest at an early age but then, influenced by Brent, his attention was turned to the Baggies, the affectionate name of West Bromwich Albion Football Club.

I have had my ups and downs financially, but I don't measure the success and failure of my life in terms of wealth, the misguided philosophy of many. Rather, I know the pleasure a loving family and friends can bring. I have not been easy to live with, but Coleen is still by my side after 53 years. I still talk to my children and their children. My friends still phone and share a glass with me from time to time, and I treasure my loyalty to others. Those are the things that matter most in my life.

*

I liked playing for England and enjoyed my five matches. I would have loved to have played more, but in some ways playing just the once would have been enough to have satisfied my need. It would also have been great to have taken five wickets in a Test match innings at Lord's and to have got on the honours boards; my four-for-25 got pretty close but was just not good enough. I could also have done without the shin soreness I experienced throughout my Test career; it was okay when bowling but agony when in the field. I suppose, like any good workhorses, we quick bowlers were expected to suffer the pain in return for the occasional glory!

The years I spent with the Lord's Taverners were some of the best of my life. I chose the charity as the perfect vehicle to put something back into the game that had provided me with so much pleasure. The trouble was that I enjoyed the Taverners just as much as playing first-class cricket, leaving me without a cause for which I was making a sacrifice. I do hope that the modern Taverners take as much care in maintaining a club atmosphere as they do in raising funds, or they could be in danger of losing that wonderful aura that draws the public to them.

top:
(left to right)
Harriet, Emma,
Philippa, Warren,
Charlotte, Coleen

middle:
Brent, Jacob,
Claire

bottom:
Scarlett, Kasia,
Matthew

My only reflection on the PCA, a body which has crossed the t's and dotted the i's of its original philosophy, is that it must never forget who it represents. It is important that it discusses future cricket policy with the ECB but not after that authority has created a fait accompli.

Having said that, I know that the PCA is currently in good hands. Daryl Mitchell, the Chairman, and David Leatherdale, the Chief Executive, have their hearts in the right place, and so too have their managers and staff. I find it a pleasure to talk to everyone in the organisation but in particular, in my case, I would single out Alison Prosser, the extremely able player membership services manager.

At Cheltenham – 50 years on from the first PCA meeting
Mike Smedley, Don Shepherd, Fred Rumsey, Eric Russell, auditor Harold Goldblatt

It was mostly by choice that I followed my destiny. I have an innovative mind that will not stop until a new or better way of doing something can be created. The whole of my life has been a mixture of activities, from banking to building, public relations to travel, charity to cricket, and all have offered the challenge of the need to change. Quite a number of my solutions ended up on the scrap heap, where they belonged, but a few have made a difference.

From the day, prior to the Second World War, when my father gave me the coal shovel and a worn tennis ball, only the well-being of one thing has run through the whole of my active life – Cricket. As you are aware, I have had my differences with the MCC and my criticisms still stand, but I must admit that I admire them for their age-long devotion to all that is cricket and their desire to oppose unnecessary change.

*

The last few pages of this book have been completed from a hospital bed. I was diagnosed as having two aortic aneurysms that were in need of an operation. My stay in hospital was meant to be a two-or-three-day affair, dependent upon my healing ability. However, when I awoke after the operation, I had lost all feeling in my right leg. This was followed by other complications, making writing a little difficult but, with Mr Isaac Nyamekye's skill along with the help of Tom and his vascular care unit at the Worcester Hospital, I began to feel human again and found myself in a three-unit ward with a neighbour called Barney – 'Yabba Dabba Doo'.

Still suffering from a dead leg, I was transferred to Abbott Ward in Evesham Community Hospital, which specialises in stroke rehabilitation, where it was established by Dr Numo Ribeiro that I had not had a stroke but was suffering from a spinal pressure disorder. The nursing staff here also give a high order of care.

My room-mate here in Evesham, Alan Bagnall, has been able to keep my spirits high by vanishing from time to time, sometimes to the torture chamber, our word for the physiotherapist's gymnasium, sometimes to the day room. One evening we both went to bed but, when I awoke, he was not in his. He didn't write, he didn't phone, just turned up five days later with some cock-and-bull story about having to go to Worcester. He also cracked the whip by making me put the finishing touches to this book, which I now do.

A BRIEF STATISTICAL DIGEST

FIRST-CLASS CRICKET

BATTING AND FIELDING

M	I	NO	Runs	HS	Ave	ct
180	204	84	1015	45	8.45	91

BOWLING

Year	Overs	M	Runs	Wkts	Best	Ave	5wi	10wm
1960	109.2	22	280	12	2-21	23.33		
1961	82	13	211	1	1-55	211.00		
1962	93.2	30	170	18	7-50	9.44	2	1
1963	794.1	176	1989	102	7-39	19.50	7	2
1964	703.5	158	1617	80	7-34	20.21	3	
1965	823.4	233	1926	119	8-26	16.18	7	1
1966	812.1	199	1911	100	7-35	19.11	4	
1967	702.4	163	1765	73	6-41	24.17	5	1
1968	661	159	1807	73	7-63	24.75	2	
1970	30.5	5	97	2	1-34	48.50		
Total	**4813**	**1158**	**11773**	**580**	**8-26**	**20.29**	**30**	**5**

SEVEN OR MORE WICKETS IN AN INNINGS

20.1	6	26	8	Somerset v Hampshire	Bath	1965
25	5	34	7	Somerset v Kent	Tunbridge Wells	1964
17.4	8	34	7	Somerset v Essex	Westcliff	1965
18.1	4	35	7	Somerset v Warwickshire	Taunton	1966
21.5	10	39	7	Somerset v Nottinghamshire	Taunton	1963
29	7	48	7	Somerset v Hampshire	Bristol (Imperial)	1966
23	10	50	7	Worcestershire v Derbyshire	Chesterfield	1962
22	6	63	7	Somerset v Leicestershire	Leicester	1968

TWELVE OR MORE WICKETS IN A MATCH

48	13	104	13	Somerset v Nottinghamshire	Taunton	1963
34.5	10	59	12	Somerset v Glamorgan	Neath	1963

TEST CRICKET

BATTING

M	I	NO	Runs	HS	Ave
5	4	3	30	21*	15.00

BOWLING

Overs	M	Runs	Wkts	Best	Ave
190.5	29	461	17	4-25	27.11

BEST BOWLING FIGURES

13	4	25	4	England v New Zealand	Lord's	1965

ONE-DAY (LIST A) CRICKET

BATTING AND FIELDING

M	I	NO	Runs	HS	Ave	ct
95	45	21	114	16*	4.75	20

BOWLING

Overs	M	Runs	Wkts	Best	Ave	4wi
800.2	161	2185	130	4-8	16.80	7

BEST BOWLING FIGURES

8	3	8	4	Derbyshire v Worcestershire	Derby	1970

MOST ECONOMICAL BOWLERS IN LIST A CRICKET

Qualification: 400 overs

		Overs	Runs	Runs per over
1	F.E. Rumsey	800.2	2185	2.730
2	V.A.P. van der Bijl	872.5	2385	2.732
3	T.W. Cartwright	1248.5	3481	2.787
4	J. Garner	2226.3	6598	2.963

The agenda for the inaugural meeting of the Cricketers' Association

INAUGURAL MEETING OF THE COUNTY CRICKETERS' ASSOCIATION

LONDON PRESS CLUB MONDAY 4th SEPTEMBER, 1967.

Chairman: Jim Parks (Sussex)

AGENDA

1. Opening address by Fred Rumsey (Somerset).

2. Jimmy Hill (Manager of Coventry City Football Club and former Chairman of the Professional Footballers' Association).

3. Cliff Lloyd (Secretary of the Professional Footballers' Association).

4. John Davies (Daily Express sportswriter).

5. John Gardner (Marketing Director-Supporters Magazines Ltd.).

- - - - - - X - - - - - -

The meeting will now go into private session for the purpose of:-

(a) Formal launching of the County Cricketers' Association and adoption of an Association Memorandum and Articles.

(b) Election of Officers and Executive Committee.

(c) Future plans.

(d) Any other business.

(e) Dates of next Executive Committee Meeting and Full General Meeting.

The original memorandum of the Cricketers' Association

PROPOSED MEMORANDUM AND ARTICLES OF ASSOCIATION OF

THE ████████ CRICKETERS' ASSOCIATION

MEMORANDUM

1. The name of the Association to be "THE ████████ CRICKETERS' ASSOCIATION".

2. The objects for which the Association is established are:-

    (a) To foster, encourage and help the cricketer and the game of cricket in general.

    (b) To represent the collective view of County cricketers' and at all times work for the cause of cricket.

    (c) To impress on the members of the Association a code of conduct to be observed at all times.

    (d) To ascertain and research ways that players can best help the game.

    (e) To find ways and means of offering more security to players thereby making County cricket a more attractive livelihood.

    (f) To create a better liaison between the players and the County Club committees particularly in times of dispute.

    (g) To set up an out-of-season employment exchange for the purpose of placing players in need of winter employment in suitable positions.

    (h) To find and contact business houses who are prepared to train the younger cricketer during the winter for a career once his cricketing days are over.

    (i) To offer help in the organisation of a players benefit/testimonial year. It is possible that by negotiating on a national basis that the Association would be able to help the beneficiary to cut the costs of organising his benefit/testimonial year.

    (j) To generally act as the cricketers' agent.

3. To provide an organisation to which members can turn to for advice and help.

BARBADOS CRICKET FESTIVAL

Winning teams

1978	Barbados Cricket League XI	1995	David Bairstow XI
1979	Richard Edwards XI	1996	Barbados Masters XI
1980	Brian Close XI	1997	Combined Schools XI
1981	Fred Rumsey XI	1998	Bill Athey XI
1982	Barbados Cricket League XI	1999	Bill Athey XI
1983	David Gower XI	2000	Mark Ramprakash XI
1984	Nick Cook XI	2001	Chris Adams XI
1985	Nick Cook XI	2002	Bill Athey XI
1986	Barbados Cricket League XI	2003	Steve Rhodes XI
1987	Graham Roope XI	2004	Nick Knight XI
1988	Barbados Cricket League XI	2005	Combined Schools XI
1989	Barbados Cricket League XI	2006	Steve Rhodes XI
1990	Barbados Cricket League XI	2007	Chris Silverwood XI
1991	David Bairstow XI	2008	Combined Schools XI
1992	Barbados Cricket League XI	2009	Brian McMillan XI
1993	Combined Schools XI	2010	Brian McMillan XI
1994	Fred Rumsey XI		

Festival records

BATTING

159	Calvin Hope	David Holford XI v Reg Simpson XI	1982
147	Collis King	Colin Milburn XI v David Gower XI	1980
138	Neil Philllips	Brian Close XI v Fred Rumsey XI	1980
136*	David Holford	David Holford XI v Richard Edwards XI	1980
132	Collis. King	Reg Simpson XI v Don Wilson XI	1982

BOWLING

6-3	Terry Connell	Barbados Cricket League XI v Fred Rumsey XI	1983
6-13	Broderick Estwick	Don Wilson XI v Brian Close XI	1980
6-13	D. Harewood	Barbados Cricket League XI v Chris Adams XI	2003
6-14	R. Foster	Barbados Cricket League XI v Keith Medlycott XI	1990
6-23	R. Spellman	Hugh Morris XI v David Bairstow XI	1992

WICKET-KEEPING

5	D. Knight *(3c, 2s)*	Colin Milburn XI v Don Wilson XI	1980
5	Brian Close *(5 s)*	Brian Close XI v Barbados Cricket League XI	1981

103 Test and one-day international cricketers in the Festival

England

Chris Adams	Godfrey Evans	Peter Martin	Ian Salisbury
Bill Athey	Paul Franks	Martin McCague	Ryan Sidebottom
Rob Bailey	Angus Fraser	Colin Milburn	Chris Silverwood
Trevor Bailey	Jason Gallian	Hugh Morris	Reg Simpson
David Bairstow	Ed Giddins	John Morris	Gladstone Small
Ian Blackwell	Darren Gough	Martyn Moxon	David Smith
Richard Blakey	Ian Gould	Tim Munton	John Snow
Chris Broad	David Gower	Paul Nixon	Peter Such
Dougie Brown	Gavin Hamilton	Min Patel	Paul Taylor
Roland Butcher	Warren Hegg	Derek Pringle	Alex Tudor
David Capel	Alan Igglesden	Mark Ramprakash	Phil Tufnell
Glen Chapple	Paul Jarvis	Derek Randall	Shaun Udal
Brian Close	Richard Johnson	Chris Read	Ian Ward
Denis Compton	Chris Jordan	Dermot Reeve	James Whitaker
Nick Cook	Nick Knight	Steve Rhodes	Craig White
Norman Cowans	Mal Loye	Graham Roope	Peter Willey
Chris Cowdrey	Darren Maddy	Fred Rumsey	Neil Williams
Phillip DeFreitas	Devon Malcolm	Martin Saggers	Don Wilson
Richard Ellison			

West Indies

Sulieman Benn	Pedro Collins	Desmond Haynes	Norman Marshall
Carlisle Best	Richard Edwards	Roland Holder	Ezra Moseley
Tino Best	Joel Garner	David Holford	Floyd Reifer
Keith Boyce	Alvin Greenidge	Tony Howard	Kemar Roach
Ian Bradshaw	Adrian Griffith	Collis King	Garfield Sobers
Henderson Bryan	Charlie Griffith	Peter Lashley	Patterson Thompson
Sylvester Clarke	Wes Hall		

Other

Nolan Clarke (Holl)	Bob Cowper (Aus)	Farokh Engineer (Ind)	Brian McMillan (SA)

51 further first-class cricketers in the Festival

England

Martyn Ball	Duncan Fearnley	Steven Marsh	Trevor Penney
Stephen Booth	Mark Feltham	David Marshall	Alan Richardson
Kevin Brooks	David Graveney	Keith Medlycott	Mike Roseberry
Joshua Cobb	Simon Hughes	Ashley Metcalfe	David Sales
Russell Cobb	Paul Hutchinson	Chris Nash	Russell Spiers
Kevin Cooper	Bill Jones	Mark Nicholas	Darren Stevens
Graham Cowdrey	Bill Kirby	Dominic Ostler	Graeme Welch
Richard Doughty	Steve Kirby		

West Indies

Anthony Alleyne	Dane Currency	Neal Phillips	Franklyn Stephenson
Hartley Alleyne	Stephen Farmer	Ahmed Proverbs	Kevin Stoute
Sean Armstrong	Teddy Foster	Leslie Reifer	Dexter Toppin
Ruel Brathwaite	Steve Hinkson	Henderson Springer	Emmerson Trotman
Duncan Carter	Shane Julien	Clinton St Hill	Ryan Wiggins
Wendell Coppin			

Rumsey steers Border to moral victory

Daily Dispatch Correspondent

PORT ELIZABETH — Eastern Province's batting hopes were knocked firmly on the head over the week-end by the former England left arm opening bowler Fred Rumsey, who piloted Border to a moral victory in the drawn two-day friendly.

Rumsey's lively spells ruffled the batsmen in both innings, and he finished with the commendable match figures of nine for 66, with Graeme Pollock (twice) and Eddie Barlow among his victims.

Rumsey bowled extremely well throughout and, alert and sometimes acrobatic Border fielding, had Eastern Province struggling for runs.

Only Graeme Pollock, with his almost faultless and delightful 92 in the first innings, and Eddie Barlow, who hit a typically pugnacious 50 in the second, threatened Border's tight hold on the game.

There is no denying that Border, generally speaking, gave Eastern Province a sharp lesson in batting, bowling and fielding, despite the fact that Rumsey was something of a lone wolf where the attack was concerned.

CONSOLATION

One can only hope that the old adage of a poor dress rehearsal means a good first night holds good for Eastern Province. A vast improvement is necessary if Natal are to be matched in the Currie Cup game in Durban 12 days from now.

There is some consolation in the fact that Natal have no opening bowler to match Rumsey.

But there is also the thought that the Border batsmen had to cope with Peter Pollock. This they did rather well, particularly the highly promising Tony Greig, whose 46 in the first innings pales into insignificance when compared with the 78 not out he hammered in 81 minutes in the second.

Greig came in when Border were 86 for five, and for the first time in the match it looked

as though Eastern Province were about to seize the initiative.

Almost disdainfully, Greig partnered Ian Harty in a stand of 69 in 48 minutes, and he and Heger put on 54 in 35 minutes in an unbeaten seventh-wicket partnership.

Greig hit 12 sparkling fours, and it was an eye-opener to see him punching Peter Pollock through the covers off the back foot.

RIGHT DIRECTION

This tall Border and South African Nuffield batsman is headed in the right direction, and his progress will be watched with great interest.

Buster Farrer batted competently in both innings, Chris Wilkens brightly in the second after his duck in the first, but Peter Haxton with big slices of luck for his half century.

The only crumb of comfort in the Eastern Province batting, apart from Barlow and Graeme Pollock, was the fact that Lorrie Wilmot looked more composed than in recent games.

A final word about Dassie Biggs, who will be 12th man in Durban. He batted quite well in the first innings, deputised satisfactorily as an off-spinner despite one or two lapses in control, and was easily the most energetic and efficient fielder in the side.

BORDER (First Innings)

Haxton, c G. Pollock, b Biggs	..	50
Wilkins, b Hector		0
Milburn, lbw, b P. Pollock	..	12
Farrer, c and b Biggs		37
Harty, c Harty, b Barlow	..	8
Groves, st Harty, b Biggs	..	19
Greig, c Harty, b P. Pollock	..	46
Heger, c Harty, b Biggs	..	9
Price, b Hector	..	22
Rumsey, not out	..	33
Scott, lbw, b P. Pollock	..	17
Extras		9
Total		**262**

Fall of wickets: 1/2, 2/38, 3/93,
4/123, 5/124, 6/144, 7/184, 8/210, 9/212.
Bowling: P. Pollock, 16.4-0-49-3; Hector, 18-4-45-2; Barlow, 15-2-47-1; Wilmot, 1-1-0-0; Biggs, 25-5-98-4; Mallett, 6-2-14-0.

EASTERN PROVINCE (First Innings)

Barlow, lbw, b Rumsey	..	3
Van Rensburg, lbw, b Rumsey	..	0
Fenix, lbw, b Heger	..	18
G. Pollock, c Milburn, b Rumsey	..	92
Wilmot, c Price, b Rumsey	..	24
Gradwell, c Heger, b Rumsey	..	9
Mallett, b Rumsey	..	0
Biggs, b Greig	..	14
P. Pollock, c Wilkins, b Heger	..	22
Harty, not out	..	0
Extras		14
Total (for nine wkts. dec.)		**201**

Fall of wickets: 1/3, 2/19, 3/76,
4/149, 5/154, 6/155, 7/165, 8/194, 9/201.
Bowling: Rumsey, 13-5-27-6; Scott, 14-3-42-0; Greig, 16.2-4-49-1; Heger, 19-3-56-2; Milburn, 4-0-13-0.

BORDER (Second Innings)

Haxton, c Harty, b P. Pollock	..	4
Wilkins, b P. Pollock	..	37
Milburn, c Harty, b Hector	..	4
Farrer, b Mallett	..	19
Groves, c Barlow, b Biggs	..	20
Harty, c Gradwell, b Biggs	..	27
Greig, not out	..	78
Heger, not out	..	12
Extras		8
Total (for six wkts. dec.)		**209**

Fall of wickets: 1/16, 2/45, 3/48,
4/86, 5/86, 6/155.
Bowling: P. Pollock, 12-2-45-2; Hector, 9-2-48-1; Mallett, 17-5-48-1; Barlow, 4-1-16-0; Biggs, 13-0-44-2.

EASTERN PROVINCE (Second Innings)

Barlow, c Haxton, b Heger	..	50
Van Rensburg, c Harty, b Rumsey	..	1
Fenix, c Price, b Rumsey	..	10
G. Pollock, c Greig, b Rumsey	..	26
Wilmot, not out	..	3
Mallett, not out	..	4
Extras		3
Total (for four wickets)		**97**

Fall of wickets: 1/12, 2/24, 3/81, 4/91.
Bowling: Rumsey, 9-1-39-3; Scott, 6-0-42-2; Heger, 4.3-2-9-1; Milburn, 2-1-

INDEX